How to Code .NET

Tips and Tricks for Coding
.NET 1.1 and .NET 2.0
Applications Effectively

■ ■ ■

Christian Gross

Apress®

How to Code .NET: Tips and Tricks for Coding .NET 1.1 and .NET 2.0 Applications Effectively

Copyright © 2006 by Christian Gross

ISBN-13 (pbk): 978-1-59059-744-6

ISBN-10 (pbk): 1-59059-744-3

Printed and bound in the United States of America 9 8 7 6 5 4 3 2 1

Trademarked names may appear in this book. Rather than use a trademark symbol with every occurrence of a trademarked name, we use the names only in an editorial fashion and to the benefit of the trademark owner, with no intention of infringement of the trademark.

Lead Editor: Ewan Buckingham
Technical Reviewer: Jason Lefebvre
Editorial Board: Steve Anglin, Ewan Buckingham, Gary Cornell, Jason Gilmore, Jonathan Gennick, Jonathan Hassell, James Huddleston, Chris Mills, Matthew Moodie, Dominic Shakeshaft, Jim Sumser, Keir Thomas, Matt Wade
Project Manager: Richard Dal Porto
Copy Edit Manager: Nicole Flores
Copy Editors: Candace English, Nicole Abramowitz
Assistant Production Director: Kari Brooks-Copony
Production Editor: Kelly Gunther
Compositor: Gina Rexrode
Proofreader: Linda Seifert
Indexer: Michael Brinkman
Artist: April Milne
Cover Designer: Kurt Krames
Manufacturing Director: Tom Debolski

Distributed to the book trade worldwide by Springer-Verlag New York, Inc., 233 Spring Street, 6th Floor, New York, NY 10013. Phone 1-800-SPRINGER, fax 201-348-4505, e-mail orders-ny@springer-sbm.com, or visit http://www.springeronline.com.

For information on translations, please contact Apress directly at 2560 Ninth Street, Suite 219, Berkeley, CA 94710. Phone 510-549-5930, fax 510-549-5939, e-mail info@apress.com, or visit http://www.apress.com.

The information in this book is distributed on an "as is" basis, without warranty. Although every precaution has been taken in the preparation of this work, neither the author(s) nor Apress shall have any liability to any person or entity with respect to any loss or damage caused or alleged to be caused directly or indirectly by the information contained in this work.

The source code for this book is available to readers at http://www.apress.com in the Source Code/ Download section.

Contents at a Glance

Contents

About the Author

Many people say that by looking at a person's dog, you can tell what the person is like. Well, the picture of me is my dog Louys, an English Bulldog. And yes, my English Bulldog and I have many common characteristics.

But what about my biography? It's pretty simple: I am guy who has spent oodles of time strapped to a chair debugging and taking apart code. In fact, I really enjoy this business we call software development. I have ever since I learned how to peek and poke my first bytes. I have written various books, including *Ajax and REST Recipes: A Problem-Solution Approach*, *Foundations of Object-Oriented Programming Using .NET 2.0 Patterns*, and *A Programmer's Introduction to Windows DNA*, all available from Apress.

These days I enjoy coding and experimenting with .NET, as it is a fascinating environment. .NET makes me feel like a kid opening a present on Christmas morning. You had an idea what the gift was, but you were not completely sure. And with .NET there is no relative giving you socks or a sweater. It's excitement all the way!

About the Technical Reviewer

■**JASON LEFEBVRE** is vice president and founding partner of Intensity Software, Inc. (http://www.intensitysoftware.com), which specializes in providing custom Microsoft .NET applications, IT consulting services, legacy system migration, and boxed software products to a rapidly growing set of clients. Jason has been using Microsoft .NET since its Alpha stages in early 2000 and uses Visual Studio and the Microsoft .NET Framework daily while creating solutions for Intensity Software's clients. Jason has been a participating author for a number of books and has written numerous articles about Microsoft .NET-related topics.

Acknowledgments

This book would not be complete without you, the reader. I came upon the idea for this book after I realized that I had a number of "canned" solutions to problems that readers of my articles, clients, or attendees of my conference sessions posed to me. For example, Andreas Penzold, a reader of my materials, worked with me to figure out what you can expect of `GetHashCode` and `Equals`.

Introduction

The title of this book may seem odd; you probably already know how to write code in .NET. But you can always benefit from knowing more. Coders, architects, and developers always strive to do their best, and if given the choice to do something correctly or incorrectly they will do it correctly. So why do we have so many bugs in our code? I could say, "Heck, it's all the managers making bonehead decisions." It would be a popular answer, but it would not be fair. We have bugs because humans and the communication between humans are imperfect.

The other major reason why code has bugs is that people do not have the time or energy to pour resources into specific problems. When you are working on an application, you are confronted with thousands of specific problems, and you have to assign a priority. This is where this book is aimed. I take the time to investigate the specific problems and figure out how to solve them. Your responsibility is to read the solutions and implement them as appropriate.

This is not a patterns book, even though I reference patterns. It is not a book meant to solve all problems, because like you I have to assign priority to the problems I want to solve. This book is the first of a series, and subsequent volumes will solve more problems. This book aims to look at a problem, feature, or fact and then figure out what that problem, feature, or fact implies. As a quick example .NET 2.0 introduced the `yield` keyword. Cool use of technology, but what does `yield` really imply? Is `yield` buggy? Is `yield` the future of all iterators? After reading this book you'll know all of `yield`'s implications and ramifications.

If you read this book and disagree with me, let me know why you disagree. Tell me what you think I did wrong. Sometimes I will correct you, but other times, we'll both learn something. Or if you want me to figure out a solution to a specific problem you are having, tell me. If I end up writing about our discussion, I will credit you and give you a free copy of my next book. Send your love or hate to christianhgross@gmail.com.

Source Code

The source code is available in the Source Code/Download section of the Apress website (http://www.apress.com). Additionally, you can visit http://www.devspace.com/codingdotnet to download the code.

CHAPTER 1

■■■

Testing Your Code

This book will introduce a series of techniques for how to write code in .NET. The best way to learn is to run a series of tests, and thus most of the examples in this book use a utility called NUnit[1] because I want to implement *test-driven development (TDD)*. In a nutshell the idea behind TDD is to architect, develop, and test your code at the same time. Additionally, it helps me write pieces of code that you can verify. In general development, the benefit of testing and developing code at the same time is that when your code is finished you know that it is tested enough to make you reasonably sure that stupid errors will not happen. The quality assurance department at your company will not complain about the lack of quality.

This chapter will take you through the steps for writing your own test routines. You'll learn about publicly available testing tools and their uses. Then you'll move on to topics such as how to define tests, why contexts are important, and how to implement mock objects.

Quick Notes About TDD

When implementing TDD, purists advise a top-down development approach in which the test is written before the code. However, due to the nature of the development environments that use IntelliSense, a developer will tend to write the code first, and then the test. When using IntelliSense, code is developed using a bottom-up approach, thus not adhering to the TDD purists' approach. It does not matter which approach you take.

What matters is the cycle: write some code and some tests or vice versa, and then run the tests. To keep TDD effective, those cycles might be a few minutes, a half hour, or (for a complex algorithm) a couple of hours. Your TDD cycle is not time-dependent, but feature-dependent. When I speak of features I don't mean high-level "create invoice"–type features. I mean features that are lower-level, like "initialized array." The key to TDD is to implement and test a small piece of functionality before moving on to the next functionality. When writing code using TDD, you will pick a feature to implement, which then allows another feature to be implemented, and so on. Eventually the application will be completely implemented with associated tests.

If you develop your code using TDD, you will experience the following benefits:

- Code and tests that are written simultaneously expose integration, data, and logic problems early.

- Code is broken down into smaller chunks, making it easier to maintain an overview of the contained logic.

---

1. http://www.nunit.org/

- Code that is tested has its logic verified, making an overall application stabler.

- You will rely less on a debugger because you can analyze a bug mentally, thus making it faster and simpler to fix a bug.

The benefits seem almost too good to be true. They do exist, however; to understand why, consider the opposite of TDD. Imagine if you wrote thousands of lines of code without any tests. When you finally do get around to writing the tests, how do you know which tests to write? Most likely because you used IntelliSense you will have written your code in a bottom-up fashion. And most likely the code that you best remember is the last bit of code, which happens to be the highest-level abstraction. Therefore you end up writing test code for the highest-level abstraction, which is the wrong thing to do. Your code will have bugs regardless of whether you use TDD. But by testing the highest level of abstraction, you are also testing every layer below that abstraction level. Simply put, with one test you are testing a complete source-code base. This is a recipe for disaster because you will be figuring out where the errors are, and most likely resorting to a debugger. At that level you can't analyze the bug mentally because there is too much code to remember. The only solution you have is to tediously debug and figure out what code you wrote and why it failed.

If you use TDD when you write your test, write your code, and test your code, the code is fresh in your mind. You are mentally alert and if something returns `true` when it should have returned `false`, and you can fix it easily because the number of permutations and combinations is small enough to figure out in your head. Having tested and implemented one functionality, your next step is to implement some other functionality. If the second functionality uses the already implemented functionality, then you don't need to waste brain cycles on guessing whether the implemented functionality works. You know the existing functionality works because it is already tested. That doesn't mean you ignore the already implemented functionality, because bugs can still pop up. What it means is that you do not need to care as much as you would otherwise, and you can concentrate on other issues.

Getting Started with TDD and NUnit

NUnit is both a framework and application; it is a framework that you use to write tests, and it is an application to run the tests that you wrote. NUnit is simple, and there is very little imposed overhead. What NUnit does not do is write the test for you. Thus the effectiveness of NUnit depends on you. If you write complete tests, then NUnit provides complete test results. Metaphorically speaking, NUnit is your hammer, and how you use the hammer is your responsibility. If you use your hammer to dig holes in the ground, then you are not going to be effective. However, if you know how to swing the hammer and position nails, then your hammer can be extremely effective.

Assuming you decided to download the NUnit distribution from `http://www.nunit.org/`, the expanded downloaded distribution file contains a number of subdirectories: `bin`, `doc`, and `samples`. The purpose of each subdirectory is explained here:

- `bin` contains the assemblies and applications that are needed to use NUnit.

- `doc` contains HTML files that provide the documentation on how to use NUnit as both an application and a framework. This book covers much of the information in the HTML files; refer to the NUnit documentation for specific details.

- `samples` contains a number of NUnit samples in different languages (VB.NET, C#, and Managed C++).

When you're using NUnit as a framework in your code, your tests use NUnit-specific classes and attributes. To be able to compile and run the tests you will need to set a reference to one or more NUnit assemblies. The references that you need are the assemblies in the `bin` directory. Looking in the `bin` directory, you will see dozens of assemblies. Using a brute-force approach you could reference all assemblies and your code would compile and run. However, a brute-force technique does not get you any closer to understanding NUnit.

For basic testing purposes you set a reference to the assembly `nunit.framework.dll`, which contains the base testing .NET attribute definitions, and assertion classes. You can use two programs to run your tests in your assemblies: `nunit-console.exe` and `nunit-gui.exe`. The difference between the programs is that `nunit-console.exe` is console-based, and `nunit-gui.exe` is GUI-based. If you intend to run a build server or you wish to automate your test, `nunit-console.exe` will serve you best. For immediate feedback and ease of retesting specific tests, `nunit-gui.exe` is your best choice.

In a test-code environment `nunit-gui.exe` is good choice, but a better choice is to use a development environment. I code with X-develop,[2] and its development environment has integrated NUnit tests. That allows me to run a collection or an individual test with a single click. Figure 1-1 shows the single-click technique.

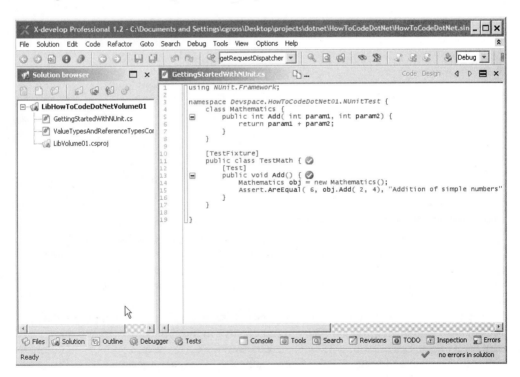

Figure 1-1. *Integration of NUnit with X-develop*

---

2. `http://www.omnicore.com/`

In X-develop, you'll see a graphical circular marker on the right side of each recognized test. The color of the marker indicates the state of the test. If the marker is a gray check mark, then the test has not been run. If the marker is a red letter *X*, then the test failed. A green check mark indicates that the test completed successfully.

Visual Studio .NET offers similar functionality. Though to use NUnit you have to install TestDriven.NET.[3] When TestDriven.NET is installed, you have similar capabilities to the ones X-develop provides, but a different look and feel. Figure 1-2 illustrates how to test the exact same source code as shown in Figure 1-1 using TestDriven.NET and Visual Studio.

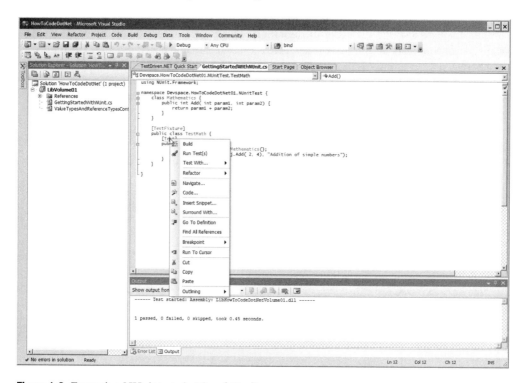

Figure 1-2. *Executing NUnit tests in Visual Studio*

To run a test in Visual Studio using TestDriven.NET, you move your mouse over the attribute `TestFixture`, or anywhere in a class that has the attribute `TestFixture`. Once you have moved the mouse to the proper location, do a context-sensitive click. From the menu that appears, click the item Run Test(s) to run the tests; the test results are generated in the Output window of Visual Studio.

Regardless of whether you use X-develop, Visual Studio .NET, or your own personal development environment, it is not necessary to run the tests in the context of a development environment; you can use the `nunit-gui.exe` and `nunit-console.exe` programs, as mentioned earlier. I've illustrated the IDEs here because you'll have a simpler time coding, compiling, and testing when you don't have to leave the comfort of the IDE.

---

3. `http://www.testdriven.net/`

One last item to note regarding writing tests and the location of the tests: If you look closely at Figures 1-1 and 1-2 you will see that the test code and the code to be tested are in the same file. When writing production tests, that is not the case. In a production setting the code to be tested and the tests are in two separate assemblies. You want separate assemblies because test code is debug code and you don't want to ship a final product that contains debug code. However, there is one notable exception: types declared with the `internal` attribute need to have the tests embedded in the assembly. When you have to combine tests and code in a single assembly, take advantage of conditional compilation, allowing debug builds to contain the tests and release builds to have the test code stripped out. Again, you don't want to ship production assemblies with embedded debug code.

■**Note** The examples in this book illustrate how to use NUnit, but Microsoft offers Visual Studio Team Systems, which has testing capabilities. The test details might be different, but the concepts are identical.

In summary, when getting started writing tests, keep the following points in mind:

- Implementing TDD results in a stabler and robuster application. If you think TDD takes time that you don't have, and that the TDD time is better spent coding, that must mean your code is perfect and bug-free. If this is what you are saying please tell me ahead of time if I ever have to look at your code, because I will want to jack up my consulting rates—I have been eying a Porsche for quite a while.

- Every program starts with a single line of code, and every test bed starts with a single test. The objective with TDD is to write some code and test code at the same time. By doing each a bit at a time, very quickly you will have a comprehensive test bed.

- Using NUnit and test-driven development is not about testing each method individually. Test-driven development is about testing scenarios, and defining what all the possible scenarios are. For reference, scenarios that fail are just as important as scenarios that succeed. As much as we would like to have shortcuts to develop test scripts using autogenerated code, it neither works nor helps the test.

- Autogenerated test code is good if you are testing mathematical algorithms or programming languages. It generates a large amount of test code that can be used as a check mark to indicate success or failure. Those thousands of test cases sound good from a talking-at-a-meeting perspective, but generally fail from an application-stability perspective. I would rather have three well-defined scenario tests than one hundred autogenerated tests that are not targeted.

- There is no best way to write tests. Essentially, tests need to provide coverage and be realistic. The best way to start writing tests is to pick a problem that the assembly or application attempts to solve. From there, determine the overall operation, define the correct parameters, and then test the generated outputs when the operation has been called.

Writing Tests Using Contexts and Results

When writing a test the objectives are to establish a context and verify the results that the context generates. Writing a test is not just about instantiating a type, calling a method, and ensuring that everything worked. If you think a test is about types with methods and the parameters necessary to call those methods, then you are missing the point of writing tests. When you write a large number of tests without considering the context, you are using brute force to verify the correctness of an implementation. Brute-force verification will test functionality and allow you to check-mark your code as being tested, but the question is, which functionality has been tested? Metaphorically speaking, brute-force testing is like making a baseball glove and testing how well the glove can catch a beach ball, a baseball, and a soccer ball. It might be able to catch all those ball types, but the test is pointless—it is a *baseball* glove, after all. Always consider the context.

Let's examine what the code in our applications represents. When we write code in our minds, the code is meant to execute in a certain context. The context could be to instantiate an invoice, create a sales total for the month, or what have you. Each context tends to be business-related. The disjoint between code and context happens in the creation of the lower-level classes. We become preoccupied with how classes instantiate other classes. When we try to figure out all of the permutations and combinations of how to instantiate a class, we become wrapped up in technical details. And with more classes we become more detailed about the technical ramifications and problems. We have lost sight of the actual problem; we are writing code that forces baseball gloves to catch beach balls. The same is true when the tests are written for the lower-level classes.

So why do we care so much about technical details? Because we are striving for completeness, but completeness involves too many permutations and combinations. What we should strive for is complete code for the context. If a context that we did not account for is created, the proper action is to generate an exception. So if somebody actually does decide to use a baseball glove to catch a beach ball, you can have an error appear: "Dude, this is a baseball glove, you know?" Generating a general exception does bother some programmers because it means writing incomplete code. Some developers might think that you are copping out of implementing some code and generating an exception to say "out of order." But an exception is not an "out of order" sign. An exception makes you write code that works for a context and only that context. Writing code for a context means you are focusing on creating baseball gloves to catch baseballs, and you are not getting distracted by the people who prefer to catch beach balls. Again, never lose sight of the context.

Switching from the theoretical to the practical, we'll now look at some code and then write some tests for it. The following is an example of a piece of source code that needs to be tested:

Source: /Volume01/LibVolume01/GettingStartedWithNUnit.cs

```
class Mathematics {
    public int Add( int param1, int param2) {
        return param1 + param2;
    }
}
```

The source code has implemented the functionality to add two integer-based numbers together. The class Mathematics has one method, Add, which has two parameters, param1 and param2. The method Add will add two numbers together and return the sum.

To test a class you need to create a class. When using NUnit to define a test class, the .NET attribute TestFixture is prefixed to the class identifier. Within a test class, tests are defined by prefixing the .NET attribute Test with a method. The standard test-method signature has no parameters and returns no values. When defining a test class and a test method, you must define both as public scope. Not using public scoping results in the NUnit test framework being unable to access the test class and method. A test class may have multiple tests and can be embedded in a namespace. What you name the class or method does not matter so long as the name is prefixed with the appropriate .NET attribute.

When you're wondering what test to write, write the test for the first thing that comes to mind. With Mathematics that would be the addition of two numbers, and the first test would be written as follows:

Source: /Volume01/LibVolume01/GettingStartedWithNUnit.cs

```
[TestFixture]
public class TestMath {
    [Test]
    public void TestAdd() {
        Mathematics obj = new Mathematics();
        Assert.AreEqual( 6, obj.Add( 2, 4), "Addition of simple numbers");
    }
}
```

In the test method TestAdd, the class Mathematics is instantiated and then the method Add is called. How you instantiate and call the code is important and must resemble the code you would write in an application. Again using the baseball glove metaphor, creating a test situation where a baseball is fired at 145 kilometers per hour at a glove is a good test of stressing a glove, but it's not realistic. Most likely a ball of that speed would be thrown by a pitcher, and hence the appropriate glove is a catcher's mitt.

The preceding test code is an example of using Mathematics in an application scenario, which is a context. The return value from the method Add is passed directly to the method Assert.AreEqual. The method Assert.AreEqual is used to verify that the result Add returns is correct.

The method Assert.AreEqual, and in particular the Assert class, play a very important role when writing tests. A test is a context of the code to be tested. When the code is being executed, there is no difference between the test bed and the production environment. The test bed needs to verify what was executed and does this using the verification class Assert. The production environment uses the same code and assumes what was executed produced a correct result. Tests verify that everything worked correctly, and Assert is used to perform the verification. For reference purposes, the class Assert has other methods that can be used to verify if a state is true or false, null or not null, and so on.

In the testing of Mathematics, the verification is the testing of the result generated by calling Add with the values of 2 and 4. The addition should return the result of 6 that is verified by the method Assert.AreEqual. If the verification fails, Assert will generate an exception and the test will be deemed to have failed. NUnit runs all tests regardless of whether they fail or succeed. A failed test is marked as such and will be displayed as failed at the end of the test run.

If your test is successful, you might write more tests, like adding 1 and 3 returning the result 4, or adding 10 and 20 returning the result 30. Yet writing these tests does not exercise the functionality of Add. It simply makes you feel good because you have written three tests and that took some time to write. The problem with the three tests is that they are exercising the same context.

You might think, "The method Add can only add two numbers, and there is no other context." However, the original context was too broadly defined. I should have said that the context is to add two numbers that are not so large. Another context would be to test two numbers that are very large.

The context of adding two numbers that are very large is the testing of an overflow situation. The method Add adds two int values, and int values on the .NET platform have a range of −2,147,483,648 to 2,147,483,647. So imagine that values 2,000,000,000 and 2,000,000,000 were added together; what would be result? We must expand the test class to include this second context.

```
[TestFixture]
public class TestMath {
    [Test]
    public void TestAdd() {
        Mathematics obj = new Mathematics();
        Assert.AreEqual( 6, obj.Add( 2, 4), "Addition of simple numbers");
    }
    [Test]
    public void TestAddLargeNUmbers() {
        Mathematics obj = new Mathematics();
        Assert.AreEqual( 4000000000, obj.Add( 2000000000, 2000000000),
            "Addition of large numbers");
    }
}
```

The added test is TestAddLargeNumbers, and again the method Assert.AreEqual is used. The numbers 2,000,000,000 and 2,000,000,000 are added together and tested to see if the return value is 4,000,000,000. We know that 4,000,000 will not be the result, but for illustration purposes we write the test as if it would work. Take a moment to look at the code again, and then look at the output. Notice something? The oddity is that the code could be executed, meaning that the code can be compiled without any errors. If you ignore the oddity for now and run the test, you'll get the following result:

```
NUnit.Framework.AssertionException: Addition of large numbers
    expected: <4000000000>
     but was: <-294967296>
    at NUnit.Framework.Assert.AreEqual(Decimal expected, ➥
Decimal actual, ➥
String message, Object[] args)
    at NUnit.Framework.Assert.AreEqual(Decimal expected, ➥
Decimal actual, String message)
```

```
    at Devspace.HowToCodeDotNet01.NUnitTest.TestMath.AddLargeNUmbers() ➡
in c:\Documents and Settings\cgross\Desktop\projects\HowToCodeDotNet\
Volume01\LibVolume01\GettingStartedWithNUnit.cs:line 20
```

We expected that the test would not work, but did we expect the result? I am not referring to the overflow (–294,967,296), because that was expected. What I am referring to is that `Assert.AreEqual` tested for 4,000,000,000. Add generates an overflow, and thus `Assert.AreEqual` should also generate an overflow because Add returns an `int`; thus the value 4,000,000,000 would be converted to –294,672,296. The generated text clearly shows that `Assert.AreEqual` is testing for the value of 4,000,000,000. Now alarm bells should be going off in your head. The limit of an `int` is approximately –2,000,000,000 to approximately 2,000,000,000. An `int` cannot reference a value of 4,000,000,000. Yet in `Assert.AreEqual` the test was against the number 4,000,000,000. What happened (and this is a hidden gotcha) is the autoconversion of the `obj.Add` method from an `int` to a `long`.

When the compiler encounters the number 4,000,000,000, it generates not an `int`, but a `long`. Thus when the compiler searches for an overloaded `AreEqual` method, it finds not the `int` version, but the `long` version because the number 4,000,000,000 is a `long`. When the comparison was executed the `obj.Add` value was converted and we were misled.

Getting back to the test method, the test failed and that is good. But the test failed in an unpredictable fashion that we do not want. We need to convert the test so that the Add method handles the overflow situation gracefully. The Add method needs to verify its data so it will not overflow. The overflow situation is special— how do you verify that the addition of two numbers will result in an overflow? Do you subtract one number from the max value before overflow and see if the other number is less than the subtracted result? And if you find that an overflow situation will occur, do you return –1 or 0 as a value? In the context of the method Add, returning –1 or 0 is useless because –1 and 0 are valid values.

The overflow problem is an example of a failing context, and it is as important as testing a successful context. Failing contexts illustrate that bad data will be marked as bad and that the program will tell you so. When you have a failing context your code must beep very loudly to tell the caller that something went wrong. Not testing failing contexts can have dire consequences. Imagine being Bill Gates and depositing $2 billion in an account that has $2 billion. Using the Add method that we currently have, it would seem that Bill Gates owes the bank $29 million. Bill Gates would not be a happy camper, whereas the bank might be thrilled.

NUnit has the ability to test failing contexts using the attribute `ExpectedException`. The attribute `ExpectedException` expects that for a failing context the tested code will generate an exception. The current implementation Add adds two numbers and generates an overflow, but no exceptions are raised. Had the current implementation of Add been tested with the `ExpectedException` attribute, the test would have failed because no exception was generated. An exception can be generated for an overflow situation by using the `checked` keyword in the implementation of Add. The rewritten code and associated test code is as follows (with modified pieces appearing in boldface):

```
class Mathematics {
    public int Add( int param1, int param2) {
        checked {
            return param1 + param2;
        }
    }
}
```

```
}

[TestFixture]
public class TestMath {
    [Test]
    public void TestAdd() {
        Mathematics obj = new Mathematics();
        Assert.AreEqual( 6, obj.Add( 2, 4), "Addition of simple numbers");
    }
    [Test]
    [ExpectedException( typeof( System.OverflowException))]
    public void TestAddLargeNumbers() {
        Mathematics obj = new Mathematics();
        obj.Add( 2000000000, 2000000000);
    }
}
```

In the implementation of the method Mathematics.Add, the checked keyword is a block that encapsulates the code that might generate an overflow situation. If an overflow has occurred, then the exception OverflowException is thrown. In the test TestAddLargeNumbers, an overflow exception expectation is created by using the NUnit attribute ExpectedException with the exception that is to be thrown. The ExpectedException and associated test is successful if the exception OverflowException is thrown. If no exception is thrown then the test is deemed to have failed.

This process of finding contexts and testing the result is how you write your tests. Notice how everything is started with one test and then incrementally built up to include more contexts. A test bed is built incrementally with one test at a time. Don't make the mistake of trying to create all tests at once. That results in the first set of tests being well-written, and the last set of tests being borderline useful. The problem with writing tests all at once is that often writing tests is tedious, and boredom causes attention to wane, thus causing the tests to suffer.

When writing tests, remember the following points:

- For each test define a context and the result associated with that context. As a rule, each context will have one to two tests. You would write two or more tests if you want to cross-verify a context. The problem is that sometimes one test for a context happens to give the correct result, whereas having a second and perhaps a third test provides assurance that the code does actually work as expected. The point is not to create an exhaustive battery of tests for one context, because they all test a single context.

- Each test has two parts: execution in a context, and verification of the state that results from the context.

- The difficult part of defining a context is being specific enough; a general context will miss tests. It is difficult to find the various contexts because that requires a good understanding of the code you are testing.

- If two contexts generate identical results, then you may have a bug. The problem is that two contexts identify two different operating conditions, and generating the same result may indicate missing functionality or improperly implemented functionality.

- When something fails, let it fail with an exception. Don't expect the consumer of your component to call another method to check if the results were generated properly.

- If a test fails, don't change the context of the test when fixing the source code. Changing the context is the same as writing multiple tests for the same context. Most likely the context that you "fixed" still exists and is a bug waiting to happen.

- If the context does not generate any return data, you need to use a mock object (discussed later in this chapter).

- When defining a context and a test result, don't just verify a simple result like "True" to indicate that an operation worked. A simple result does not indicate validity of the context. This type of situation often results in multiple contexts generating the same results, which indicates a poor test bed.

Writing Tests for Code Pieces That Have No Tests or Few Tests

Inheriting code from another developer is not an enjoyable experience, especially if you are required to fix the bugs in the inherited code. There is no fun in cleaning up a mess if you were not the one that created it. When confronted with sloppy code, you know that any tests you write will find the bugs and that you will need to fix the bugs. Some people might look on this as a challenge. Others will think that the code is more hassle than it's worth. Most programmers will consider this an extremely big hassle if the code is in production and works most of the time. Your tests and your bug-finding abilities may cause the code to cease working, and you'll be labeled as the person who broke a working application.

This solution illustrates how to write tests for code pieces that do not have tests, and not have the tests explode in your face. (The tests *could* still explode in your face, but at least you will have an audit trail indicating that it was not your fault.) The idea behind this solution is to go through the steps that you would when trying to untangle a piece of code. The example presented is a two-class solution in which one class calls another class. Combined, the two classes represent a two-tier programming approach. The example classes are two mathematical operators. Think about the mathematical operation exponentiation; it is nothing more than the same number multiplied by itself a number of times. In algorithmic terms an exponentiation operator could be implemented by using a multiplication operator. Following is the source that implements the exponentiation and multiplication operators.

Source: /Volume01/LibVolume01/TestingLargeCodePieces.cs

```
class Mathematics {
    public int Multiply( int param1, int param2) {
        checked {
            return param1 * param2;
        }
    }
}
```

```
class HigherMath {
    public int Power( int number, int power) {
        Mathematics cls = new Mathematics();
        int result = 0;

        for( int c1 = 0; c1 < power; c1 ++) {
            result += cls.Multiply( number, number);
        }
        return result;
    }
}
```

In the example source code there are two classes: Mathematics and HigherMath. Mathematics exposes a method Multiply that is used to multiply two numbers together. Notice how the checked keyword checks for an overflow condition. The class HigherMath has a method called Power that is used to calculate the mathematical exponentiation of a number. The method HigherMath.Power uses the operator Multiply in its calculation.

The example mathematical classes represent (in simplified form) the code that is a mess, and we need to figure out what is going on. Notice how one class calls the other, the arbitrary splitting of functionality of the two classes, and odd naming that makes us believe that this is real-live spaghetti code. The first step is to figure out what test to write. You could write a test for the class Mathematics or the class HigherMath. I am going to start with HigherMath because in most cases where you have unknown code you will test what you are first exposed to. The first test, being our first context, will test the Power method:

Source: /Volume01/LibVolume01/TestingLargeCodePieces.cs

```
[TestFixture]
public class TestClass {
    [Test]
    public void TestPower() {
        HigherMath cls = new HigherMath();
        Assert.AreEqual( 27, cls.Power( 3, 3));
    }
}
```

Running the test, we calculate 3 to the power of 3, which returns the result of 27; the context has been tested and all is OK. However, we need to find more contexts and implement more tests.

I mentioned earlier that when you test untested code, the first reaction is to test the higher-level code. And testing the higher-level code without testing the lower-level code is the wrong thing to do because you end up testing all of the code. Testing all of the code makes no sense because it will confuse more than help. However, that's true only if you are testing code that you wrote. But when you are testing code that someone else wrote, it is the only way to figure out what is going on—you don't know what code works or does not work until you test the higher level. If your test code fails because of code you have not tested directly, then the next set of tests will be for the code that failed. The idea is to go for the low-hanging fruit first and get those bugs out of the way. Then when you go for the very hard bugs you will have isolated the untested code and reduced the combinations and permutations of where the error could lie.

In this example finding more contexts is absolutely vital because the test that ran successfully is in fact wrong. You might think the test was successful because 3 to the power of 3 is 27. But the code is implemented in such a way that it just happens to calculate the right value for 3 to the power of 3. Had I by chance chosen 4 to the power of 6, the test would have failed. This is what can happen when you are confronted with unknown buggy code—you choose a set of conditions that happens to work, but in fact are buggy. Following are the problems of the current test class:

- HigherMath has more than one context; for example, any number to the power of 0 is 1, 0 to the power of anything is 0, and any number to the power of 1 is the number itself.

- Even though it would seem that the bug in the code would have been found with multiple tests of one context, it is very important to define more contexts. A bug that happens to work in one context will be revealed as a bug in another context. The likelihood that you will encounter a situation in which all context tests can succeed with a buggy implementation is remote.

- Even if the code has tests, when you encounter a piece of code for the first time, do not assume that either the code or the tests are correct or maintained. You need to look at the code and the associated tests.

To identify more contexts, you must look beyond the parameters of a single method. You need to identify the individual layers and what those layers do. How you find those layers depends on you. It can be by code inspection, by looking at the assemblies, or by writing a test that finds failures (resulting in more tests). When the layers are clearly defined, you write or organize your tests for each layer. You want to identify the layers so that your tests are organized and result in a clear testing strategy. Remember that you are facing code that you don't know about and that has no clear testing strategy.

In your testing strategy, the lowest layer is the first test set, the next lowest layer is the second test set, and so on until all layers have been tested. Applying the logic to our mathematical example, the testing layers would appear similar to those in Figure 1-3.

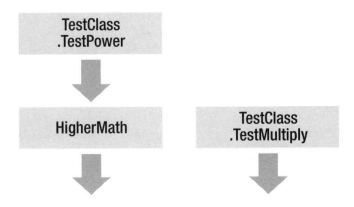

Figure 1-3. *Layered testing architecture*

In Figure 1-3 the base layer is Mathematics, and the method TestMultiply is used to test Mathematics. Logically speaking, if TestMultiply is successful, then Mathematics is considered correct. Assuming that Mathematics is correct, then anything that calls Mathematics and generates errors means that the caller of Mathematics is buggy. The class HigherMath calls Mathematics, resulting in the method TestPower testing HigherMath. If TestPower fails, then the bug lies in HigherMath, and not Mathematics, since the first set of tests gave Mathematics a passing grade.

The logic of starting at the bottom and working our way up the layers works so long as the tests for Mathematics are complete. If the tests are not complete, then a bug found at a higher layer could be because of a context that was not tested in a lower layer. The more contexts you define, the more tests you will create, and the less likely that your lower layer is responsible for a bug at a higher layer. I am talking quite a bit about layers, but the discussion could just as easily be about modules. What is essential is the granularization of the code and the associated tests. Granular code is modular code, which is easier to control and maintain.

Sometimes when writing granular code, you want to test a piece of code on its own. However, most pieces of code call other pieces of code, and if the other pieces of code are not tested or even executable, your tests are useless as the problem may not be in your code. To be able to test your granular code in isolation, you must create a piece of code that looks, feels, and behaves like the real code but is not the real code. You are creating pretend code.

When testing using Unit testing terminology, that pretend code is called a *fake object*[4] or *fake method*. The idea behind a fake object or method is to insert a layer that can be used to verify and control the data that is being passed around. The concepts are applied to the example math classes and illustrated in Figure 1-4.

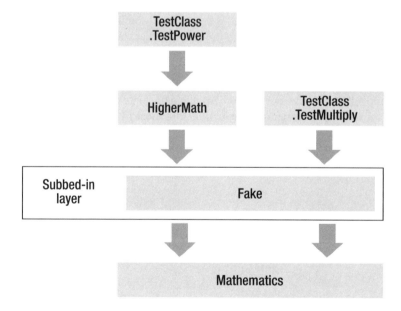

Figure 1-4. *Layered approach with fake object*

---

4.   Michael C. Feathers, *Working Effectively with Legacy Code* (Upper Saddle River, NJ: Pearson Education, 2004), p. 21.

In Figure 1-4 the class HigherMath (representing the second layer) calls the fake object, which calls Mathematics (representing the first layer). The second layer calls the first layer through the fake object, but the second layer has no idea what is happening. Likewise, the first layer is being called by the fake object instead of the second layer and does not. The fake object has become a wedge between HigherMath and Mathematics. When properly implemented, the fake object separates two layers into distinct modular pieces of functionality. From a legacy-code perspective this is fantastic because you have managed to separate two code bases without affecting the functionality. In effect you have created check points, making it possible for you to figure out what each piece of code is doing.

What is important about the fake object is that HigherMath cannot know that it is calling the fake object. If we were using interfaces, then the fake object would be implementing the Proxy pattern. Fake objects can also implement mock objects, which we will get to shortly. Rewriting the original source code to use fake objects, we get the following results:

```
namespace Original {
    class Mathematics {
        public int Multiply(int param1, int param2) {
            checked {
                return param1 * param2;
            }
        }
    }
}
class Mathematics {
    private void LogMultiply(int result, int param1, int param2) {
        System.Console.WriteLine("Result (" + result +
            ") from multiplying (" + param1 + ") and (" + param2 + ")");
    }
    public int Multiply(int param1, int param2) {
        Original.Mathematics cls = new Original.Mathematics();
        int result = cls.Multiply(param1, param2);
        LogMultiply(result, param1, param2);
        return result;
    }
}

class HigherMath {
    public int Power(int number, int power) {
        Mathematics cls = new Mathematics();
        int result = 0;

        for (int c1 = 0; c1 < power; c1 ++) {
            result += cls.Multiply(number, number);
        }
        return result;
    }
}
[TestFixture]
```

```
public class TestClass {
    private Mathematics _cls;

    [TestFixtureSetUp]
    public void Initialize() {
        _cls = new Mathematics();
    }
    [Test]
    public void TestMultiply() {
        Assert.AreEqual( 4, _cls.Multiply( 2, 2));
        Assert.AreEqual( 0, _cls.Multiply( 10, 0));
    }
    [Test]
    [ExpectedException( typeof( System.OverflowException))]
    public void TestOverflow() {
        _cls.Multiply( 2000000000, 10);
    }
    [Test]
    public void TestPower() {
        HigherMath cls = new HigherMath();
        Assert.AreEqual(27, cls.Power( 3, 3));
        Assert.AreEqual( 1, cls.Power( 34, 0));
        Assert.AreEqual( 0, cls.Power( 0, 6));
        Assert.AreEqual( 1, cls.Power( 1, 3));
        Assert.AreEqual( 5, cls.Power( 5, 1));
    }
}
```

Notice that the HigherMath class was not modified and is a prerequisite when implementing a fake object. You don't want the higher layers to know that you added a layer.

■**Note** Looking at how the fake object is implemented, you may think that the solution is a bad one. However, it was the only other possibility because the code used hard-coded classes, which in itself is a bad programming habit. Had the code been properly written, I would have used interfaces and the Proxy pattern. But, if the code had been properly written, you probably would not need to read this solution because the properly written code would be modular and have all the tests to make the layer complete.

New to the rewritten code is the attribute TestFixtureSetUp, which provides a way of initializing data before running the tests. This is useful when tests operate on stateful objects. Stateful objects require some calls to be made before tests can be executed (for instance, opening a database connection). For reference purposes, Mathematics and HigherMath are stateless, but to simplify the code Mathematics is instantiated in the setup function instead of every time a test is run. The attribute TestFixtureTearDown is called after all tests have been executed and destroys any data members that have been initialized. In the case of the example, it is unnecessary to destroy any data or close any resources because the garbage collector will take care of our objects automatically and there are no resources to close.

In TestClass the bolded code represents the added tests for the additional contexts used to test Mathematics. There are three contexts: simple number, overflow, and multiplication by 0. The method TestPower has been extended to include other contexts related to choosing a number. For example, any number to the power of 0 is 1, 0 to the power of any number is 0, 1 to the power of any number is 1, and any number to the power of 1 is that "any" number. From a coding perspective, the tests are considered complete, or as complete as a developer can think. All that remains is to run the tests.

When running the tests, the first generated failure is the line cls.Power(34, 0), and the associated output is as follows:

```
Result (9) from multiplying (3) and (3)
Result (9) from multiplying (3) and (3)
Result (9) from multiplying (3) and (3)
NUnit.Framework.AssertionException:
    expected: <1>
    but was: <0>
   at NUnit.Framework.Assert.AreEqual(Int32 expected, Int32 actual, ➥
String message, Object[] args)
   at NUnit.Framework.Assert.AreEqual(Int32 expected, Int32 actual)
   at Devspace.HowToCodeDotNet01.TestingCodeThatIsAMess.PickedApart.TestClass.➥
TestPower() in c:\Documents and Settings\cgross\Desktop\projects\➥
HowToCodeDotNet➥
\Volume01\LibVolume01\TestingCodeThatIsAMess.cs:line 79
```

The first three lines represent the output generated by the fake object. The output was added to see how the multiply functionality is called, and the response that is returned. By having the fake object generate output, we have a quick way to see what data is transferred between the two layers. And if there is a problem we can quickly see if the fault is the caller or the called layer. In the example, we can see if the fault lies at the Mathematics or HigherMath layer.

After three lines of output is an NUnit failure indicating that an Assert.AreEqual failed. From the perspective of NUnit, the method Power caused the failure. But we don't know if the origin of the failure is correct. We know that in the other tests TestMultiply and TestOverflow did not fail, thus hinting at the bug in Power. To quickly get an idea of what is at fault, we look at the output generated by the fake object. The calculation of 3 times 3 is 9, indicating that all seems to be working. But look closely at the generated output; 3 times 3 is called three times. If Power were working correctly, the first multiplication is 3 times 3, and the second calculation is 9 times 3, yielding 27. The Power method is multiplying 3 and 3 three times and adding the total of the three multiplications, which is 27. Ironically, it happens to be the correct answer.[5] What we should have expected is the following trace:

```
Result (9) from multiplying (3) and (3)
Result (27) from multiplying (9) and (3)
```

---

5. This actually happened to me. To demonstrate a calculation I wrote a single test and just happened to choose 3 to the power of 3, and the test worked. The fact that I hit a fluke that worked made me believe everything was OK. Too bad I did not play the lottery that day.

By inspecting the generated output of the fake output, you can verify the correctness of a contract (by verifying the correctness of the data being sent in the contract). In general, by looking at the data that is passed between layers you can very quickly verify if bad data is being sent, or if good data is being processed incorrectly.

Now we return to my claim that one context is not enough; you now have proof. In the first assertion (or context) of the method TestPower, 3 to the power 3 returned the correct result, but the second assertion failed. From the generated output and the failed second context you know that you need to fix the class HigherMath, as shown here:

```
class HigherMath {
    public int Power(int number, int power) {
        Mathematics cls = new Mathematics();
        int result = 1;

        for (int c1 = 1; c1 <= power; c1 ++) {
            result = cls.Multiply(result, number);
        }
        return result;
    }
}
```

The solution is almost identical to the buggy version, with a few items tweaked. When we rerun all of the tests there are no failures, indicating everything is OK. The trace logs generated by the fake object support our impression that everything was correct, letting us be comfortable in the fact that our code is now bug-free.

This finished class with tests illustrates that we have understood our code, partitioned it the best we could, and we're ready to make changes. Of course, this does not mean that the code is properly partitioned or uses the correct naming conventions. The correctness of the algorithms is part of the development cycle. This solution only provides a means to figure out what the algorithms are doing and if they are performing their calculations properly.

When writing tests in the context of larger code bases, remember the following points:

- Tests are layer-based or modular, and complete tests of one layer or module indicate the correctness of that layer or module.

- Writing complete tests for a layer or module is pipe dream, as more often than not you will forget some contexts.

- Fake objects or methods make it possible to insert a wedge between two layers or modules, allowing the fake object or method to trace the data being sent and received. Tracing the data makes it possible to understand what data is being transferred and thus recognize the problems or additional contexts used to test lower layers.

- You can use the trace log to implement mock objects. When presented with a certain data set, the mock objects would respond with the results generated in the trace log.

- Layers or modules are best implemented using interfaces and the Proxy pattern.

Writing Tests for Code Pieces That Don't Give Information Back

You already know about the concept of a fake object, which acts as a wedge layer between two other layers. Fakes are not limited to objects; there are also fake methods. When a consumer calls a fake method, the fake method calls the actual method. The caller of the fake method has no idea that the method being called delegates to another method. In this solution you will learn about *mock objects*, which are fake objects with a given purpose. In a nutshell mock objects are canned types that look, feel, and behave like the type they are supposed to be. Fake objects do not need to look, feel, or behave like the type they are supposed to be. In the previous section the fake object was used as a pass-through logging-type object.

The difference between the real object and the mock object is that the mock object contains canned functionality. From the perspective of the mock object's caller, there is no difference between real and mock. For a given context the answers the mock object receives are completely identical to the answers the real object receives. Using the calculator as an example, a real object would add, subtract, multiply, or divide numbers. A mock implementation would match conditions with a precalculated answer. If the client sends a 1 and a 2 and expects a multiplication, then the mock object will look for a test case and multiply and the numbers 1 and 2. Mock objects are in their truest nature garbage-in, garbage-out types. Mock objects cannot process information and are giant lookup tables.

Figure 1-5 is a visual illustration of the data flow for the aforementioned calculation.

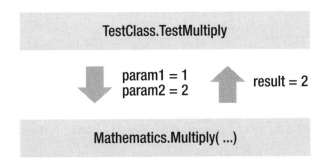

Figure 1-5. *Data flow for Mathematics.Multiply*

In Figure 1-5 the method `TestClass.TestMultiply` calls `Mathematics.Multiply` and passes two parameters: `param1` and `param2`. The method `Mathematics.Multiply` processes the two parameters' associated values. `Mathematics.Multiply` returns the result of multiplying the two parameters. Figure 1-5 illustrates that there is a data flow in and data flow out. The data flow out need not be an explicit return value, but could be the modified state of the class instance `Mathematics`. What is important is that by calling or assigning a particular method or property there is a change of state that the caller can quantify.

The calculation example shows how a mock object functions and how to manipulate the data flow. But why does the calculation need a mock object in the first place? The following source code, which generates an output to the console, shows where you need a mock object.

Source: /Volume01/LibVolume01/MockObjects.cs

```
class OutputGenerator {
    public static void WriteIt( string buffer) {
        Console.WriteLine( buffer);
    }
}

class DoTranslation {
    public void Translate( string word) {
        if( word == "hello") {
            OutputGenerator.WriteIt( "hallo");
        }
    }
}

[TestFixture]
public class Tests {
    [Test]
    public void TestTranslation() {
        DoTranslation cls = new DoTranslation();
        cls.Translate( "hello");
        cls.Translate( "goodbye");
    }
}
```

In the example, Tests has a method TestTranslation. The method TestTranslation instantiates the class DoTranslation, and calls the method Translate twice. In the implementation of DoTranslation.Translate, a decision of how to translate the word is made, followed by a method call to OutputGenerator.WriteIt. Notice the following problems in the code:

- There is no returning data flow that the test functions can use to verify whether a translation was successful.

- The tests seem similar, but they represent two different contexts (can translate word and cannot translate word). The tests are not in separate tests, where one expects success and the other expects failure.

- How does the caller of DoTranslation.Translate know whether the method was successful?

Our challenge is to figure out how to verify whether a translation was successful for a given context. The failure of not giving any feedback lies partially in the definition of the Translate method declaration. The source code reveals that the method Translate does not return anything, and a true or false value could indicate whether something is translated. By changing Translate to return a Boolean value, the following code results:

```
class DoTranslation {
    public bool Translate(string word) {
        if (word == "hello") {
```

```
            OutputGenerator.WriteIt("hallo");
            return true;
        }
        else {
            return false;
        }
    }
}

[TestFixture]
public class Tests {
    [Test]
    public void TestTranslation() {
        DoTranslation cls = new DoTranslation();
        Assert.IsTrue( cls.Translate("hello"));
        Assert.IsFalse( cls.Translate("goodbye"));
    }
}
```

In the modified sources the implementation of the method Translate returns a true value if it performed a translation and false if it did not. A cynic could say the true or false does not actually give us any feedback as to the correctness of the translation. The true or false value has indicated only that a translation has taken place, but there is no way to prove that it was the correct translation. It's like saying, "Yes, I understood what that foreigner said, but I have no idea what it means." This is an important aspect of writing tests: when verifying the truth of an assertion, make sure that your test can verify the result. Don't ever rely on status codes or success and failure flags, as they can contain errors themselves. Although we might have improved the testability of the class slightly, we did not solve the core problem, which was to check if a translation occurred properly.

The core of the translation problem is that the methods do not return the resulting translation to the caller. Adding functionality to return a value for testing purposes does not make sense, as the situation of not returning data is common. A situation in which there is no return data happens very often when you are writing database applications; you create SQL that performs some type of action, and the program cannot know if the SQL worked properly because that would require opening an explicit database connection and verifying that the modifications happened. You can do this, but it requires more work then you may have anticipated.

The solution is a mock object that captures the result of the translation, giving the test a chance to verify that the translation is in indeed correct. The code that will be mocked is OutputGenerator because it called by DoTranslation.Translate and is a lower-level class. Mock objects are always lower-level classes, except when recursion is involved. The recursion exception will be discussed at the end of this section.

A mock object, like a fake object, can be created manually or by using dynamic proxy generators like the library Nmock,[6] or DotNetMock[7] objects. For simplicity I'll use the Nmock library for illustration; it operates almost identically to DotNetMock.

---

6. http://nmock.org/
7. http://dotnetmock.sourceforge.net/

Both Nmock and DotNetMock call objects and methods based on virtual methods. Consider the following modified Output class.

```
public class OutputToBeMocked {
    public virtual void Message( string message) {
        Console.WriteLine( "Message (" + message + ")");
    }
}
```

The class OutputToBeMocked has a method Message that has the virtual keyword added. The mock libraries generate proxies and wrappers using dynamic intermediate language (IL) and generate classes that override methods. Thus, to be able to subclass an existing type, the method must be virtual; otherwise, the override does not work. Following is an example of how the source code for mocking the class OutputToBeMocked would look:

```
[TestFixture]
public class NMockFixture {
    [Test]
    public void SimpleTest() {
        NMock.Mock mock = new NMock.DynamicMock( typeof( OutputToBeMocked));
        mock.Expect( "Message", new NMock.Constraints.IsEqual( "message"));

        ((OutputToBeMocked)mock.MockInstance).Message( "message");
    }
}
```

The method SimpleTest is marked to be tested, and contained within the method is the code that creates a dynamic mock object. The class DynamicMock accepts as a single parameter that will have a generated mock object. The returned class instance is converted into the type Mock, which references a type-identical mock object. In the preceding example, the instance calls the method of the mocked object. Dynamically generated mock objects are useful if you are testing against interfaces. With a dynamically generated interface you don't need to provide a default implementation.

If you don't want to use an autogenerated mock object, then you can create a mock object by converting a fake object. The following source code illustrates how to convert a fake object into a mock object for the translation-code example:

```
class OutputGenerator {
    static public string CompareValue;

    public static void WriteIt( string buffer) {
        if( CompareValue != buffer) {
            throw new Exception( "Does Not Match");
        }
        Original.OutputGenerator.WriteIt( buffer);
    }
}
class DoTranslation {
    public bool Translate( string word) {
```

```
        if( word == "hello") {
            OutputGenerator.WriteIt( "hallo");
            return true;
        }
        else {
            return false;
        }
    }
}
[TestFixture]
public class Tests {
    [Test]
    public void TestTranslation() {
        OutputGenerator.CompareValue = "hallo";
        DoTranslation cls = new DoTranslation();
        Assert.IsTrue(cls.Translate("hello"));
        Assert.IsFalse(cls.Translate("goodbye"));
    }
}
```

In the source code the class OutputGenerator has been converted into a fake object, and calling the fake object calls the real object (Original.OutputGenerator.WriteIt). In the example the boldface code illustrates how it is possible to test the generated output. The fake object has a public data member CompareValue. When the method WriteIt is called, the parameter buffer is compared to CompareValue. If the values are not identical, then the translation did not work properly.

What makes the mock object work in this context is the fact that the test knows what data to send and what data to expect. The data to expect is assigned in the test TestTranslation by assigning the static data member CompareValue. Mock objects let you isolate the layer to be tested by controlling what is fed to the layer and what is passed on to the lower layer.

The preceding example is relatively simple because the test routines can get direct access to lower-level layers called by DoTranslation. It is not always possible to control which types are instantiated, as sometimes the instantiation of the type to be mocked is embedded in a type. Consider the following source code, which is very difficult to mock.

```
class Mathematics {
    private void LogMultiply(int result, int param1, int param2) {
        System.Console.WriteLine("Result (" + result +
            ") from multiplying (" + param1 + ") and (" + param2 + ")");
    }
    public int Multiply(int param1, int param2) {
        Original.Mathematics cls = new Original.Mathematics();
        int result = cls.Multiply(param1, param2);
        LogMultiply(result, param1, param2);
        return result;
    }
}
```

```
class HigherMath {
    public int Power(int number, int power) {
        Mathematics cls = new Mathematics();
        int result = 1;

        for (int c1 = 1; c1 <= power; c1 ++) {
            result = cls.Multiply(result, number);
        }
        return result;
    }
}
```

In the example source code a fake object has been created, but the fake object cannot be mocked because the test cannot isolate the class HigherMath to control the input data and the data that is passed to the lower layer. That's because the lower layer, as represented by the class Mathematics, is instantiated in HigherMath. A test cannot validate how Mathematics is being used because HigherMath is keeping the instance of Mathematics all to itself.

One solution would be to hack in a static variable like in DoTranslation. The problem with a static variable is that if the test involved multiple threads or multiple states, a consistent state cannot be ensured. A better solution would be to declare Mathematics as an interface and instantiate an instance using a factory. Another alternative is to pass in the Mathematics instance, as illustrated by the following source code:

```
class HigherMath {
    Mathematics _math;
    public HigherMath( Mathematics math) {
        _math = math;
    }
    public int Power(int number, int power) {
        int result = 1;

        for (int c1 = 1; c1 <= power; c1 ++) {
            result = _math.Multiply(result, number);
        }
        return result;
    }
}
```

In the modified source code HigherMath has a constructor that accepts a Mathematics instance as a single parameter. The Mathematics instance is assigned to the data member _math, which method Power then references. The use of the constructor or a method to associate one instance with another is a preferred approach because it makes sure that the class hierarchy contains no hidden dependencies. The exception to this rule is if the instance is an interface and a factory is used to instantiate the instance. In that case the "hidden" dependency is not hidden because the factory hides the instantiation of the type.

To understand why hidden dependencies are bad, imagine using Mathematics in two scenarios. The first is the production scenario, and the second is the mock-object scenario.

When Mathematics is instantiated in a production scenario it needs a database configuration. HigherMath provides the database-configuration information through the use of a configuration file that only HigherMath knows about. In the mock-object scenario, Mathematics is now a mock object and HigherMath is being executed in the context of NUnit. The first problem that HigherMath is going to run into is figuring out how to get the configuration information for the database connection. Because that configuration information was hidden in the implementation of HigherMath, the test script has no idea that it needs to provide such information. Hence HigherMath fails if tested. Imagine that somewhere somehow this configuration information magically appears; the Mathematics mock object has no idea what to do with the configuration information since the mock object is providing a mocked execution context. In a nutshell, by creating hidden dependencies you are digging your grave.

Earlier in this chapter I mentioned that situations involving incursion also require the use of a mock. The following piece of source code illustrates that scenario:

```
class A {
    B _reference;
}
class B {
    A _reference;
}
```

In the preceding example there are two classes: A and B. Class A has a data member that references B, and B has a data member that references A. For you to test A, B has to be considered tested and correct. But to consider B tested and correct, A has to be tested and correct. You are caught in a recursive loop because neither A nor B can be tested since they depend on each other.

The solution to testing A or B is to create a mock object for each. So if you are testing A, then B is a mock object. And if you are testing B, then A is a mock object. By using mock objects you are enforcing a contract that A and B must support.

You may think you would never write code that creates reverse dependencies. But consider the XML Document Object Model (DOM). In the XML DOM there are parents and children. The parents reference the children, and vice versa. In that case it is even worse because to test an XML element for correctness you need to mock the XML element. Another example is when callbacks are involved.

When writing tests that cannot evaluate the correctness of an object, remember the following:

- Mock objects are fake objects, but fake objects need not be mock objects.

- Mock objects are necessary when you need to isolate a layer by controlling what data is fed to the layer and what data is generated by the layer.

- Mock objects are necessary when recursive references are generated.

- Interfaces and factories between layers make it simpler to implement mock objects using the Proxy pattern.

Verifying the Correctness of an Object Instance Without Having Access

There is a contradiction between object-oriented programming (OOP) and test-driven development (TDD). The contradiction is that OOP does not expose the internal state of the class, but to verify that everything is working correctly you do need access to some data members. This goes back to the earlier point that having a method return a status flag of success or failure does not cut it; you want the test method to be able to verify an object state's correctness or lack of correctness. Consider the following code:

Source: /Volume01/LibVolume01/VerifyingTheCorrectness.cs

```
class OrderManager {
    public bool GenerateOrder( string value) {
        return true;
    }
}
[TestFixture]
public class Tests {
    [Test]
    public void TestMethod() {
        Order cls = new Order();
        Assert.IsTrue( cls.GenerateOrder( "tires"));
    }
}
```

In the preceding example the class OrderManager has a single method GenerateOrder that accepts a string buffer as a parameter. The string buffer represents the item to order. If an order was added, a Boolean true value is returned. What makes this case unique is that OrderManager will not call a lower layer and all of the functionality is contained within the OrderManager layer. With no lower layers, to verify the data the mock-object solution cannot apply, and you must use a different solution.

One solution is to rewrite GenerateOrder to return a piece of state, and in particular the generated order. Following is the rewritten code (the bolded elements are new code pieces):

```
class Order { }

class OrderManager {
    public Order GenerateOrder(string value) {
        return null;
    }

}
[TestFixture]
public class Tests {
    [Test]
    public void TestMethod() {
        OrderManager cls = new OrderManager();
```

```
        Order order = cls.GenerateOrder( "tires");
        // Verify the state of Order
    }
}
```

The method `GenerateOrder` does not return a Boolean value, but returns an instance of `Order`. The `OrderManager` might manage the `Order` internally, but a reference is returned to the caller as evidence of an order. With an `Order` instance at hand the test can verify the correctness of processing an order.

Returning an `Order` instance exposes an object's internal state. You might consider returning an order. But let's say that both the order and the total number of orders being processed are returned. The total number of orders is internal state information that the client does not need to know about. But for test-verification purposes we do need to know if the total number of orders has increased. However, returning the total number of orders is a solution for the test only; otherwise that information is not needed. Another design pattern–oriented solution is to use the Visitor pattern.

The purpose of the Visitor pattern is to enable an external object to view a class's internal state without accessing the internal state. The Visitor pattern transfers the state that defines the object's state into another structure that can be manipulated by an external piece of code. For the purposes of testing the correctness of an object instance, you need only to verify the state of the structure. The Visitor pattern is the implementation of two interfaces, which are defined as follows:

```
public interface ISupportVisitor {
    void Accept( IVisitor visitor);
}

public interface IVisitor {
    void Process< Type>( Type parameter);
}
```

The type that will copy its state to another structure implements the interface `ISupportVistor`. A type that wants to receive and inspect the state of another type implements the `IVisitor` interface. The `IVisitor` interface is a .NET Generics type, so multiple types can process the method `Process`. Remember that each type has its own state, and therefore its own structure. If Generics were not used, then the method `Process` would have to define the type for `parameter` to be an `Object`.

■**Note** If you are not well-versed in .NET Generics, I advise getting some basic understanding before reading many of the solutions in this book. In particular, you need a mechanical understanding of .NET Generics. Over the course of this book, I'll explain why you want to understand .NET Generics and provide some interesting techniques for using them.

When applying the Visitor pattern, and in particular the `ISupportVisitor` interface, the original code `GenerateOrder` would be modified to the following source code:

```
struct OrderManagerState {
    public OrderManagerState( string orderid) {
        OrderId = orderid;
    }
    public string OrderId;
}
class OrderManager : ISupportVisitor {
    public void Accept(IVisitor visitor) {
        visitor.Process( new OrderManagerState( _orderId));
    }
    private string _orderId;

    public bool GenerateOrder( string value) {
        _orderId = "ORDER1234";
        return true;
    }
}
```

The implementation of ISupportVisitor is minimal and illustrates the essence of transferring the internal state of OrderManager to the structure. An external entity calls the method Accept, which is a request for the state of OrderManager. A request for the state results in the instantiation of the structure OrderManagerState. The structure OrderManagerState contains a single reference to the order ID (OrderId) that is being managed. It is very important that another type is defined to transfer the state. The other type would be responsible for transferring the state from the owner (OrderManger) to itself (OrderManagerState).

The transfer of state must be value-based, and that means all references are cloned using the clone method. Otherwise, when the internal state is extracted another class that manipulates OrderManagerState could be modifying the internal state of OrderManager. That is the last thing that you want to happen with your source code. Therefore, when copying the state, use Clone whenever possible. Once the internal state has been copied, the visitor.Process method is called, passing the state to the caller. The testing routines would need to implement the IVisitor interface; the modified tests are as follows. The bolded code is the code used to implement the Visitor pattern:

```
[TestFixture]
public class Tests {
    class VisitorImpl : IVisitor {
        public string OrderId;

        public void Process< Type>(Type parameter) {
            if( parameter is OrderManagerState) {
                OrderId = ((OrderManagerState)(object)parameter).OrderId;
            }
        }
    }
```

```
    [Test]
    public void TestMethod() {
        OrderManager cls = new OrderManager();
        Assert.IsTrue( cls.GenerateOrder( "tires"));
        VisitorImpl impl = new VisitorImpl();
        cls.Accept( impl);
        Assert.AreEqual( "ORDER1234", impl.OrderId);
    }
}
```

For the scope of the testing routines, VisitorImpl is used to receive the state generated by OrderManager. The received state is extracted for a particular identifier that is then referenced after the method cls.GenerateOrder has been called. The test code has two verifications to test whether the method returns true and whether the internal state has been modified properly.

There is a way to verify the correctness of the internal state using the "partial classes" feature of .NET 2.0. With partial classes you can access the internal data members directly. Normally I do not condone the use of partial classes, as I find them a kludge with a couple of exceptions—one being testability of an internal data member. The following is an example of testing an internal data member without affecting the original structure of a class.

Source: /Volume01/LibVolume01/VerifyingTheCorrectness.cs

```
public partial class MyClass {
    public MyClass() {
        dataMember = 0;
    }
    int dataMember;
}


[TestFixture]
public partial class MyClass {
    [Test]
    public void IsCorrect() {
        MyClass cls = new MyClass ();
        Assert.AreEqual( 0, cls.dataMember);
    }
}
```

The class MyClass is defined as partial, meaning within the context of the source code for the assembly, MyClass can be extended. The problem with this approach is that you are creating a maintenance nightmare. There are two cooks mixing the same pot. If somebody updates the internal state MyClass, then that person needs to update the tests. This flies directly in the face of good object-oriented design. Even though the Visitor pattern extracts the internal state, the extracted state is separate from the class implementation and does not affect the declaration or execution of the class implementation. The person who updates the internal state does not need to care what happens to the extracted state. With partial classes this is not the case and thus adds to the burden of maintaining a class.

When verifying the correctness of an object where it is not possible to directly access the internal state, remember the following:

- The straightforward solution to verifying whether a context created a correct state is to require methods to return the state as either out parameters or return values.

- The Visitor pattern is a standardized pattern approach to extracting the internal state of an object instance. When copying the state, remember to do a full copy of the objects and copy only items that constitute an object's state. Transitory objects such as database connections are not part of a state.

- Don't use partial classes to test an object's internal state. It is a bad design and bad practice.

- When verifying the correctness of the defined contexts, test code needs to perform two tests: it must make sure that the methods were successful, and verify any manipulated state directly in the context of a test method to be correct.

CHAPTER 2

■■■

.NET Runtime- and Framework-Related Solutions

The solutions covered in this chapter relate to the .NET runtime and are not particular to any specific language. Of course, it is not advisable to present the bulk of the solutions using Microsoft Intermediate Language (MSIL), and a language must be used. For the scope of this chapter and book, I've chosen C# as the language.

Keeping Value Types and Reference Types Straight

The .NET documentation states that a class is a reference type, and a struct is a value type. Generally speaking, the difference between the two seems irrelevant from a coding perspective. Both a value type and a reference type use memory space. One of the features that differentiates them is where each type stores its memory space. An instantiated reference type is stored on the heap, and an instantiated value type is stored on the stack. Sounds good, right? Next question: what are a heap and a stack? The heap is like a global variable in that all objects stored on the heap are accessible by all other objects. However, it does not behave as a global variable because .NET manages the access of the references. The stack is a memory space that is private between the caller and callee. In Figure 2-1 a method call uses a stack that contains a value and a reference type.

In Figure 2-1 two types are declared: MyStruct is declared as a struct and hence a value type, and MyObject is declared as a class and hence reference type. The method Example.Method has two parameters, where the first is a value type and the second is a reference type. When the method is called, the calling stack contains the two parameters, but how they are stored in the stack is different. In the case of the structure the complete state of the value type is stored on the stack. If the structure required 10 bytes of memory, then the stack would make room for the 10 bytes of memory. For the reference type, the state is stored in the heap, and a reference to the memory on the heap in stored on the stack.

Let's look at how each type can be manipulated in a function call. For example, one ramification of using a value type is that any change in the stack value will not travel from callee to caller. Consider the following source code, which is an implementation of a function that has a number of modified value parameters; what interests us is to know which parameters are modified.

Source: /Volume01/LibVolume01/ValueAndReferenceTypeConfusion.cs

```
class ValueExample {
    public void InputOutput( long input, long out1, out long out2) {
        out1 = input + 10;
        out2 = input + 10;
    }
}
```

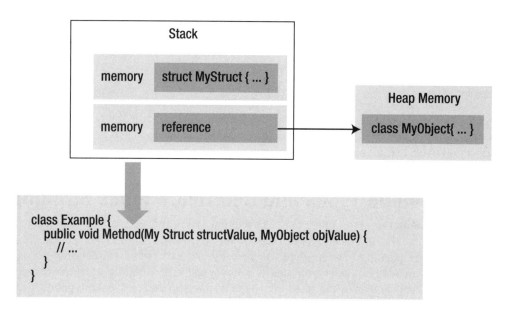

Figure 2-1. *How reference and value types are stored when making a method call*

In the example the class ValueExample has a single method, InputOutput, with three parameters. All three parameters are value types, but each serves a different purpose. The idea behind InputOutput is to create a method in which some of the parameters are input values, and some of the parameters are output values. When coding, you use input parameters to generate data, and output parameters to hold the generated content. (You might also use return values for output parameters, but that approach does not illustrate the point here.) The first parameter is the input value that will be used to assign the values for the second and third output parameters. In the implementation of InputOutput the parameter out1 is assigned the value of input plus 10, and the parameter out2 is assigned the value of input plus 10. The caller of InputOutput would expect the values of out1 and out2 to be 20.

To understand what we would get as a value, we must understand the behavior variables out1 and out2. The variable out1 is assigned, but because it is a value type and stored on the stack, the variable is modified but the caller does not see the changes because of how the stack operates. A stack is allocated, sent to the method, and then discarded. The variable out2 is also a value type and is also assigned, but it is associated with the keyword out. The keyword out makes a world of difference because the value modified on the stack is carried back to the caller. The following test code represents the calling code and verifies which variables appear altered.

Source: /Volume01/LibVolume01/ValueAndReferenceTypeConfusion.cs

```
[TestFixture]
public class TestValueExample {
    [Test]
    public void TestCall() {
        ValueExample cls = new ValueExample();
        long out1 = 0, out2 = 0;
        cls.InputOutput( 10, out1, out out2);
        Assert.AreEqual( 0, out1);
        Assert.AreEqual( 20, out2);
    }
}
```

Running the test results is a success; out1 is not modified, and out2 is modified. This tells us we can manipulate value parameters on the stack without having to worry about the caller seeing the manipulations. Of course, the exception is when the out parameter is used.

Reference types follow the rules of the stack, except the caller can see a modification of an object. A reference type stores on the stack a reference to the memory on the heap. Thus if a caller changes data on the heap, the callee will see the changes. However, there is a "gotcha" element, illustrated here:

Source: /Volume01/LibVolume01/ValueAndReferenceTypeConfusion.cs

```
private void AppendBuffer( String buffer, String toAppend) {
    buffer += toAppend;
}
[Test]
public void TestStringBuffer() {
    String original = "hello";
    String toAppend = " world";
    AppendBuffer( original, toAppend);
    Assert.AreEqual( "hello", original);
}
```

Look at how AppendBuffer is declared, and notice the two parameters. The first parameter is a buffer, and the second parameter is also a buffer that will be appended to the first parameter. In the implementation of AppendBuffer the += operator is used to append data to the first parameter. Knowing what we know regarding value types and reference types, we must ask whether the caller sees the modified value in the first parameter.

The answer is that the caller does not see the changes, but that's not because String is either a value type or a reference type. Rather, it's because the += operator used in conjunction with the immutable String type reassigns the value of the reference, not the memory pointed by the reference. Reassigning the value of the reference is like changing contents of a value type parameter, meaning you are changing the contents of a stack. This is why methods like AppendBuffer usually use the return keyword, sending the changed reference value to the caller. Another option would have been to add the out keyword to the first parameter variable buffer.

There is another "gotcha," and that relates to using interfaces in conjunction with structures and classes. Consider the following interface declaration:

Source: /Volume01/LibVolume01/ValueAndReferenceTypeConfusion.cs

```
public interface IRunningTotal {
    int Count { get; }
    void AddItem( int value);
}
```

The interface IRunningTotal has a single property Count, and a method AddItem. The objective of the interface is to provide a way to add items to a collection, and then figure out how many items are in the collection. Egg boxes are an example of a collection to which you can add items and then count them. The following example shows the implementations of an egg box using class and struct declarations:

Source: /Volume01/LibVolume01/ValueAndReferenceTypeConfusion.cs

```
public struct StructEggbox : RunningTotal {
    public int _eggCount;
    public StructEggbox( int initialCount) {
        _eggCount = initialCount;
    }
    public int Count    {
        get {
            return _eggCount;
        }
    }
    public void AddItem( int value) {
        _eggCount += value;
    }
}


class ClassEggbox : RunningTotal {
    private int _eggCount;
    public ClassEggbox( int initialCount) {
        _eggCount = initialCount;
    }
    public int Count    {
        get {
            return _eggCount;
        }
    }
    public void AddItem( int value) {
        _eggCount += value;
    }
}
```

The implementation of each type is completely identical, except for the type identifier (ClassEggbox vs. StructEggbox). In each implementation there is a data member _eggCount that keeps track of the number of eggs in the box. The method AddItem adds to the data member _eggCount the number of eggs as defined by the parameter value. And the property Count returns the current number of eggs stored in the variable _eggCount.

Both types implement the IRunningTotal interface, which makes it possible to decouple and modularize software. Using the interface, a caller could add and count eggs without having to know if he is dealing with the type ClassEggBox or StructEggbox. For example, we may want to generalize the operation of adding a dozen eggs to the egg carton, and therefore would use the IRunningTotal interface and call the method AddItem, as in the following source code:

```
public void AddEggs( RunningTotal rt) {
    rt.AddItem( 12);
}
```

The method AddEggs has a single parameter that is the interface IRunningTotal. In the implementation of the AddEggs method a dozen eggs are added. This outlines what we are intending to do, and all that remains is to put everything together in the form of tests. The tests will instantiate the class or structure, call AddEggs, and test how many eggs are in the egg carton.

Source: /Volume01/LibVolume01/ValueAndReferenceTypeConfusion.cs

```
[Test]
public void RunClassTest() {
    ClassEggbox eggs = new ClassEggbox( 0);
    AddEggs( eggs);
    Assert.AreEqual( 12, eggs.Count);
}
[Test]
public void RunStructTest() {
    StructEggbox eggs = new StructEggbox( 0);
    AddEggs( eggs);
    Assert.AreEqual( 0, eggs.Count);
}
```

Our logic says that if the method AddEggs is called, then a dozen eggs are added to the eggbox regardless of the type being used. But in the tests something else happens. The types ClassEggbox and StructEggbox are instantiated with no eggs in the box. When the method AddEggs is called for each instance, we expect 12 eggs to be in the box. However, the tests for each type test for a different number of eggs. In the instance for StructEggbox (test RunStructTest) there are no eggs (Assert.AreEqual), whereas for the ClassEggbox instance (test RunClassTest) there are 12 eggs.

It seems that there is a bug in the implementation of StructEggboxAddEggs since a dozen eggs are missing. If you are skeptical that a dozen eggs are missing for StructEggbox, copy the code and run it. The result is frustrating because the method AddEggs is called and the eggs are added. Yet a dozen eggs have gone missing because value and reference types are creating an inconsistency. You could argue that the logic of the interface instance has been violated because when calling the method AddEggs, the caller expects that the eggs are added to the IRunningTotal interface instance.

The next step is to understand why StructEggbox is a problem; it is because of data being stored on the stack versus the heap. At the coding level these little details are not obvious. The only way to understand what is going on is to look at the Microsoft Intermediate Language (MSIL). The MSIL[1] is a lower-level detail that shows us where data is being allocated and stored. Since the problem is the StructEggbox, let's disassemble the method RunStructTest:

```
.method public hidebysig instance void
        RunStructTest() cil managed
{
  .custom instance void
      [nunit.framework]NUnit.Framework.TestAttribute::.ctor() = ( 01 00 00 00 )
  // Code size       50 (0x32)
  .maxstack  2
  .locals init ([0] valuetype
        StructsAndClassesCanBeConfusing.StructEggbox eggs)
```

The command .locals init initializes the variable eggs to be a value type and is an automatic variable in the scope of a method. The result is that calling RunStructTest will automatically allocate and initialize the variable eggs. Continuing with the details of the RunStructTest method:

```
  IL_0000:  nop
  IL_0001:  ldloca.s    eggs
  IL_0003:  ldc.i4.s    0
  IL_0005:  call        instance void StructsAndClassesCanBeConfusing.➥
StructEggbox::.ctor(int32)
```

The command call calls the constructor of the StructEggbox directly and assigns a value of 0. Notice that the new keyword (or in the case of MSIL, the newobj instruction) is missing. You don't need a new keyword because the memory space for the value type is already allocated using the .locals init instruction. Had the variable egg been a class type, then the command .locals init would have initialized the space needed for the value of the reference. Initializing a reference type means that space for the reference to the heap has been allocated, but the space does not contain any reference. To have the reference point to something, the object would have to be initialized on the heap and thus would require calling the MSIL newobj instruction to instantiate a new object.

Continuing with the details of RunStructTest, after the IL calls the structure's constructor, the AddEggs method is called. In the following code piece you'll see why we are being haunted with missing eggs in the egg carton:

```
  IL_000a:  nop
  IL_000b:  ldarg.0
  IL_000c:  ldloc.0
  IL_000d:  box         StructsAndClassesCanBeConfusing.StructEggbox
  IL_0012:  call        instance void StructsAndClassesCanBeConfusing.Tests::➥
AddEggs(➥
class StructsAndClassesCanBeConfusing.RunningTotal)
```

---

1. To investigate the MSIL of a compiled .NET assembly use ILDASM.exe, which is distributed with the .NET Framework SDK. You could use reflector, but that will not help you since reflector has a tendency to generate source code form the MSIL thus hiding the information that you are interested in.

In the MSIL, the box command is bolded because it is the key to our problem. The MSIL before the highlighted box is not relevant and involves a series of stack operations. What is important is the box command and how it interoperates with the stack. The method AddEggs requires an instance of RunningTotal. However, StructEggbox is a value type and RunningTotal is a reference type. .NET boxes the value type and then performs a cast. This is called *autoboxing*, in which the contents of the value type are copied to the heap, and a reference of the copied contents is stored on the stack. After the boxing, the method AddEggs is called. We missed the autoboxing because compiler knows about boxing and will inject it automatically.

What is still puzzling is why the box command is problematic. The answer is in the Microsoft documentation:[2]

> ***box<token> (0x8c)*** *Convert a value type instance to an object reference. <token> specifies the value type being converted and must be a valid Typedef or TypeRef token. This instructions [sic] pops the value type instance from the stack, creates a new instance of the type as an object, and pushes the object reference to this instance on the stack.*

That says it all; the cause of the missing eggs is the stack not being copied back to the caller. When a boxing operation happens, the content of the value type is copied from the stack to the heap. The missing eggs are the result of the boxing because the egg count on the heap is manipulated and not copied back to the original value type stored on the stack in the function RunStructTest.

How can we avoid the autoboxing while still using value types? A solution is to autobox the structure instance from the beginning and not assign the value type to a variable of type value. By our assigning a value type directly to a reference type, the autoboxing will create a reference type that can be typecast to another reference type without autoboxing occurring. Following is an example in which the structure value is autoboxed and assigned to a reference type:

```
Object eggs = new StructEggbox( 0);
AddEggs( (IRunningTotal)eggs);
Assert.AreEqual( 12, ((IRunningTotal)eggs).Count);
```

In the source code the newly allocated StructEggbox instance is immediately assigned to a variable of type Object. As in the MSIL, the new keyword does nothing, but the assignment to the heap is important and will result in autoboxing. In this case the autoboxing is to our advantage. But because the variable eggs is of type Object, whenever we need a specific type we must use a typecast. The typecasts do not alter the functionality of the boxed type, and they produce the correct number of eggs in the box, but they also make the code uglier. Instead of defining eggs as being of type Object, I could have defined the original variable eggs as being of type IRunningTotal. The source code would have functioned just as well; once the eggs are autoboxed, doing reference typecasts does not affect the state of a value type.

Assuming that eggs is of type Object, meaning that an autoboxing has occurred, you could cast back to the original value-type structure StructEggbox. The interface IRunningTotal gives us access to some information of StructEggbox, but only with StructEggbox can we

---

2.   .NET IL Assembler, p. 264.

access all of the data members. Typecasting with an autoboxed type is not as simple as it seems; the following source code illustrates it:

```
((StructEggbox)eggs)._eggCount += 12;
```

In the example, eggs is typecast to StructEggbox and enclosed in parentheses. After the last paren the type is StructEggbox, and the source code can access the data member _eggCount directly. From a programmatic perspective, the typecast performed is like any other typecast. Yet from a compiler the perspective it is not the same; you will see problems when the compiler attempts to compile the source code. The following error results:

```
ValueTypesAndReferenceTypesConfusion.cs(129,14): error CS0445: Cannot modify the ➥
result of an unboxing conversion
Done building project "LibVolume01.csproj" — FAILED.
```

The error indicates that we cannot typecast and modify data of an autoboxed variable. The alternative is to assign another variable using a typecast, as the following source code illustrates:

```
StructEggbox copied = (StructEggbox)eggs;
copied._eggCount += 12;
Assert.AreEqual( 0, ((RunningTotal)eggs).Count);
```

In that example, the variable eggs is typecast to StructEggbox and assigned to copied. The variable copied has its data member eggCount incremented. Yet the verification by Assert illustrates that there are still no eggs in the egg box in the variable eggs.

The problem with this source code is not boxing, but unboxing, as this MSIL code shows:

```
IL_0037:  nop
IL_0038:  ldloc.0
IL_0039:  unbox.any  StructsAndClassesCanBeConfusing.StructEggbox
IL_003e:  stloc.1
IL_003f:  ldloca.s   copied
IL_0041:  dup
```

In the preceding code the command unbox.any unboxes an autoboxed type. The content of the unboxing is pushed on the stack. The command dup copies the content from the unboxed reference type to the variable copied. The MSIL code clearly illustrates a copy, and hence any modification of copied will result in nothing being altered in the original memory referenced by the boxed value type.

The conclusion of this boxing, autoboxing, value type, and reference type is that value types have their contents copied, and reference types have the reference to the heap memory copied. Remember that value and reference types are two different kinds of types with different purposes.

At the beginning of this section you saw an example where the MSIL new keyword was missing from the initialization of the structure data type. Yet in the C# source code a new keyword was required. The question is, does the C# source code need a new keyword? From the perspective of the MSIL, using the new keyword on a value type would have no effect. Is this just an idiosyncrasy?

To see if there is anything behind the use of the new keyword, let's take a closer look at two previous code pieces that instantiated a value type at the MSIL level. The first MSIL is the allocation of a value type that is assigned to a value-type variable. The second MSIL is the allocation of a value type that is assigned to a reference type, causing an automatic boxing. The objective is to see if there is any difference in how the same value type is instantiated and stored.

The following source code instantiates the value type StructEggbox and assigns the instantiated type to a variable of type StructEggbox:

```
.locals init ([0] valuetype StructsAndClassesCanBeConfusing.StructEggbox eggs)
IL_0000:  nop
IL_0001:  ldloca.s    eggs
IL_0003:  ldc.i4.s    12
IL_0005:  call        instance void StructsAndClassesCanBeConfusing.➥
StructEggbox::.ctor(int32)
```

When a value type is declared, the space for the value type is automatically created on the stack. The command .locals init is responsible for creating the space on the stack. Knowing that the space has been allocated, it is not necessary to allocate the space again. Thus when instantiating the value type the MSIL calls the constructor to initialize the structure (::ctor(int32)).

The second example is the allocation of the value type and assigning the value type to a reference type, causing an autoboxing.

```
.locals init ([0] object eggs)
IL_0000:  nop
IL_0001:  ldc.i4.s    12
IL_0003:  newobj      instance void ➥
StructsAndClassesCanBeConfusing.➥
StructEggbox::.ctor(int32)
IL_0008:  box         StructsAndClassesCanBeConfusing.StructEggbox
```

This time .locals init does allocate a value type, but it allocates space for reference value. This means when calling a method for a reference type, the space for a reference value is allocated on the stack. A reference type takes up less space than a value type. In the calling of the constructor (::ctor(int32)), a different command is used. Instead of using the call command, the command newobj is called. This means the value type is being allocated and then the constructor is being called. Right after the allocation, a boxing operation is carried out. If you want to delay the instantiation of a value type, the best approach is to assign it to a reference type.

So far this seems like an academic exercise that gives you some interesting (if not all that useful) information. However, a ramification of using a value type is clearly illustrated using an if block:

```
public void WhenIamCalled( bool flag) {
    if( flag) {
        StructEggbox eggs = new StructEggbox( 12);
        AddEggs( eggs);
    }
}
```

Only if the flag is `true` will the variable eggs be declared and allocated. Here's what the MSIL does with the code:

```
WhenIamCalled(bool flag) cil managed
  {
    // Code size       25 (0x19)
    .maxstack  2
    .locals init ([0] valuetype StructsAndClassesCanBeConfusing.StructEggbox eggs)
    IL_0000:  ldarg.1
    IL_0001:  brfalse.s  IL_0018

    IL_0003:  ldloca.s   eggs
    IL_0005:  ldc.i4.s   12
    IL_0007:  call       instance void ➥
StructsAndClassesCanBeConfusing.➥
StructEggbox::.ctor(int32)
    IL_000c:  ldarg.0
    IL_000d:  ldloc.0
    IL_000e:  box        StructsAndClassesCanBeConfusing.StructEggbox
    IL_0013:  call       instance void StructsAndClassesCanBeConfusing.➥
Tests::AddEggs(class StructsAndClassesCanBeConfusing.RunningTotal)
    IL_0018:  ret
  } // end of method Tests::WhenIamCalled
```

In the code there are two boldface MSIL instructions. The second one is the start of the decision block. The first boldface code block instantiates the value type. Notice the order of the instantiation and the decision block. The order is inverse of the way the code allocated the data. As per the MSIL specification, whatever is declared in the `.locals init` command must be initialized by the just-in-time the compilation before the method executes. Looking back at the original code, this means the value variable eggs is allocated at the beginning of the method no matter what the value of `flag` is. (Remember that allocation does not mean instantiation.)

Now you can put all of this together and think about what it means. Do you care? For the most part, no. When a value type is instantiated, memory is allocated for the value type on the stack even if you do not need to use the memory. The value type is not initialized (in other words, the constructor's value type is not called). If a value type contains references to reference types, they are not instantiated.

■**Note** With value types, you must use the constructor to initialize a reference type. So the hit of initialization does not happen until the new keyword is used. Where a value type might make a difference is if the value type results in the instantiation of 4MB of memory; allocating that amount of memory requires some time. Where this barrier can be reached is if you are using code generators (such as Web Services Description Language [WSDL] utilities), as often they generate classes without regard to complexity. However, an exception to the allocation problem is when an array is created. An array is a reference type; thus an array of value types is a reference type that references a collection of value types.

When using value and reference types, remember the following:

- Autoboxing can hit you when you least expect it. Autoboxing occurs whenever structure types implement interfaces. Therefore, you must very clearly understand the differences between value and reference types.

- Don't mix types. Keep value types as value types, and reference types as reference types.

- Just because you can do something like implement interfaces using a struct does not mean you should.

- Using a struct means using a value type, which is useful for storing data. Do not implement a struct in such a way that it behaves and is manipulated like a class.

- Due to the completely different behavior of value and reference types a struct should generally reference only other value types. It is acceptable to reference a value type from a reference type.

Using Delegates

Delegates are a mainstay of the .NET programming environment and they solve many problems very elegantly. A *delegate* is a strongly typed function pointer that has the ability to call class methods at runtime. The consumer of the delegate does not know what class method is being called, and sees only the function pointer.

It is important to understand the ramifications of using a delegate. If a class instance has a method associated with a delegate, do you need to keep a reference to the class instance? If you don't keep a variable reference, does the garbage collection mistakenly remove the instance? Consider the following code, in which the class SomeClass is instantiated and the method DelegatedMethod is associated with the delegate:

```
new MyDelegate( new SomeClass().DelegatedMethod);
```

I am uneasy about this code because an instance of SomeClass is created but not assigned to anything. The method of the instance is passed to the delegate, and it leaves me wondering whether the garbage collector puts the unassigned instance right on the to-be-collected list. Or is there something more happening here? The garbage collector is based on instances of types, and a method is not a type. I recommend rewriting the code to the following:

```
value = new SomeClass().Calculate();
myDelegate = new MyDelegate( new SomeClass().DelegatedMethod);
```

In the example I know what the references are and I know when those references will be garbage-collected. What bothers me is that I don't know what is happening. The following code helps me understand what happens with a delegate:

Source: /Volume01/LibVolume01/WhatAreDelegates.cs

```
public delegate void MyDelegate( string parameter);
```

The definition of the delegate is very similar to that of a method except that the keyword delegate is used, and that there is no implementation of the method. The delegate MyDelegate has a single parameter, and no return value.

MyDelegate could be used as in the following example:

Source: /Volume01/LibVolume01/ WhatAreDelegates.cs

```
[TestFixture]
public class Tests {
    public static void ImplDelegate(
        string parameter) {
        Console.WriteLine( "Hello (" + parameter
            + ")");
    }
    [Test]
    public void RunDelegate() {
        MyDelegate callme = new MyDelegate(
            ImplDelegate);
        callme( "hello");
    }
}
```

The class Tests contains two functions: ImplDelegate and RunDelegate. The function ImplDelegate is a static method that can be called without instantiating Tests. The method RunDelegate contains the code to instantiate the delegate MyDelegate. What is peculiar about the instantiation of the delegate is that someone who did not know that MyDelegate is a delegate might believe it is a class instantiation that needs a constructor parameter. However, the line after the delegation instantiation makes the class behave like a function or method call.

So far it seems that a delegate is part function and part class. I don't intend to call into question the delegate's syntax. Instead, I am trying to illustrate how a delegate is implemented so that the behavior becomes clear. The generated MSIL provides a clue; with the MSIL the exact structure and calling sequence can be traced. The abbreviated MSIL that is generated for the delegate is as follows:

```
.class public auto ansi sealed WhatAreDelegatesReally.MyDelegate
        extends [mscorlib]System.MulticastDelegate
```

As you can see, a delegate is nothing more than a class that inherits from System. MulticastDelegate, and MulticastDelegate inherits from the class Delegate. For experimentation purposes. let's define a class and subclass System.MulticastDelegate. Compiling the code results in the following error:

```
WhatAreDelegatesReally.cs(8,18): error CS0644: 'WhatAreDelegatesReally.TryDerive' ➥
cannot derive from special class 'System.MulticastDelegate'
Done building project "Main01.csproj" — FAILED.
```

The compiler error means that a delegate at the MSIL level is a class that derives from the special class MulticastDelegate, which cannot be derived from at the C# level. MulticastDelegate is a special class that is not seen, but its implementation is felt. The next question is whether the subclassing restriction is a language design or a .NET design.

Using the .NET Framework SDK–provided tool ILASM, you can define a class and let it derive from MulticastDelegate. So you could define your delegates at the MSIL level by subclassing `MulticastDelegate`. The next experiment is to figure out if it is possible to subclass a class that subclassed `MulticastDelegate`. The code is trivial, and ILASM compiles the code. However, the code still needs to be executed. And the execution is the problem, as the following error message illustrates:

```
Unhandled Exception: System.TypeLoadException: Could not load type ➥
'AllAlone.SingleDelegate' from assembly 'SingleDelegate, Version=0.0.0.0, ➥
Culture=neutral, PublicKeyToken=null' because delegate classes must be sealed.
    at Program.Main(String[] args)
```

By putting the exception into context with the other delegate implementation aspects, you'll get a clear picture of what a delegate is—a special class that at the MSIL level follows the resource conventions of a class. Going back to my previous concern of the garbage collector, I am now at ease when allocating unassigned class instances because the instance is stored as a reference in the special delegate class.

When using delegates, remember the following:

- Delegates follow the resource conventions of a class. This means if a delegate references a class instance, the referenced class instance will be garbage-collected once the delegate is garbage-collected.

- Delegates are by default multicastable, which means a single delegate could reference dozens of method or class instances using the += operator. The dozens of method and class instances use up resources and are released once the delegate is released.

- Delegate instances are class instances, and therefore you can call the methods associated with the abstract classes `Delegate` and `MultiCastDelegate`.

Versioning Assemblies

In the packaged-software market the concept of the version number has disappeared for the most part. Take, for example, Microsoft and the Windows operating system—the names Windows 95, Windows 98, Windows 2000, Windows XP, and Windows Vista illustrate that there is little consistency to the versioning of many pieces of software. Version numbers are a way to control the features and robustness of an application. But who needs version numbers? End users do not *need* version numbers even though they probably would like them. It is developers who need version numbers.

In open source, version numbers are used extensively and are considered very important. The version numbers in open source very often resemble the numbers of a lottery ticket, but they have a convention, and understanding the convention makes it easier to select open source packages; but more important, understanding the convention makes it simpler to understand your assemblies.

Let's say I am confronted with the version number capivara: 0.7.2. The version number contains a *major number*, a *minor number*, and a *patch number*:

Major number. In the capivara example, 0 is the major number. It is used to define major functionality changes in a piece of software. If the software has not reached the number 1, then the version is considered a beta. A beta identifier does not mean the software is unusable. Many packages prefer to wait to see if all of the bugs are ironed out before releasing the final product. For example, the Wine project has been an alpha release for a decade, yet people still use Wine. Changing major version numbers does indicate a major change of functionality, however—what worked in version 1 may not work in version 2. For instance, in the Apache HTTPD server project, the 1.x and 2.x series are two different implementations.

Minor number. In the capivara example, 7 is the minor number. It is used to define minor functionality changes in a piece of software. Changing version numbers indicates new features, but old functionality is still supported. Changes may include bug fixes or patches.

Patch number. In the capivara example, 2 is the patch number. It is used to define a patched version of the software, which includes bug fixes or other changes. The changes do not affect the software's features, and the functionality does not change.

When you attempt to download a package, usually you are confronted with multiple versions. For example, consider the version numbers 4.23 and 4.29 (beta). Because you want the latest and greatest, you might be tempted to download version 4.29. But before you download anything, remember that open source applications make multiple versions available. And the example version numbers are unique in that the beta identifier is associated with version 4.29 (meaning that version 4.29 is a beta). You'll likely be better off downloading version 4.23, because 4.29 might not work properly. Version 4.23 is considered stable and therefore usable.

The open source community often uses the following terminology for software releases:

Stable. A version that can be used in a production environment and should not crash.

Unstable. A version that should not be used in production, but will probably work despite some crashes.

Nightly. A version will all bets off—the version may or may not work. The reason for using a nightly build is to monitor progress and check specific issues. Nightly versions are not intended only for developer use.

Alpha. A version that illustrates the concepts that will make up a future version of the software. What is available one day might be completely gone the next.

You are probably wondering is why I am talking about open source and not .NET. Open source provides a high-level description of how to version software. .NET continues that by providing the technical support to implement versioning. Following is an example of versioning an assembly:

```
[assembly: AssemblyVersion("1.1.0.0")]
[assembly: AssemblyFileVersion("1.1.0.0")]
```

The attributes `AssemblyVersion`, and `AssemblyFileVersion` can be added anywhere in the assembly or application. If you're using Visual Studio, you'll most likely add the attributes to the file `AssemblyInfo.cs`. The versions of the file have four significant parts: major version, minor version, build number, and revision.

The significance of version numbers in .NET is slightly different from significance of version numbers in open source. The major and minor number serve the same purpose as in open source. The build number can (but does not have to) represent a daily build number.

The revision identifier can (but does not have to) represent a random number. Visual Studio's built-in mechanisms update the build number and revision number automatically. Otherwise you can use a tool, or you can increment the numbers manually. I use a revision number of 0, and consider the build number as a patch number. Regardless of how an assembly is versioned, a version number should exist and be used, especially if you plan on distributing your assemblies.

Additionally, I recommend defining a strong name in conjunction with the version number. In .NET, that means creating a cryptographic unique identifier that can distinguish one assembly from another—if you happen to have an assembly called "book" from vendor A, and another "book" assembly from vendor B, a strong name will see that the assembly names are identical but will identify them as unique assemblies. If an assembly is considered as shared and copied to the global assembly cache, *you must* create a strong name. A strong name is not required for unshared private assemblies. To create a strong name, you use the sn command, as the following command line illustrates:

```
sn -k mykey.snk
```

The command line generates a key (mykey.snk) that the .NET cryptographic routines use to fingerprint an assembly. In years gone by, you would have used an assembly attribute identify which key to combine with the assembly. The preferred way these days is to use the C# compiler command-line option /keyfile:mykey.snk. The resulting assembly can be added to the global assembly cache (GAC):

```
gacutil /I [assembly name]
```

When the gacutil command is used for the first time, the assembly is copied from the local directory to the cache. The gacutil command can be executed multiple times with multiple versions, as the Figure 2-2 shows.

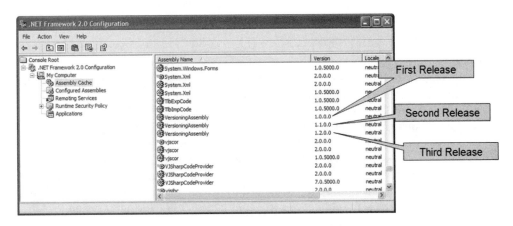

Figure 2-2. *Example assembly added to the GAC three times with three different versions*

In Figure 2-2 the assembly called VersioningAssembly has been added to the GAC three times with three different versions (1.0.0.0, 1.1.0.0, and 1.2.0.0). With the GAC in this state, an application or another assembly has the option to reference three different versions of the same assembly.

An application that uses types located in another assembly employs what .NET calls a *reference* to identify and load the required types. When the application or assembly that uses the types is compiled, a specific version number of the referenced assembly is identified. So, for example, if a reference to the version 1.1.0.0 of VersioningAssembly is defined, when the compiled assembly loads and executes VersioningAssembly, the assembly will search for version 1.1.0.0.

Let's say VersioningAssembly is upgraded and the application or assembly needs to use a new version of VersioningAssembly. The old application will not be aware of the new assembly and will attempt to load the version of the assembly that was referenced at the application's compile time. To make the application or assembly aware of the new assembly, the application or assembly configuration file must be updated. The configuration file update provides a redirect to the version of VersioningAssembly that needs to be loaded. The redirection says that if a certain version of an assembly is requested, then the new version should be loaded. Following is an example of an assembly redirection:

```xml
<?xml version="1.0"?>
<configuration>
  <runtime>
    <assemblyBinding
        xmlns="urn:schemas-microsoft-com:asm.v1">
      <dependentAssembly>
        <assemblyIdentity name="VersioningAssembly"
        publicKeyToken="bd42f9cb12b40d1b"
        culture="neutral" />
        <bindingRedirect oldVersion="1.1.0.0"
        newVersion="1.2.0.0"/>
      </dependentAssembly>
    </assemblyBinding>
  </runtime>
</configuration>
```

In the example configuration, the assemblyBinding XML element defines a collection of assemblies that will be redirected. A single redirection of an assembly is embedded within the dependentAssembly element. Within the dependentAssembly element are two child elements: assemblyIdentity and bindingRedirect. The element assemblyIdentity identifies the assembly that application requests and for which a redirection will be provided.

When a redirection is matched to make the redirection work the element bindingRedirect is searched for (bindingRedirect defines to what assembly the reference is redirected). The element bindingRedirect contains two attributes: oldVersion and newVersion. The attribute oldVersion identifies a reference to the old assembly in the calling assembly or application. In the example the old-version reference is 1.1.0.0, and the new-version reference is 1.2.0.0. Thus if the application has a reference to VersioningAssembly version 1.1.0.0, VersioningAssembly version 1.2.0.0 will load. The new version has an incremented minor number, indicating a version of an assembly that has compatible interfaces, but changed implementations. However, the binding redirection does not care whether the newVersion attribute references a new version or an old version. The version identifiers are just that—identifiers. You could redirect a new version to an old version and .NET would not complain one iota.

You should now understand how an application or assembly can define and use version numbers. Remember the following points when using your own version numbers:

- For organizational purposes, use version numbers that include a major number, a minor number, and a patch number. When using Visual Studio, you can also manage the version number.

- Make it a habit to use strong names. Even if the assembly will be kept private and thus does not require a strong name, using strong names is a good programming practice in case an assembly is converted into a shared assembly in the GAC.

Loading and Unloading Assemblies Dynamically

If you are building a component-oriented application, then most likely you will have assemblies referencing other assemblies. When an assembly is referenced using direct references that are compiled into the application, it is not possible to load any assembly other than the referenced one. Of course, you can load different versions of the assembly, but if an assembly with a specific strong name is identified, then only that assembly will be loaded.

Sometimes at runtime you would like to have the option of loading a different assembly. Maybe you defined a number of interfaces and have decided to change the implementation that is loaded. If you want your assemblies to have plug-and-play functionality, you need a plug-in. When programmers hear the word plug-in, the first thing that springs to mind is the definition of a contract that is implemented by different assemblies. ADO.NET database drivers are examples of plug-ins, as they all define the same interfaces. When an application loads an ADO.NET plug-in, implementations specific to a database are loaded.

In this solution I will illustrate two approaches to loading plug-ins. The first approach is the simpler one; it can load an assembly but cannot unload the assembly during application execution. The second approach is more complicated, but it allows you to hot-plug assemblies.

Loading Assemblies Dynamically

Loading an assembly dynamically using .NET is straightforward programming, and involves calling two methods: `Assembly.Load` and `assembly.CreateInstance`. You can call those two methods and consider the plug-in architecture finished. Using the two methods meaningfully requires some forethought, however.

For illustration purposes I'll use a class in an application that is defined in a separate assembly:

```
public class Implementation { }
```

The methods for `Implementation` have been omitted, and what is important is the declaration of `Implementation` in its own assembly. In the application the following code dynamically loads and instantiates the class `Implementation`:

```
Implementation cls = Assembly.Load( ➥
@"c:\MyImplementation.dll").➥
CreateInstance( "Implementation") as Implementation;
```

The code will work, and it will do everything expected of it. But the code is meaningless because you are dynamically loading a class that has a static assembly reference, as Figure 2-3 illustrates.

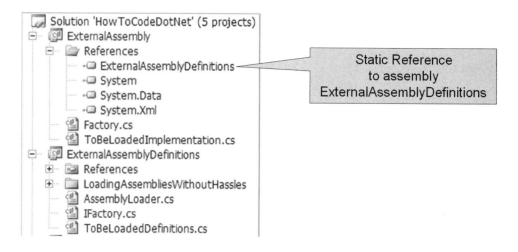

Figure 2-3. *Static reference of an assembly*

You need a static reference because the compiler needs to know about the `Implementation` definition. The compiler will create an internal reference to the type, which will implicitly load the assembly when the application is started. With a static reference the assembly will be implicitly loaded into the running application of the calling assembly. Thus, using the `Assembly.Load` and `CreateInstance` methods to load the assembly dynamically makes no sense since the assembly will already be loaded.

The solution is to not allow a static reference to the `Implementation`, but have `Implementation` implement an interface. Then when the `CreateInstance` is called, instantiated is the implementation, but referenced is the interface. In the Implementations assembly `Implementation` would be defined as follows.

```
class Implementation : IInterface { }
```

And the application that uses `Implementation` is rewritten to the following.

```
IInterface cls = Assembly.Load( "MyImplementation.dll" ).➥
CreateInstance( "Implementation") as IInterface;
```

In the modified code there is no reference to `Implementation` other than a string identifier. A string identifier does not implicitly load an assembly. By using the interface and implementation in combination with the string identifier, we've separated the application and assembly cleanly. When the application and assembly are compiled they do not need to know about each other—both simply need to know about the interface.

Our solution seems to work, but there is a missing detail—the declaration for `IInterface` was omitted. How the interface's methods or properties are declared is not important. What is important is where the interface is declared. There are multiple places to put the interface declaration. If you put it in the application, then the assembly containing the implementation will have a static reference to the application. If instead you put the declaration in the Implementations assembly, the application will implicitly load the assembly, making the dynamic loading useless. The solution is to create a third assembly, and Figure 2-4 illustrates the resulting architecture.

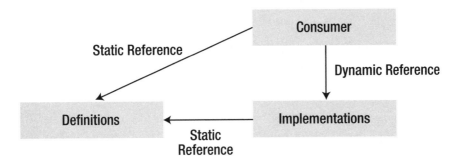

Figure 2-4. *Three-assembly architecture for loading assemblies dynamically*

The three assemblies in Figure 2-4 are defined as follows:

Consumer. The application assembly is the higher-level code that uses the plug-in architecture represented by the Implementations assembly. The Consumer assembly has a dynamically generated reference to the Implementations. The Consumer assembly statically references the Definitions assembly.

Definitions. This assembly contains the interface definitions shared by the Consumer and Implementations assemblies. The Definitions assembly does not reference either of the other assemblies, as that would create an undesired implicit loading of those other assemblies.

Implementations. This assembly contains class definitions that implement the interfaces defined in the Definitions assembly. The Implementations assembly has a static reference to the Definitions assembly.

The Consumer assembly can reference the Definitions assembly, and the Implementations assembly can reference the Definitions assembly. This referencing model makes it possible to dynamically load and unload the Implementations assemblies. The only ramification with this architecture is that the Consumer and Implementations assemblies load definitions, making it impossible to dynamically load and change the Definitions assembly.

Now that we've outlined the architecture, let's implement it. The following source code shows the declaration of IInterface in the Definitions assembly:

Source: /Volume01/ExternalAssembliesDefinitions/IInterface.cs

```
public interface IInterface {
    void Method();
}
```

The class Implementation defined in the Implementations assembly is as follows:

Source: /Volume01/ExternalAssemblies/Implementation.cs

```
class Implementation : IInterface {
    public void Method() {
        Console.WriteLine( "Called the implementation");
    }
}
```

The code for the definitions and Implementations assembly it is minimal and thus needs no helper functionality to simplify the code. The same cannot be said for the consumer; it needs to include the following source code:

Source: /Volume01/LibVolume01/LoadingAssembliesWithoutHassles.cs

```
Assembly assembly = Assembly.Load(
    AssemblyName.GetAssemblyName( @" c:\ExternalAssembly.dll"));
Object @object;

@object = assembly.CreateInstance("Implementation");

Assert.IsNotNull(@object);
IInterface impl = @object as IInterface;
if (impl != null) {
    impl.Method();
}
```

The consumer code uses the two assembly loading and instantiating methods, and the code is straightforward. But if an application were to dynamically load multiple assemblies, it would get tedious because you would have to copy and paste the loading code to multiple places. Instead, you should create a generic class that would reduce the tedious work.

Following is a .NET Generics class declaration that wraps the dynamic loading of an assembly:

Source: /jaxson.commons.dotnet /Loader/SimpleLoader.cs

```
public class AssemblyLoader {
    Assembly _assembly;

    public AssemblyLoader(string path) {
        _assembly = Assembly.Load(AssemblyName.GetAssemblyName(path));
    }
    public type Instantiate< type>(string typeidentifier) where type: class {
        return _assembly.CreateInstance(typeidentifier) as type;
    }
}
```

The class AssemblyLoader has one method, and a constructor that expects as a parameter the path of the assembly. The AssemblyLoader class will execute the two methods (Assembly.Load and assembly.CreateInstance) and perform a typecast of the dynamically loaded type. The consumer code used to load the assembly can be abbreviated to the following:

```
IInterface impl = new AssemblyLoader( @" c:\ExternalAssembly.dll")
    .Instantiate<IInterface>(" Implementation");
impl.Method();
```

The abbreviated code is not littered with extra instantiations and variable references. The AssemblyLoader class makes is trivial to load an assembly and instantiate a type. In the preceding code sample there are two hard-coded references: the assembly identifier (c:\ExternalAssembly.dll) and the implementation identifier (Implementation). You could avoid having the two hard-coded references by storing the identifiers in a configuration file.

Regardless of how the identifiers are stored, one thing is for sure: you don't want the consumer code hard-coding the identifiers. Instead you want to add one more abstraction level and use a Factory,[3] as the following code illustrates.

```
IInterface impl = Factory.CreateInstance();
impl.Method();
```

As you can see, the code has been abbreviated even further and now the consumer code has no idea whether the instance is local, remote, or dynamically loaded from an assembly. This is exactly what we want, because it allows the underlying code to algorithmically determine where the location of the implementation is at runtime. The use of Factory completely decouples the consumer assembly from the implementation assembly.

The following code shows the implementation of a factory (in either the consumer or definitions assembly):

Source: /Volume01/LibVolume01/LoadingAssembliesWithoutHassles.cs

```
public class Factory {
    static public IInterface CreateInstance() {
        return new AssemblyLoader(@" ExternalAssembly.dll")
            .Instantiate<IInterface>("Implementation");
    }
}
```

In the implementation of CreateInstance the code is identical to the previous abbreviated example that used AssemblyLoader. The fact that the two code samples are identical is not a problem. In fact, that is what we want. The main purpose of Factory and the method CreateInstance is to provide a wedge between the consumer and instantiation of the implementation. In the Factory example, the paths and identifiers are still hard-coded because the code is for illustration purposes only. Ideally the configuration file would define the identifiers, but you could also use a database or an LDAP server.

---

3. For more details on factories, consult Chapter 4.

When working with dynamically loaded assemblies, remember the following:

- When you plan on loading assemblies dynamically, always use interfaces or base classes.

- Three assembly types make up a dynamic loading assembly architecture: Consumer, Definitions, and Implementations. You must remember how each assembly type references the other, as illustrated in Figure 2-4. Not following that pattern will result in assemblies being implicitly loaded.

- In the Consumer assembly type you do not want the code knowing how the implementation was instantiated or retrieved; thus you want to use the Factory pattern to hide those details.

- Your Factory pattern implementations should use a configuration file or some other external information to enable a user or administrator to update the configuration without requiring any sources to be recompiled.

- Using the approach in this section the `Factory` implementation could do a static reference instantiation, local dynamic load, remote dynamic load, or even a Web service call. The consumer code does not know nor care which method is used.

Loading and Unloading Assemblies Dynamically

You've seen how using a `Factory` in conjunction with the `AssemblyLoader` class loads an assembly. Using those classes it is not possible to unload the assembly during the execution of the application. Unloading an assembly was not illustrated earlier because doing so is not possible using the illustrated techniques. Using the methods `Assembly.Load` and `CreateInstance` loads the assembly into the current *application domain* (AppDomain), which is a container for an assembly. In .NET if you wish to unload an assembly you must unload the application domain, and hence you must unload the current application.

For many scenarios, dynamically loading an assembly into the current AppDomain and then exiting the application to replace the dynamically loaded assemblies with new assemblies is not a problem. But if you were to write a server-side application that wants to load and unload assemblies dynamically without exiting the application, then there is a problem. Exiting the application means stopping the server, which means being unable to process requests. No administrator would accept such a situation.

To unload an assembly, an AppDomain is unloaded. In .NET terms, an AppDomain is a construct, loosely defined, used to represent a process in .NET. The words "loosely defined" apply because an AppDomain is specific to .NET and represents a way of isolating assemblies, security descriptors, and so on. In the early days of Java, when two Java applications were "executing" each could see the static data of the other application because Java applications were not shielded and were all executed in the context of one operating-system process. This was problematic because it meant that when two Java applications were using the same class with a static data member, each would see the same data. AppDomains solve this problem and then some.

AppDomains provide separate execution spaces for .NET assemblies so that a loaded assembly sees its own security descriptors, fault protection, and set of assemblies. Having multiple AppDomains would be a good idea in the aforementioned server application because one assembly cannot take down an entire server. A server application would create multiple AppDomains and then load the assembly dynamically within the individual AppDomains. There is a complication, though, involving cross-AppDomain calls. When a loaded assembly attempts to make a cross-AppDomain call, it requires serialization and proxying. It is not as simple as when an assembly calls another assembly within the same AppDomain.

There are many advantages to managing a separate AppDomain (robustness and security among them). The one downside is its communications complexity. I will not address all of the complexity issues here, but I will address the basic issues involved with loading and unloading an assembly.

In regard to the Consumer assembly, using the AppDomain code should be no different than using the simple dynamic loading code. The Consumer assembly code must remain identical to the following code:

```
IInterface impl = Factory.CreateInstance();
impl.Method();
```

In the example, `Factory` has a method `CreateInstance` that will instantiate the implementation and return an interface instance to `IInterface`. The entire solution should look and behave like the sample code. In the implementation there is still an `AssemblyLoader` class, but instead of that class being implemented using the two assembly method calls, it contains the logic to instantiate, load, and unload AppDomains. You'll still need three assembly types: Consumer, Definitions, and Implementations. And each of the three assembly types still serves the same purpose. What is different is `AssemblyLoader`.

Consider the `Factory.CreateInstance` method, which is implemented as follows:

```
public class Factory {
    private static AssemblyLoader _loader;

    static Factory() {
        _loader = new AssemblyLoader( "Test");
        _loader.AssignRemoteAppDirectory( @"C:\..\Debug");
        _loader.Load();
    }
    static public IInterface CreateInstance() {
        return _loader.Instantiate<IInterface>(
            new Identifier( "ExternalAssembly, … PublicKeyToken=null",
            "Implementation"));
    }
}
```

In the implementation of `Factory`, the new identifiers appear in boldface. Previously to load an assembly you specified the path of the assembly and the type that you wanted to instantiate. With AppDomains, you need the root path that contains the assemblies that will be loaded dynamically, and the identifier of the assembly. Unlike in the previous section, the filename does not reference the assembly's name, but instead references the identifier that is returned when the property `Assembly.FullName` is queried.

In the example the identifier is hard-coded and should be retrieved dynamically. One way to retrieve the information dynamically is to load the assembly and then query for the full name using the `FullName` property. But dynamically retrieving the full name of the assembly loads the assembly in the current AppDomain, defeating the purpose of being able to unload an assembly dynamically. Another technique would be to instantiate a remote AppDomain and have it iterate a particular directory and catalog the found types. Then when the `Instantiate` method call is made, the remote AppDoman is cross-references the identifier against the cataloged type. This saves the developer from having to figure out which assembly contains which type. The technique makes configuration trivial, because all that is necessary is the identification of a directory of assemblies and the type that you want to load.

Before we delve into the code, examine Figure 2-5, which shows how the three assemblies are mapped in the AppDomains.

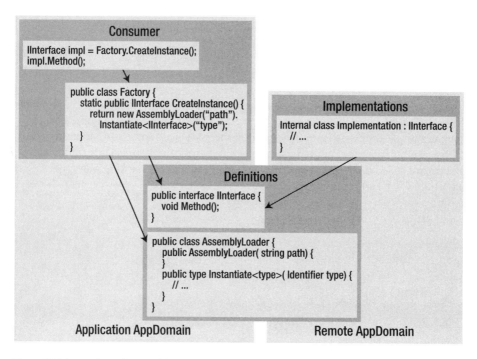

Figure 2-5. *Mapping of assemblies into their AppDomains*

In Figure 2-5, the consumer assembly is loaded into the Application AppDomain, which is the local AppDomain that is created when a .NET application starts up. To unload the Application AppDomain, you must exit the application. The Application AppDomain controls the Remote AppDomain, which can be loaded and unloaded dynamically. The implementations assembly is loaded into the Remote AppDomain.

The Definitions assembly is loaded into both the Remote AppDomain and the Application AppDomain. This is necessary because both the Consumer and Implementations assemblies need information (such as interface definitions) from the Definitions assembly. The downside to having the Definitions assembly loaded in both AppDomains is that the assembly cannot be updated unless both AppDomains are shut down. Therefore, when creating a Definitions assembly, make sure that it changes very little—otherwise you will be forced to start and stop the server.

To create the Remote AppDomain, you must use the method `AppDomain.CreateDomain`. Once you have the other AppDomain, you can instantiate an object in it using the method `[remote AppDomain instance].CreateInstanceAndUnwrap`.

The class `AppDomain` has a method `CreateInstance`, but you cannot use it since you are instantiating an object in one AppDomain but referencing the object in another. If you were to use `CreateInstance` to instantiate an object from another AppDomain, it would return an `ObjectHandle`, and not the object itself. To be able to call the object, you must call the method `ObjectHandle.Unwrap`. Alternatively, you can combine the two steps and call `CreateInstanceAndUnwrap`.

The unwrapping part is necessary because when you are calling across AppDomains you are making a .NET remoting call,[4] which changes the application's dynamics immensely. In a nutshell, it means using the .NET remoting attributes and deriving from the appropriate classes. As part of .NET remoting, when making cross-AppDomain calls, .NET generates proxies to the objects dynamically. Not having those proxies will result in runtime errors related to the serialization and deserialization of the types you are referencing.

Now let's return to the `AppDomain.CreateDomain` method call. .NET 2.0 offers six overloaded versions of this method, but each one is attempting to accomplish the same goal of instantiating a remote AppDomain. For now we are interested in one variation that was introduced in .NET 2.0, and simplifies the instantiation of a Remote AppDomain. The method signature is as follows:

```
public static AppDomain CreateDomain (
        string friendlyName,
        Evidence securityInfo,
        string appBasePath,
        string appRelativeSearchPath,
        bool shadowCopyFiles,
        AppDomainInitializer adInit,
        string[] adInitArgs
)
```

This variation is the friendliest because it has all of the flexibility you need without getting bogged down in details. The parameters are as follows:

`friendlyName`: This is the name given to an AppDomain as a unique identifier.

`securityInfo`: This defines the security descriptor for the AppDomain to be instantiated. If no `securityInfo` is given, the security information from the current AppDomain is used.

`appBasePath`: This defines the base execution directory of the AppDomain that is being created.

`appRelativeSearchPath`: This defines the path where assemblies can be found relative to the `appBasePath` directory.

`shadowCopyFiles`: This specifies whether assemblies will be shadowed when loaded.

---

4. The details of .NET remoting are beyond the scope of this book; if you are not familiar with .NET remoting, I advise reading some .NET remoting documentation before you apply the solutions in this section.

adInit: This is a delegate that is called when the other AppDomain is being initialized.

adInitArgs: This is an array of strings that, when called, is passed to adInit.

Now that you know the foundations, we can begin to implement an alternative AssemblyLoader class. The distributed source code contains two versions of the AppDomain assembly loaders: detailed[5] and simplified.[6] For the scope of this section, I'll explain the simpler of the two versions. The detailed solution is like the simplified one, but uses a variation of the CreateDomain method that allows for more fine-tuning.

The following source code shows the base declaration with data members of AssemblyLoader2 (the other methods declared in AssemblyLoader2 are discussed later in this solution):

Source: /jaxson.commons.dotnet/Loader/AssemblyLoader2.cs

```
public abstract class AssemblyLoader2 : IFactory< Identifier> {
    public AssemblyLoader2() {
    }

    protected AppDomain _unloadable;
    protected string _applicationName;
    protected string _remoteDomainAppDirectory;
    protected string _appRelativeSearchPath;
    protected bool _shadowCopyFiles;
    protected Evidence _securityInfo;
    protected AppDomainInitializer _initializer;
    protected string[] _initializerArgs;
}
```

The class AssemblyLoader2 implements the IFactory interface, allowing the assembly loader to be used generically. The data member _unloadable references the Remote AppDomain from Figure 2-5, which is used to instantiate an object. The other data members are a one-to-one cross-reference to the simplified CreateDomain method variation.

Notice that AssemblyLoader2 is marked as abstract, which means that anybody who wants to use AssemblyLoader2 must implement a class. The implemented class will fill in the specific details for finding, loading, and unloading assemblies. The class implementation overrides specific methods that are used to assign the data members for the CreateDomain method. The methods that a class could implement are defined as follows.

```
protected abstract string GetAppDomainName();
protected virtual string GetRelativeSearchPath() {
    return "";
}
protected virtual string GetAppDomainBaseDirectory() {
    return AppDomain.CurrentDomain.BaseDirectory;
}
```

---

5. /jaxson.commons.dotnet/Loader/AssemblyLoader.cs
6. /jaxson.commons.dotnet/Loader/AssemblyLoader2.cs

```
protected virtual bool GetShadowCopyFiles() {
    return false;
}
protected virtual Evidence GetSecurityInfo() {
    return AppDomain.CurrentDomain.Evidence;
}
protected AppDomainInitializer GetInitializerFunction() {
    return new AppDomainInitializer(
        AssemblyLoader2.LocalAppDomainInitialize);
}
protected string[] GetInitializerArgs() {
    return new string[]{ };
}
protected virtual AppDomain CreateApplicationDomain() {
    return AppDomain.CreateDomain(
        _applicationName, _securityInfo, _remoteDomainAppDirectory,
        _appRelativeSearchPath, _shadowCopyFiles,
        _initializer, _initializerArgs);
}
```

All of the overridable methods have a default implementation, with the exception of
GetAppDomainName. The parameter friendlyName is the only mandatory one, and thus must be
specified. The other method overloads all have optional default values such as null, false,
and AppDomain.CurrentDomain.Evidence. From a programmatic perspective, you would override the respective method if you wanted to do the following:

GetAppDomainBaseDirectory: This returns the base directory of the new AppDomain. You
will need to specify this path either to the directory of the assembly you want to load, or
to a parent of that directory. Not doing so could lead to "assembly not found" errors.
When managing this directory, do not point it to the same directory of the Application
AppDomain—during development you might inadvertently reference or load an assembly that you don't want referenced, causing loading errors during runtime.

GetRelativeSearchPath: This returns a number of paths relative to the path defined by
GetAppDomainBaseDirectory, where assemblies to be loaded reside. Each path is separated
by a semicolon in Windows, or a colon in UNIX. To ensure that your code is cross-
platform, use the PathSeparator property when concatenating paths.

GetSecurityInfo: This returns a security descriptor that you can use to define how the
Remote AppDomain behaves. For example, you can define which assemblies are fully
trusted.

GetShadowCopyFile: This enables shadowing, and will be detailed later in this section.

GetInitializerFunction, GetInitializerArgs: These methods work together to return
the AppDomain initializer function and arguments.

CreateApplicationDomain: This method is used to instantiate a domain using a particular
version of the CreateDomain method. You can override the method if custom tweaking of
the parameters is necessary, or if you want a different variation of the CreateDomain
method.

Let's think about dynamic loading and unloading a bit more. The application starts, and two AppDomains are created: Application and Remote. When the Application needs the functionality from the implementation, the Remote AppDomain loads the implementation and offers the functionality to the application. The connection between the application AppDomain and the remote AppDomain is .NET remoting. If the implementation needs to be updated, then the remote AppDomain is unloaded.

You know about the process method of loading an assembly, but now think a bit more about the communications and unloading of the assembly, or more accurately put, unloading of the AppDomain. What is the trigger to unload the AppDomain? Does an administrator push a button? Does an algorithm manage the assemblies based on a time or maximum-size cache? The most likely reason why you would want to unload an assembly is so that you can replace it. If you were to try to replace an assembly that is dynamically loaded, most likely you wouldn't be able to because it is locked in place. If you are using a remote AppDomain, the lock does not go away. If you want to replace the assembly, you must explicitly unload the AppDomain; if there are no other outstanding references, the assembly will be unlocked. This approach is acceptable if you are writing an application and the assemblies are replaced when the application is not running. But it won't work when the application is running. An administrator does not want to shut down part of a server application to replace an assembly. An administrator would like to replace the old assembly and let the server figure out when to unload the AppDomain and load the new assembly.

The shadow-copy flag solves the file-lock problem by copying an assembly to another location. Then when a reference is made to the assembly the reference is in fact from the shadow location, and the method original assembly reference is unlocked and can be replaced freely. When shadow copying is in action, the cache looks similar to Figure 2-6.

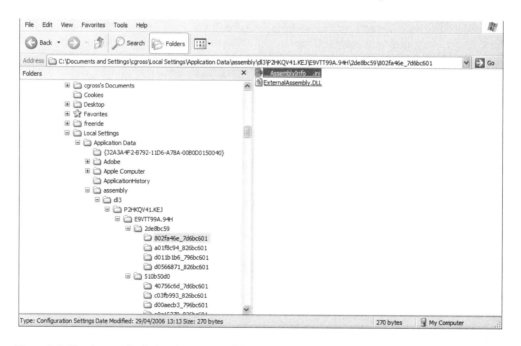

Figure 2-6. *Shadow cache being investigated from Windows Explorer*

The default location for the shadow cache when you don't specify its location is the directory [user identifier]/Local Settings/Application Data/assembly/[dynamically generated directory]. The dynamically generated directory makes it so you don't know what the subdirectories are, nor do you care. This is not to confuse the user, but to make sure that multiple versions of an assembly do not conflict. The default shadow cache is for you to know about, but not touch. You can define a custom location, but generally it is not necessary.

After all of the parameters have been initialized, the modified AssemblyLoader code calls the method CreateDomain. A new AppDomain that can be used to instantiate an object is returned. Any object instantiated in the new AppDomain is subject to all of the rules of the new AppDomain. If you have global information stored in a singleton that is defined in the Application AppDomain, it will not be viewable in the new AppDomain. You will need to reload and reinitialize all configuration information. This aspect of AppDomains is often forgotten.

To be able to unload the AppDomain and the assemblies it contains, you call the method Unload, as the following source code illustrates.

```
private void pUnload() {
    AppDomain.Unload(_unloadable);
    _unloadable = null;
}
```

As the code illustrates, unloading an AppDomain is trivial. As the AppDomain is unloaded, so are the assemblies. However, remember that having an AppDomain unloaded does not mean that the assembly is unlocked. If you have multiple AppDomains loading the same assembly, then all AppDomains must unload the assembly. If you are using shadow copying, some AppDomains may have newer versions of an assembly than other AppDomains do.

With a new AppDomain it is possible to instantiate objects using the AssemblyLoader2. Instantiate method, which is implemented as follows:

```
public ObjectType Instantiate<ObjectType>(Identifier identifier)
    where ObjectType : class {
    if (identifier.DoesExist(Identifier.ID_type) &&
        identifier.DoesExist(Identifier.ID_assembly)) {
        string typeIdentifier = identifier[Identifier.ID_type];
        string assemblyIdentifier = identifier[Identifier.ID_assembly];

        return _unloadable.CreateInstanceAndUnwrap(
            assemblyIdentifier, typeIdentifier) as ObjectType;
    }
    return default( ObjectType);
}
```

In the implementation Instantiate is the important bit. The boldface portion illustrates how the object is instantiated using CreateInstanceAndUnwrap and then cast to the desired class type. The other code relates to defining the type and identifier using a structure instead of simple strings.

Finally, when implementing a custom AppDomain-based assembly loader, you must subclass AssemblyLoader2 and implement the required parameters. The following is an example of implementing a new assembly loader class:

Source: /Volume01/LibVolume01/DynamicallyLoadUnload.cs

```
class MyLoader : AssemblyLoader2 {
    protected override String GetAppDomainName() {
        return "Test2";
    }
    protected override string GetAppDomainBaseDirectory() {
        return @"c:\...\assemblytoload";
    }
    protected override bool GetShadowCopyFiles() {
        return true;
    }
}
```

In the example implementation three parameters were implemented: an application name, a base directory, and a shadow copy. In most cases these are the three methods that you will implement. You will probably not implement security because you will use the security restrictions established by whoever loaded the consumer assembly. However, if you were writing a server application that managed its own resources, implementing security would be a good idea.

Because making cross-AppDomain calls requires the use of .NET remoting techniques, your objects must be .NET remoting–friendly. This means using the .NET attributes or, as the following source code shows, subclassing a specific .NET remoting class:

Source: /Volume01/ExternalAssemblies/Implementation.cs

```
class Implementation : System.MarshalByRefObject, IInterface {
    public void Method() {
        Console.WriteLine("Called the implementation");
    }
}
```

In the example the .NET remoting–required identifier is MarshalByRefObject. Not having that identifier would generate an exception because the .NET runtime would not know what to do. When using MarshalByRefObject as a base class you are saying, "Please do not serialize this object, but pass the reference of the object to the other AppDomain and generate a proxy that will call me."

Be very careful about using marshal by value, which copies the object's state to the Application AppDomain, and instantiates the object. By instantiating the object in the Application AppDomain you are defeating the purpose of this solution because the assembly will have to be loaded into the Application AppDomain. Serialize only types that are defined in the definitions assembly.

The following source code shows how to use MyLoader to instantiate the types that previously we used the simple dynamic loading techniques to instantiate:

Source: /Volume01/LibVolume01/DynamicallyLoadUnload.cs

```
MyLoader loader = new MyLoader();
loader.Load();
```

```
IInterface impl = loader.Instantiate<IInterface>(
    new Identifier("ExternalAssembly, …, PublicKeyToken=null",
                   "Implementation"));
impl.Method();
```

Instantiating the types is like the simple dynamic loading examples, except that the type
Identifier is used to identify the assembly and the type to instantiate. When the type is
instantiated, we can call the methods just like any other object.

When you are using AppDomains to dynamically load and unload, it's very important that
you know what to instantiate. There are four possible approaches to resolving the identifier
into a type and assembly:

Configuration file. A configuration file is loaded and processed by AssemblyLoader2.
When a specific type needs to be instantiated, AssemblyLoader2 cross-references the
requested type with the configuration information. This lets you configure the application
at runtime and use versioning information to load specific versions in specific contexts.
However, the administrator needs documentation from the developer on available plug-
in implementations, and an improper configuration file can wreak havoc when you're
debugging a production issue.

Assembly directory. Using a configuration file a directory is specified that contains a
number of assemblies. AssemblyLoader2 reads the directory and iterates the available
assemblies. Each assembly has its type information extracted and saved in a list. The list
is used to cross-reference identifiers to types and assemblies whenever a type instantiation request is made. The advantages of this approach are that minimal configuration
information is required since dynamic resolution occurs, and that the application can
heal itself if the appropriate version routines are kept. But the disadvantages of this
approach are that loading and instantiation logic is hard-coded within the dispatcher,
meaning a logic change requires an application restart; additionally, the application
developer has to know which plug-in implementation identifiers to use at development
time.

Factory delegation. The assemblies are referenced as a directory, or individually in a configuration file. The assemblies are dynamically loaded, but the type information is not
extracted. AssemblyLoader2 searches for a Factory pattern implementation in the individual assemblies that hooks itself to AssemblyLoader2. When a piece of code makes an
instantiation request, AssemblyLoader2 delegates to the Factory pattern. In this approach
instantiation is delegated to the plug-in implementations, which allows the implementation to decide which logic to use when instantiating a type. Additionally, the microkernel
or internal server does a delegation, allowing the assembly to handle its own versioning or
identifier cross-reference. The disadvantages of this approach are that each assembly
must implement a standard type used as an entry point for type instantiation, and each
assembly is responsible for figuring out which to instantiate—which means extra coding
requirements for the developer.

Server registration. In this approach `AssemblyLoader2` knows nothing, and it is the server's responsibility to register its type information with `AssemblyLoader2`. In this approach, types will be switched automatically whenever the server requires it. The problem with this approach, though, is that some program has to start the servers and indicate where `AssemblyLoader2` resides. This is an additional level of overhead. The other resolution techniques are not quite as flexible as this one, even though they are simpler.

As you can tell, each approach has its advantages and disadvantages. You have to decide for yourself what the best solution is. For illustration purposes, throughout this book I will reference the assemblies and type identifiers directly (a technique not detailed in this book). Would I use this technique in my daily development? Sure, when I am prototyping and trying to figure out how to structure my application.

Now let's consider a complication where you are making a Web service call. Web services use a neutral technology so that multiple technologies can talk to the Web service. In .NET to be able to make Web service calls you would use a tool to generate a proxy. However, the proxy might change. Therefore, we want to be able to load and unload the proxy. This would imply using a remote AppDomain. But there is a "gotcha" with the current .NET implementation of Web services: the problem is how .NET 2.0 generates proxies. Consider the following interface as being a Web service:

```
public interface ITestServiceSoap {
    string Echo(string a);
    int Add(int a, int b);
}
```

The Web service `ITestServiceSoap` has two methods: `Echo` and `Add`. They are simple methods that echo a sent buffer and add two numbers together. To call a Web service in .NET a proxy has to be generated. Using the console, the following command generates a proxy (Visual Studio offers wizards that do it automatically):

```
$ wsdl http://jupiter:8008/1.1/webservice/TestService.asmx?page=wsdl
```

```
Microsoft (R) Web Services Description Language Utility
[Microsoft(R) .NET Framework, Version 2.0.50727.42]
Copyright (C) Microsoft Corporation. All rights reserved.
Writing file 'TestService.cs'.
```

The `wsdl` command converts a Web Services Description Language (WSDL) file into a proxy. A WSDL file is the equivalent of an interface in Web-service speak.

The generated `wsdl` file will appear similar to the following (please note that I've cut most of the file to simplify the explanation):

```
[System.CodeDom.Compiler.GeneratedCodeAttribute("wsdl", "2.0.50727.42")]
[System.Diagnostics.DebuggerStepThroughAttribute()]
[System.ComponentModel.DesignerCategoryAttribute("code")]
[System.Web.Services.WebServiceBindingAttribute(➥
Name="TestServiceSoap", Namespace="http://tempuri.org/")]➥
public partial class TestService : ➥
    System.Web.Services.Protocols.SoapHttpClientProtocol {
```

The problem with the generated code is that the type TestService is a class. This is a problem for our remote AppDomain solution because cross-AppDomain calls expect an interface, or at least an abstract base class. It seems our only choice is to use the simple dynamic loading techniques and stop the application whenever a new proxy is generated.

You could hand-code an interface, but that is tedious and error prone. Another solution is to get the WSDL generator to create an interface. This is possible because the WSDL generator can generate the server stubs, which use interfaces. So the solution is to generate the client stubs, then generate the server stubs, copy the generated server interface, and tweak the client stubs to implement an interface.

Here is the generated output of running the WSDL generator twice:

```
$ wsdl /serverInterface ➡
http://jupiter:8008/1.1/webservice/TestService.asmx?page=wsdl
```

```
Microsoft (R) Web Services Description Language Utility
[Microsoft(R) .NET Framework, Version 2.0.50727.42]
Copyright (C) Microsoft Corporation. All rights reserved.

Writing file 'TestServiceInterfaces.cs'.
```

```
$ wsdl http://jupiter:8008/1.1/webservice/TestService.asmx?page=wsdl
```

```
Microsoft (R) Web Services Description Language Utility
[Microsoft(R) .NET Framework, Version 2.0.50727.42]
Copyright (C) Microsoft Corporation. All rights reserved.

Writing file 'TestService.cs'.
```

In the first instance of running the wsdl command, the command-line option /serverInterface is used. It generates a file that contains an interface that implements a Web service on the server. The trick lies in removing all of the attributes from the generated file and then subclassing the type TestServiceInterface in the type TestService. The resulting code will appear similar to the following:

```
[System.CodeDom.Compiler.GeneratedCodeAttribute("wsdl", "2.0.50727.42")]
  [System.Diagnostics.DebuggerStepThroughAttribute()]
[System.ComponentModel.DesignerCategoryAttribute("code")]
[System.Web.Services.WebServiceBindingAttribute(Name="TestServiceSoap", ➡
Namespace="http://tempuri.org/")]
public partial class TestService :
    System.Web.Services.Protocols.SoapHttpClientProtocol, ITestServiceSoap {
}
```

This redefined type can be encapsulated in a Factory:

```
namespace Chap04.Webservice {
    public static class Factory {
```

```
    public static ITestServiceSoap Create() {
        TestService srvc = new TestService();
        return srvc;
    }
  }
}
```

The three pieces of code, `TestService`, `TestServiceInterface`, and `WebService.Factory`, are compiled into an assembly that can be loaded and unloaded into a remote AppDomain.

The last item to cover in this section is the loading of assemblies. There are three types of assemblies: Consumer, Implementations, and Definitions. To make everything work smoothly, it is important to keep the Consumer and Implementations assemblies in separate directories because of the way .NET resolves assembly references. Consider the `RemoteLoader` class, which has built-in functionality to generate its list of loaded assemblies. Following is the source code that displays the loaded assemblies:

Source: `/jaxson.commons.dotnet/Loader/AssemblyLoader.cs`

```
public class RemoteLoader : MarshalByRefObject {
    public RemoteLoader() {
    }
    public override string ToString() {
        return new ToStringTracer()
            .Start(this)
            .Variable("Base Directory", AppDomain.CurrentDomain.BaseDirectory)
            .Variable("Application directory", ➡
AppDomain.CurrentDomain.SetupInformation.ApplicationBase)
            .Variable("Application bin directory", ➡
AppDomain.CurrentDomain.SetupInformation.PrivateBinPath)
            .StartArray("Loaded Assemblies")
            .Delegated(new ToStringTracerDelegate(
                        delegate(ToStringTracer instance) {
                            foreach (Assembly assembly in ➡
AppDomain.CurrentDomain.GetAssemblies()) {
                                instance.Variable("Assembly", assembly.FullName);
                            }
                        }))
            .EndArray()
            .End();
    }
}
```

Take special note of the `ToString` implementation. Within `ToString` are references to three `CurrentDomain` properties and methods: `ApplicationBase`, `PrivateBinPath`, and `GetAssemblies`. The properties `ApplicationBase` and `PrivateBinPath` determine the paths that .NET will use when trying to load an assembly. The method `GetAssemblies` generates the currently loaded AppDomain assemblies. These three pieces of information can give you an idea of what is loaded and from where. The same sort of `ToString` implementation is created for `AssemblyLoader2`.

The Consumer-type assembly is called `LibHowToCodeDotNetVolume1`, the Implementations-type assembly is called `ExternalAssembly`, and the Definitions-type assembly is called `ExternalAssemblyDefinitions`. Examine the following generated output, in which the assemblies are partitioned into separate directories:

```
Type:MyLoader
  Variable: application name (Test2)
  Variable: Application directory (E:\projects\HowToCodeDotNet\bin)
  Variable: Application bin directory ()
  Array Loaded Assemblies
     Variable: Assembly (mscorlib,)
     Variable: Assembly (nunit.core,)
     Variable: Assembly (System,)
     Variable: Assembly (System.)
     Variable: Assembly (System.Xml,)
     Variable: Assembly (LibHowToCodeDotNetVolume01,)
     Variable: Assembly (nunit.framework,)
     Variable: Assembly (nunit.core.extensions,)
     Variable: Assembly (ExternalAssemblyDefinitions,)
     Variable: Assembly (NCommons,)
Type: RemoteLoader
     Variable: Base Directory (E:\projects\ExternalAssembly\bin\Debug)
     Variable: Application directory (E:\projects\ExternalAssembly\bin\Debug)
     Variable: Application bin directory ()
     Array Loaded Assemblies
        Variable: Assembly (mscorlib,)
        Variable: Assembly (NCommons,)
        Variable: Assembly (ExternalAssembly,)
        Variable: Assembly (ExternalAssemblyDefinitions,)
```

The generated output contains two types: `MyLoader` and `RemoteLoader`. `MyLoader` is loaded in the Application AppDomain, and `RemoteLoader` is loaded in the Remote AppDomain. The number of assemblies loaded in each AppDomain is dramatically different because in the Remote AppDomain not as many assemblies are required for execution.

The bolded code represents where the Consumer, Implementations, and Definitions assembly types are loaded. The Consumer assembly `LibHowToCodeDotNetVolume101` is loaded into the Application Domain. The Implementations assembly `ExternalAssembly` is loaded into the Remote AppDomain. And the definitions assembly `ExternalAssemblyDefinitions` is loaded into both. This is what we wanted.

But things get funny when the implementations assembly is copied into the Application AppDomain directory. If you run the same code again, the following assembly listing is created:

```
Type:MyLoader
  Variable: application name (Test2)
  Variable: Application directory (E:\projects\HowToCodeDotNet\bin)
  Variable: Application bin directory ()
  Array Loaded Assemblies
     Variable: Assembly (mscorlib,)
     Variable: Assembly (nunit.core,)
```

```
        Variable: Assembly (System,)
        Variable: Assembly (System.)
        Variable: Assembly (System.Xml,)
        Variable: Assembly (LibHowToCodeDotNetVolume01,)
        Variable: Assembly (nunit.framework,)
        Variable: Assembly (nunit.core.extensions,)
        Variable: Assembly (ExternalAssemblyDefinitions,)
        Variable: Assembly (NCommons,)
        Variable: Assembly (ExternalAssembly,)
Type: RemoteLoader
        Variable: Base Directory (E:\projects\ExternalAssembly\bin\Debug)
        Variable: Application directory (E:\projects\ExternalAssembly\bin\Debug)
        Variable: Application bin directory ()
        Array Loaded Assemblies
            Variable: Assembly (mscorlib,)
            Variable: Assembly (NCommons,)
            Variable: Assembly (ExternalAssembly,)
            Variable: Assembly (ExternalAssemblyDefinitions,)
```

ExternalAssembly has been loaded into the Application AppDomain even though it is not necessary. The reason relates to how an assembly is referenced—via the Assembly.Fullname property that was coded using a string. When .NET resolves the assembly identifier to an assembly, it can reference either the GAC or the application base directory. If it references the application base directory, then all assemblies in the directory are loaded whenever an assembly resolution is made.

This side effect is undesired and illustrates that you need to be careful when loading and unloading assemblies. Keep the assemblies in separate directories, and be careful with the .NET APIs that perform dynamic resolution. Loading and unloading assemblies dynamically is more work than referencing an assembly directly, and it requires you to create infrastructure to be put into an assembly. You want to write the infrastructure code once and leave it.

Remember the following when implementing dynamic loading and unloading of assemblies:

- Loading and unloading an assembly uses AppDomains; you must understand what AppDomains are and how they function.

- When making cross-AppDomain method calls you are subject to the rules of .NET remoting. This means you should prefer interfaces to abstract base classes.

- To replace an assembly while the software is running, use a shadow directory so that the original assembly is not locked (which would prevent an update).

- When marking a class for execution in a remote AppDomain, don't forget to subclass System.MarshalByRefObject. If a class is serialized from the remote to local AppDomain, then use the Serializable attribute.

- Some code generators do the wrong thing (such as the WSDL generator) and require you to jump through hoops before you can load and unload the code.

- Hard-coded strings are a bad idea. When dynamically loading and unloading assemblies, look into using a resolution technique such as a configuration file.

- The success or failure of your implementation rests on how carefully you manage the storage and referencing of assemblies. These issues are administrative, but you must make sure your code does the right thing.

Implementing GetHashCode

Implementing the GetHashCode function is not much fun because you wonder what to write. The MSDN documentation doesn't help matters:

This method can be overridden by a derived class. Value classes must override this method to provide a hash function that is appropriate for the class and that ensures a better distribution in the hash table. Classes that might be used as a key in a hash table must also override this method, because objects that are used as keys in a hash table are required to generate their own hash code through this method. However, if the objects that are used as keys do not provide a useful implementation of GetHashCode, you can provide a different hash code provider, that is based on the System.Collections.IHashCodeProvider interface, when the Hashtable is constructed. —MSDN Object.GetHashCode

You can understand the words, but what does it mean? The purpose of GetHashCode is to uniquely identify the type in a collection of other types. Imagine creating a table of same-type instances. You can use the result from GetHashCode to uniquely identify one state of the object. And this is the core purpose of GetHashCode. If two object instances of one type contain the same data, then they will return the same hash code. You may want to use GetHashCode to compare two lists and see if they contain the same elements, for instance.

Implementing a hash code is best delegated to helper class that does the heavy lifting. The book *Effective Java*[7] outlines a robust technique:

1. Store some constant nonzero value, such as 17, in a variable.

2. For each data member of the type, perform a mathematical operation that results in int values that are successively multiplied and added, where the operation is specific to the type and defined as follows:

   2.1. Bool: If true return 0; otherwise return 1.

   2.2. byte, char, short, or int return the value of the type.

   2.3. Long: Return (int)(f ^ (f >>> 32).

   2.4. Float: Return Convert.ToInt32 of the value.

---

7. Joshua Bloch, *Effective Java* (Palo Alto, California: Addison-Wesley, 2001).

2.5. Object: Return the value generated by calling object.GetHashCode.

2.6. Array: Iterate and treat each element individually.

The rules are implemented in a class called HashCodeAutomater, and the following source code is an implementation in an abbreviated form:

Source: /jaxson.commons.dotnet/Automators/hashutilities.cs

```
public class HashCodeAutomater{
    private readonly int _constant;
    private int _runningTotal;

    public HashCodeAutomater() {
        _constant = 37;
        _runningTotal = 17;
    }

    public HashCodeAutomater AppendSuper(int superHashCode) {
        _runningTotal = _runningTotal * _runningTotal +
            superHashCode;
        return this;
    }

    public HashCodeAutomater Append( Object obj) {
        if (obj == null) {
            _runningTotal = _runningTotal * _constant;

        } else {
            if( obj.GetType().IsArray == false) {
                _runningTotal = _runningTotal * _runningTotal +
                    obj.GetHashCode();

            } else {
                if (obj is long[]) {
                    Append((long[]) obj);
                }
                // Other tests have been removed for clarity purposes
                else {
                    // Not an array of primitives
                    Append((Object[]) obj);
                }
            }
        }
        return this;
    }

    public HashCodeAutomater Append(long value) {
```

```
            _runningTotal = _runningTotal * _constant +
                ((int) (value ^ (value >> 32))));
            return this;
        }
    public HashCodeAutomater Append(long[] array) {
        if (array == null) {
            _runningTotal = _runningTotal * _constant;
        }
        else {
            for (int i = 0; i < array.Length; i++) {
                Append(array[i]);
            }
        }
        return this;
    }
    public HashCodeAutomater Append(Object[] array) {
        if (array == null) {
            _runningTotal = _runningTotal * _constant;
        }
        else {
            for (int i = 0; i < array.Length; i++) {
                Append(array[i]);
            }
        }
        return this;
    }
    public int toHashCode() {
        return _runningTotal;
    }
}
```

The different implementations of the method Append belong to a single grouping for a single data type, long. For example there is an Append method that accepts a long and a long array. In the full implementation of HashCodeAutomater there would be an Append method for short and short array, and all of the other data types. There is no specific group implementation for the string type, because it is treated like an object that has its own hash code calculation implementation.

Notice in the implementations of the Append methods how a calculation is performed and then added to the data member _runningTotal. The return value is a this reference, so that the methods can be chained together. This allows a client to use the HashCodeAutomater class, as in the GetHashCode implementation here:

Source: /Volume01/LibVolume01/ImplementGetHashcode.cs

```
class HashcodeExample {
    public int value;
    public string buffer;
```

```
    public HashcodeExample( int val, string buf) {
        value = val;
        buffer = buf;
    }
    public override int GetHashCode() {
        return new HashCodeAutomater()
            .Append( value)
            .Append( buffer).toHashCode();
    }
}
```

In the implementation of HashcodeExample, there are two data members: value and buffer. The two data members make up the class's state. Not all data members are used when calculating a class instance's hash code value. For example, if HashcodeExample had a data member that referenced a database connection, it should not be used when calculating the hash code. That's because the database connection is the type used to get the state, and does not influence the state—it is a means to an end.

Once the GetHashCode method has been implemented, the Equals method can be implemented:

```
public override bool Equals(object obj) {
    if( obj is HashCodeExample) {
        return obj.GetHashCode() == this.GetHashCode();
    }
    else {
        return false;
    }
}
```

Because the rule for GetHashCode is that two object instances with identical hash code values must return the same value, it makes sense to implement Equals using GetHashCode. What started out as a good idea turns out to be a bad idea, though, as illustrated in the following code.

Source: /Volume01/LibVolume01/ImplementGetHashcode.cs

```
[Test]
[ExpectedException( typeof( ArgumentException))]
void TestConflicting() {
    String s1 = "Hello";
    String s2 = "World";
    int x1 = 17 * 17 + s1.GetHashCode();
    int x2 = 17 * 17 + s2.GetHashCode();

    HashCodeExample h1 = new HashCodeExample (x2 * 37, s1);
    HashCodeExample h2 = new HashCodeExample (x1 * 37, s2);

    Hashtable ht = new Hashtable();
    ht.Add(h1, null);
    ht.Add(h2, null);
}
```

The following source code illustrates that having two objects with completely different states results in the same hash code value and generates an exception because Equals has been implemented incorrectly. In the implementation of Hashtable when an added object collides with another already existing object, an equality test is made. If the equality test returns true, then the exception is generated because Hashtable does not allow you to add an object with the same state as another object.

The solution is not to fix the GetHashCode method but, rather, to modify the Equals method:

```
public override bool Equals(object obj) {
    if (obj is HashCodeExampleWorking) {
        if (obj.GetHashCode() != this.GetHashCode())
            return false;

        // todo
        // 1. comparing element by element // hard work, not universal
        HashCodeExampleWorking toTest = obj as HashCodeExampleWorking;
        if( toTest.val == this.val) {
            if( toTest.buf == this.buf) {
                return true;
            }
        }
        // or
        // 2. comparing with reflection
        // or
        // 3. comparing the results of ToString()
        // what if not overridden or should this standard practice
        // like GetHashCode and Equals
    }
    return false;
}
```

The logic of the modified Equals method is to first test if both types are identical. If not, then false is returned. The next test determines if GetHashCode returns unequal values. GetHashCode will always return different values for objects that have different data members. If the hash-code values are equal, then comes the hard work of testing each data member individually for equality.

Rerunning the test that illustrates objects that returned the same hash code but different states will result in no exception being generated. Of course, because the code expects an exception, an error will be generated. In this case an error is good because it proves that you can add two objects to a hash table with the same hash-code values.

When implementing the GetHashCode method, remember the following:

- Don't try to come up with your own GetHashCode implementation. Use the one presented in this book.

- Whenever possible, implement GetHashCode.

- If you implement GetHashCode, also implement Equals. Equals is called when there is a hash-code-value collision.

Thinking of .NET Generics as Black Boxes

A black box in literal terms is a box that you have in your hand, but cannot open. You have no idea what is inside it, and often you do not care. For mail carriers, the letters or packages they deliver are black boxes; they contain things that they never open or read. In coding terms black boxes are extremely useful because they delegate functionality to another area of your code.

Before .NET Generics, black boxes could be represented only using the Object type. The .NET 1.x collection classes used the Object type as the basis of all objects. In .NET 2.0 the Object type has been replaced with .NET Generics. The following source code illustrates how a collection is managed using .NET Generics and the Object type.

Source: /Volume01/LibVolume01/GenericsAreBlackBoxes.cs

```
IList< int> lstNew = new List<int>();
lstNew.Add( 1);
int value = lstNew[ 0];

IList lstOld = new ArrayList();
lstOld.Add( 1);
value = (int)lstOld[ 0];
```

In the code the variable lstNew represents a list that uses .NET Generics. The variable lstOld represents a .NET 1.x list that uses the Object type. In the declaration of the .NET Generics list the angle brackets contain the type identifier int. This means that the list lstNewAdd is a collection of integers. When you want to add an integer or retrieve an integer from the list there is no autoboxing and no typecasting necessary.

In contrast, lstOld has no type indication. The collection could be integers, doubles, objects—whatever type .NET supports. Adding an integer to the list seems like adding a list to a .NET Generic collection, but there is quite a bit happening under the cover. When an integer is added to the collection a boxing operation happens, which wastes resources and CPU time. Then to extract the value from the collection a typecast is needed, which results in an unboxing operation that wastes more resources and CPU time.

So in the first order, using .NET Generics in the context of a collection saves resources and time. But .NET Generics are very powerful and make it possible to think in abstract terms. The .NET Generics collection class is saying, "I am going to manage a collection of type instances." Before .NET Generics, "Object instances" would have replaced "type instances" in that sentence. There is a world of difference between managing type instances and Objects. For example, the collection class is a type instance, and the following source code is completely legal:

```
IList< IList< IList< IList< int>>>> lst = new List< List< List< List< int>>>>();
```

The example illustrates how it is possible to embed declarations, enabling very sophisticated abstractions. As a result, the code can quickly become unreadable.

Imagine that you are implementing a Command-like pattern. You intend to create a chain of links that are executed in succession when implementing a Web server. In a Web server before a handler executes, a series of filters preprocesses the HTTP request. If we did not have Generics, the architecture could be defined as follows:

Source: /Volume01/LibVolume01/GenericsAreBlackBoxesOldWay.cs

```csharp
public interface IComponent {
    void Process(Object controldata);
}
public class Chain {
    IList _links = new ArrayList();

    public void AddLink(IComponent link) {
        _links.Add(link);
    }

    public void Process(Object controldata) {
        foreach (IComponent element in _links) {
            element.Process(controldata);
        }
    }
}
```

The bolded pieces reference the general type Object. In this case Object could be anything, and would require a typecast to be able to do anything meaningful. We have no option but to use Object if we want to keep things general.

You may wonder why we want to keep things general for a Web server. This is the crux of the argument for .NET Generics. I gave the Web server as an example, but the code could be used in other contexts. What is important about the context is that an abstract scenario is described. Without .NET Generics, everything has to be specific, or be so general that anything and everything could work in theory. We are conditioned to think in specific terms—conditioned to think of IList and not a collection of items.

.NET Generics lets us think in terms of a collection of objects, objects to be executed, and so on. And in the example the abstract scenario is the successive execution of IComponent-derived implementations that process the same data instance. From a .NET Generics perspective, the abstract scenario would be implemented as follows:

Source: /Volume01/LibVolume01/GenericsAreBlackBoxes.cs

```csharp
public interface IComponent<ControlData> {
    void Process(ControlData controldata);
}

public sealed class Chain<ControlData> where ControlData : new() {
    IList<IComponent<ControlData>> _links =
        new List<IComponent<ControlData>>();

    public void AddLink(IComponent<ControlData> link) {
        _links.Add(link);
    }

    public void Process(ControlData controldata) {
```

```
        foreach (IComponent< ControlData> element in _links) {
            element.Process(controldata);
        }
    }
}
```

In the example the interface IComponent<> is defined, where ControlData is a .NET Generics parameter that replaces the type Object. The Generic parameter is used in the method Process. In the class Chain<> the Generic parameter is ControlData. The identifiers are identical, but do not confuse this as meaning that they are the same type. The identifiers are just that: they serve as placeholders for types that are replaced when the class Chain is instantiated.

Look closely at the declaration of _links. The data member _links is a list of a Generic class embedding a Generic interface. Whoever declares Chain<> determines the specific embedded interface type. Embedding a Generic declaration within a Generic declaration gives us the freedom to determine the specifics later.

The following source code makes extensive use of Generics:

Source: /Volume01/LibVolume01/GenericsAreBlackBoxes.cs

```
class ImmutableData {
}

class Link : IComponent< ImmutableData> {
    public void Process(ImmutableData data) {
    }
}

class Accumulator< ControlData, ListProcessor> :
    IComponent< ControlData>
    where ListProcessor : IList< ControlData>, new() {
    ListProcessor _list;
    public Accumulator() {
        _list = new ListProcessor();
    }
    public void Process(ControlData controlData) {
        _list.Add(controlData);
    }
}

[TestFixture]
public class Tests {
    [Test]
    public void Example() {
        Chain<ImmutableData> chain =
            new Chain<ImmutableData>();
```

```
        chain.AddLink(new Link());
        chain.AddLink(
            new Accumulator< ImmutableData,
                List< ImmutableData>>());
        chain.Process(new ImmutableData("data1", "data2"));
    }
}
```

Ignore all of the details; they will lead you astray. Before you look at code that uses Generic libraries, make sure you understand what the Generic libraries do. If you do not, you will not understand the big picture and hence will not understand what the specifics are trying to accomplish.

Remember that the Generic library is a Command-like pattern implementation that is the successive execution of IComponent-derived implementations that process the same data instance. The Generic library implements the IComponent interface, and uses the Chain class. We could therefore work top-down or bottom-up. I've chosen to work bottom-up and therefore we must find anywhere IComponent is referenced. (If we were to work top-down, then we would need to find anywhere a Chain class is referenced.) Because we're working bottom-up, we must find both of the IComponent implementations: Link and Accumulator. Link is an example of class that leaves no options available; it has specified what the .NET Generic parameter ControlData as ImmutableData. That means that somewhere there must be a Chain class reference that has defined its .NET Generics parameter as Immutable.

Accumulator is not as obvious, and complicates everything because it is Generic class that has an additional .NET Generics parameter. However, we sort of know what the additional Generic parameter does because it has the constraint that ListProcessor must implement the IList interface.

Having investigated all of the IComponent implementation references, let's move up a layer and find a Chain reference with ImmutableData. We don't need to look far; the test case has an example. With Chain using the ImmutableData type as ControlData, all of the other references classes must define its ControlData parameter as ImmutableData.

We now know that Link is some processor that does some logic, and that Accumulator acts like a sink and collects all of the ImmutableData instances executed in the chain.

Bear the following points in mind when thinking about .NET Generics:

- .NET Generics is not just a way to manage collections as a single type.

- .NET Generics is about implementing an abstract concept and leaving the specifics as implementation details.

- To fully understand .NET Generics and how to use them, you must understand how to read and write code as abstract concepts.

- The specifics are black boxes that do something, are passed around, and are manipulated in the .NET Generic class.

- Your mechanisms of abstraction are .NET Generics, then interfaces, and then implementations.

- It is very easy to create code that becomes very difficult to understand and use. Hence it is extremely important that you write code that is verbose, and does not use tricks. Tricks make your code harder to maintain and extend.

- When reading and trying to understand more-sophisticated .NET Generic code, read and understand in layers. Start with the abstract and move to the specific, not the other way around.

Figuring Out What Generic Methods Do

For most situations developers will define classes or interfaces to use .NET Generics, but it is possible to use .NET Generics at the method level. There are two scenarios in which using Generics at the method level is the best solution: when you want to stop .NET Generics parameter explosion, and when you want flexibility of parameter types.

Unless you have used .NET Generics extensively, you probably have no idea how bad parameter explosion can be. Generic parameter explosion happens when you have types reference other types, and as a result of that referencing the types require a .NET Generics parameter that they usually would not.

Imagine implementing a Web service, but instead of implementing the search algorithm you use the Google, Microsoft, and Amazon Web service APIs. For every search request your implementation generates three requests, each of which generates some results that will be gathered and then fed back to the original request. The process of shooting off multiple requests and then waiting for the results would be implemented as follows:

Source: /Volume01/LibVolume01/WhatGenericMethodsDo.cs

```
interface ICommand< ResultType> {
    void Execute(IParent< ResultType> parent);
}
interface IParent< ResultType> {
    void AddResult(ResultType result);
}
class ExecuteHandlers< ResultType> : IParent< ResultType> {
    ArrayList _commands = new ArrayList();
    public void AddResult( ResultType result) {

    }
    public void Execute() {
        foreach( ICommand<ResultType> cmd in _commands) {
            cmd.Execute( this);
        }
    }
}
```

In the example there are two interfaces: ICommand<> and IParent<>. Both interfaces are defined using a .NET Generics parameter ResultType, which defines a general response type. In the case of the Web search example, the general response type would be a search result.

> **■Note** If you are wondering why I am talking about search, and you're thinking that the source code has absolutely nothing to do with searching, then read the section "Thinking of .NET Generics as Black Boxes." .NET Generics gives us an abstract way of expressing certain pieces of logic without using types that relate specifically to search.

Here I'll outline how to implement search using the defined .NET Generics classes. A request is received by the HTTP server, then the HTTP handler executes ExecuteHandler<> and three classes (Amazon, Google, and Yahoo search implementations) that implement the ICommand<> interface. Then the instances are added to the ExecuteHandler<>._commands data member. The search data is passed to the individual instances using constructor parameters. At this point control passes to the ExecuteHandler<> instance, and the ExecuteHandler<> instance spins off a thread for each item in the _commands list. The ExecuteHandler<> has implemented IParent<>, thus allowing the ICommand<> instances to save their results in a central location. When all of the searches are complete, the HTTP request retrieves the results and returns them to the client. The logic of this is correct and minimalist.

The source code shows an explosion of ResultType. Every class and interface is defined with a .NET Generics parameter ResultType. In the case of ICommand<>, is the ResultType .NET Generics parameter needed? In an abstract logic sense no, because ICommand<> is a reference point that the ExecuteHandlers<> class uses to execute some logic. The .NET Generics parameter is needed because the ICommand<> interface exposes a method that has as a parameter the IParent<> interface, which defines and needs the .NET Generics parameter ResultType. Because we needed to set up a callback situation, a .NET Generics parameter declared in one type had to be declared in another type to satisfy the compiler's constraints.

Generic parameter explosions occur for multiple reasons, with one example being the interfaces ICommand<> and IParent<>. The example contains only one level of explosion, but you might have two or three levels, and you might have to create *carryover Generic parameters*. A carryover Generic parameter is a Generic parameter associated with a type that serves no purpose other than being a Generic parameter for some other referenced type. You could break up the interfaces to minimize a callback situation, but that delegates the Generic parameter explosion into different interfaces or classes.

The solution is to use a method-level .NET Generics parameter. The following is the modified version of the source code that used .NET Generics parameters at the interface level:

```
interface ICommand {
    void Execute(IParent parent);
}
interface IParent {
    void AddResult< ResultTypeMethod>(ResultTypeMethod result);
}
class ExecuteHandlers< ResultType> : IParent where ResultType : class {
    IList< ICommand> _commands = new List<ICommand>();
    IList< ResultType> _results = new List< ResultType>();
    public void AddCommand( ICommand cmd) {
        _commands.Add( cmd);
    }
}
```

```
    public void AddResult<ResultTypeMethod>(ResultTypeMethod result) {
        _results.Add( result as ResultType);
    }
    public void Execute() {
        foreach (ICommand cmd in _commands) {
            cmd.Execute(this);
        }
    }
}

class Result {
}
class MyCommand : ICommand {
    public void Execute( IParent parent) {
        parent.AddResult( new Result());
    }
}

[TestFixture]
public class Tests {
    [Test]
    public void Test() {
        ExecuteHandlers< Result> handler = new ExecuteHandlers< Result>();
        handler.AddCommand( new MyCommand());
        handler.Execute();
    }
}
```

The .NET Generics parameter is applied to the method level of the interface IParent. This means that someone who wants to reference IParent does not have to account for the .NET Generics parameter. When a callback scenario is required the modified ICommand implementation does not use Generic parameters.

The tricky bit is in the implementation of ExecuteHandlers<>, because it is still defined using a Generic parameter. We want that because we want all results to be of a single type. When a Generic parameter is defined at the method level, there is no specific type defined. For the method AddResult, that means any type of result can be generated. Generally this is good, but in the case of ExecuteHandlers we want a specific type as defined by the Generic parameter ResultType. The result is the definition of two Generic parameters that have nothing to do with each other.

When you look more closely at the implementation of AddResult, you'll see that the parameter is of type ResultTypeMethod, but the list is of type ResultType. To match the two types, a typecast using the as operator is performed. The Generic parameter ResultType in .NET Generic terms is different from the .NET Generics parameter ResultTypeMethod defined on the method AddResult.

If there is a weakness in this technique, it is that if a .NET Generics parameter is defined at the class/interface and method levels, they are two different types that need a typecast. Is it not better to use the .NET Generics parameter at the type level? The answer is no, because .NET Generics parameter explosion does happen, and often it gets tedious when you need to drag .NET Generics parameters around for bookkeeping's sake. Additionally, dragging around extra .NET Generics parameters does not help the code's readability.

As you've seen, .NET Generics parameters at the method level give you flexibility. You would want that flexibility if you are dealing with different types that might need to be converted or managed, or with a situation in which there is no clear single type. For example, when declaring a list using a .NET Generics parameter declared at the type level, the list can contain only the .NET Generics declared type. Sometimes you might want a collection of mixed types. For that purpose .NET Generics parameters defined at the method level are ideal.

Now let's consider another use of .NET Generics parameters at the method level by implementing a universal data converter. Using .NET 1.x techniques, the definition of the converter would be as follows:

Source: /Volume01/LibVolume01/WhyGenericsNeedNewClass.cs

```
class UniversalDataConverter {
    public Object Convert( Object input) { }
}
```

The class UniversalDataConverter has a single method, Convert. An object is input for conversion, and an object is output. To perform a conversion from one type to another, the converter needs to know what type the Convert method should convert to. Using reflection you know the input type, but because the method is declared you don't know the return type. Using .NET 1.x you would need to provide a second parameter that defines what the return value's type should be.

Alternatively, you can use .NET Generic methods, which provides enough information to convert the input to the output type. The following is a modified declaration that uses .NET Generics at the method level:

```
class UniversalDataConverter {
    public outType Convert<outType, inType>( inType input) {
        // …
    }
}
```

The method Convert has been changed and is complete because there are type declarations for the input and output types. Based on these two .NET Generics parameters, Convert can decide how the parameter input is converted.

Before I continue explaining the method, I want to explain why method-level Generics is more appropriate than type-level Generics. To get the same effect at the type level, you'd use the following declaration:

```
class UniversalDataConverterType< inType, outType> {
    public outType Convert(inType input) {
}
```

The declaration of the Generic parameters has shifted from the method to the type and it seems that there is not much difference. But the difference is apparent when calling the types, as the following source code illustrates:

```
String buffer = new UniversalDataConverterType<
    string, string>().Convert( "buffer");
```

```
int value = new UniversalDataConverterType<
    int, string>().Convert( "123");
UniversalDataConverter converter = new UniversalDataConverter();
String buffer = converter.Convert< string, string>("buffer");
int value = converter.Convert< int, string>("123");
```

In the example conversions, the type `UniversalDataConverterType` had to be declared and instantiated for each conversion performed. In contrast, using .NET Generics at the method level allowed the client to instantiate a single instance and reuse that instance with different types. This is the big difference with method-level and type-level .NET Generics: in method-level .NET Generics a single instance can be used for multiple .NET Generics operations.

Continuing with `UniversalDataConverter`, notice that the declaration does not contain any constraints that could be declared as follows:

```
class UniversalDataConverter {
    public outType PassThrough<outType, inType>( inType input)
        where outType : string where inType : int  {
        // …
    }
}
```

In the example the constraints say that the `outType` must be of `string` type, and the `inType` must be of `int` type. The constraints are not legal and will generate compiler errors. However, I've included them here because they illustrate the error, showing that constraints are possible at the method level and that constraints are not useful in the context of type conversion because they limit the conversions.

Now let's implement some conversions. The following is the source code for two conversions (`string` to `string` and `string` to `int`).

```
class UniversalDataConverter {
    public outType Convert<outType, inType>(inType input) {
        if (input is string &&
            typeof( string).IsAssignableFrom(typeof( outType))) {
            return (outType)(object)input;
        }
        else if( input is string &&
            typeof( int).IsAssignableFrom( typeof( outType))) {
            return (outType)(object)int.Parse( (string)(object)input);
        }
        return default(outType);
    }
}
```

In the implementation the `is` operator checks the type of the `input` parameter. This is possible because `inType` has an instance defined by the parameter `input`. For `outType` there is no instance and thus it is more difficult to verify the type; in .NET there is no `is` operator for type classes. A solution would be to instantiate `outType`, but that would require adding the new constraint to `outType`, and what if `outType` were an interface or an abstract base class?

In either of those cases it is would be impossible to instantiate an instance. There are two viable solutions that let you verify the type. The first is as follows:

```
if( typeof( string).IsAssignableFrom(typeof( outType))) {
```

This solution says that an outType instance can be assigned to a string instance. Therefore, outType is either of the type, subclasses the type, or implements the type.

The second viable solution is as follows:

```
if( typeof( type).GetInterface( "User") != null) { ...
```

In this example the source says that to figure out the type we must retrieve the interface User. If the interface type information can be retrieved from the type, then the type can be cast to the interface.

Once we've established the input and output types, we can perform a conversion. This is where things become tricky; there are no constraints and therefore the C# compiler has no idea what the types are. Even though the decision block (if(typeof…) has established the types, the information is defined using runtime techniques that are not available to the compiler. So, for example, converting a string to a string requires multiple casts, as the following source code illustrates:

```
return (outType)(object)inType;
```

The trick is the double cast. The first cast is from the unknown type to an object. If inType were a class type, the cast would be implicit. If inType were a value type, that would involve some boxing. Looking at the underlying IL, the double casting is a boxing and unboxing operation so that a cast from one type to another is legal:

```
IL_0028:  ldarg.1
IL_0029:  box        !!inType
IL_002e:  unbox.any  !!outType
IL_0033:  ret
```

The double cast is required because a constraint was not defined. The compiler has to assume that both class and value types are used. Had the class constraint been defined, then we could have used the following code:

```
return input as outType;
```

For the conversion from string to int several conversions happen:

```
return (outType)(object)int.Parse( (string)(object)input);
```

The double cast (string)(object) converts the input type to a string, and the (outType)(object) converts the integer value to the return type. These casts are necessary because the compiler has no type constraints and thus has no idea what the input and output types are.

When using method-level .NET Generics, remember the following:

- Using .NET Generics at the method level or the type level does not affect how the Generic parameters behave.

- Generic parameters stop Generic parameter explosions, in which types drag around Generic parameters because of referencing issues.

- The advantage of using Generics at the method level is that the same method can be called multiple times with different Generic parameters using the same object instance. To get the same effect with Generic parameters at the type level, multiple object instances are involved. The one exception is if the methods are static.

- When using Generics at the parameter level, you will most likely need to make the method robust enough to accept a variety of types, requiring the use of some special coding techniques (reflection and the double cast).

Using the new and class Keywords with .NET Generics

As I was writing the section "Finding Out What Generic Methods Do," when I instantiated a Generic type in the context of a method I stumbled onto something that both intrigued and puzzled me. First consider the following code, which can be used to instantiate a type:

```
return new Implementation();
```

The instantiation is a direct instantiation of a type, and the underlying IL is as follows:

```
IL_0001:  newobj    instance void Implementation::.ctor()
```

The command newobj instantiates the Implementation type and calls the parameterless constructor. This way of instantiating a type is what I know and expect. Consider the following source code, which has the class and new constraints added to a Generic type defined at the method level:

Source: /Volume01/LibVolume01/WhyGenericsNeedNewClass.cs

```
type AlwaysWorks<type>() where type: class, new() {
    if( typeof( IBase).IsAssignableFrom( typeof( type)) is IBase) {
        return new type();
    }
}
// …
IBase base = AlwaysWorks< Implementation>();
```

The code looks relatively innocent; when the method AlwaysWorks is called with the method type of Implementation, it will instantiate Implementation directly, similar to the previously illustrated MSIL (or at least that's how it is supposed to happen). But look at how the generated MSIL actually looks:

```
//000028:          type obj = new type();
    IL_0001:  call       !!0
                  [mscorlib]System.Activator::CreateInstance<!!0>()
    IL_0006:  stloc.0
```

The MSIL calls the method Activator.CreateInstance, which means a late binding instantiation is happening. The type information for the Generic parameter is loaded and passed to the method `Activator.CreateInstance`. There is no direct instantiation using the keyword `newobj` even though the Generic type information is available. This is mind-boggling because the generated code implies that the Generic type does not have direct access to the type information.

The following source code is a C# representation of the MSIL:

Source: /Volume01/LibVolume01/WhyGenericsNeedNewClass.cs

```
public Object CreateType( Object type) {
    return Activator.CreateInstance( type.GetType());
}
```

The generated IL code gets even more bizarre if the `class` constraint is dropped from the constraints; the following IL code is generated for the instantiation:

```
//000020:          type obj = new type();
    IL_0001:  ldloca.s    CS$0$0001
    IL_0003:  initobj     !!'type'
    IL_0009:  ldloc.2
    IL_000a:  box         !!'type'
    IL_000f:  brfalse.s   IL_001c

    IL_0011:  ldloca.s    CS$0$0001
    IL_0013:  initobj     !!'type'
    IL_0019:  ldloc.2
    IL_001a:  br.s        IL_0021

    IL_001c:  call        !!0
            [mscorlib]System.Activator::CreateInstance<!!0>()
```

What is the C# compiler generating? Is the C# compiler doing the right thing? Indeed the C# compiler is doing the right thing, because in the declaration of `AlwaysWorks` we are not indicating a class type since the `class` constraint is missing. This means that the Generic type could be a reference type or a value type. The generated IL starts by instantiating the Generic type as if it were a value type, and if that does not work it attempts to instantiate the type as a reference type.

I decided to compile the same source code using the Mono C# compiler, and it generated the following MSIL:

```
//000020:          type obj = new type();
    IL_0005:  call class [mscorlib]System.Type class
                [mscorlib]System.Type::GetTypeFromHandle(
                valuetype [mscorlib]System.RuntimeTypeHandle)
    IL_000a:  call object class
                [mscorlib]System.Activator::CreateInstance(
                class [mscorlib]System.Type)
```

The Mono-generated code is interesting in that the method `Type.GetTypeFromHandle` is called before the method `Activator.CreateInstance`. Simply put, the Mono C# compiler uses late binding as well.

Does this mean you need to avoid instantiating types in the context of a Generic method or class? It depends on your performance needs. More important, though, using the Factory pattern in the context of .NET Generics will not slow down your application. The following code does not use the new keyword, but delegates to a Factory.

```
type AlwaysWorks<type>() where type: class {
    if( typeof( IBase).IsAssignableFrom( typeof( type)) is IBase) {
        return objFactory.instantiate();
    }
}
```

Using a Factory does require a method call, but you have complete control over how to instantiate the type. Using the new constraint, you can instantiate only the types that have parameterless constructors.

Remember the following when using the new and class constraints:

- The new and class constraints are convenience keywords to optimize the code.

- Whether you use the Factory pattern or the new constraint, there will not be much difference from a performance perspective. A Factory's advantage is that it can accept multiple constructor parameters that are not possible when using the new constraint.

- If possible use the class constraint; it tends to create slimmer code. Using the class keyword means your Generic type or method will use classes only. The compiler does not need to generate any code that must process value types.

CHAPTER 3

■■■

Text-Related Solutions

There are many countries, cultures, and languages on this planet we call home. People in each country may speak a single language or multiple languages, and each country may host cultures. In the early days of computing, you could choose any language to use—so long as it was American English. As time progressed we became able to use software in multiple languages and for multiple cultures. .NET raises the bar; it lets you mix and match cultures, languages, and countries in a single compiled application. This chapter is about processing text in a multiculture/multicountry/multilanguage situation.

Converting a String to an Array and Vice Versa

In previous programming languages like C and C++, strings were buffer arrays, and managing strings was fraught with complications. Now that .NET strings are their own types, there is still grumbling because managing a string as bits and bytes has become complicated.

To manage a string as bits and bytes or as an array, you need to use byte arrays, which are commonly used when reading and writing to a file or network stream. Let's look at a very simple example that reads and writes a string to a byte array and vice versa.

Source: /Volume01/LibVolume01/StringToBufViceVersa.cs

```
[Test]
public void SimpleAsciiConversion() {
    String initialString = "My Text";
    byte[] myArray =
        System.Text.Encoding.ASCII.GetBytes(
        initialString);
    String myString =
        System.Text.Encoding.ASCII.GetString(
        myArray);
    Assert.AreEqual( initialString, myString);
}
```

In the example the string initialString contains the text "My Text". Using the predefined instance System.Text.Encoding.ASCII and method GetBytes, the string is converted into a byte array. The byte array myArray will contain seven elements (77, 121, 32, 84, 101, 120, 116) that represent the string. The individual numbers correspond to representations of the letter from the ASCII[1] table. Byte arrays are examples of lookup tables, where the value of a byte

---

1. http://www.lookuptables.com/

corresponds to a representation. For example, the number 77 represents a capital *M*, and 121 a lowercase *y*. To convert the array back into a string, you need an ASCII lookup table, and .NET keeps some lookup tables as defaults so that you do not need to re-create them. In the example the precreated ASCII lookup table System.Text.Encoding.ASCII is used, and in particular the method GetString. The byte array that contains the numbers is passed to GetString, and a converted string representation is returned. The test Assert.AreEqual is called to verify that when the buffer was converted to a byte array and then back to a buffer no data was lost in translation. When the code is executed and the test is performed, the strings initialString and myString will be equal, indicating that nothing was lost in translation.

Let's consider another example, but this time make the string more complicated by using the German *u* with an umlaut character. The modified example is as follows:

Source: /Volume01/LibVolume01/StringToBufViceVersa.cs

```
[Test]
public void SimpleAsciiConversion() {
    String initialString = "für";
    byte[] myArray =
        System.Text.Encoding.ASCII.GetBytes(
        initialString);
    String myString =
        System.Text.Encoding.ASCII.GetString(
        myArray);
    Assert.AreEqual( initialString, myString);
}
```

Running the code generates a byte array that is then converted back into a string array; the text für is generated. In this case something was lost in translation because the beginning string and the end string don't match. The question mark is a bit odd because it was not in the original array. Let's take a closer look at the generated values of the byte array (102, 63, 114) after the conversion from the string. When the byte array is converted back to a buffer in the ASCII table referenced earlier, 63 represents a question mark. Thus something went wrong in the conversion from the string buffer to the byte array. What happened and why was the *ü* lost in translation?

The answer lies in the way that .NET encodes character strings. Earlier in this section I mentioned the C and C++ languages. The problem with those languages was not only that the strings were stored as arrays, but that they were not encoded properly. In the early days of programming, text was encoded using American Standard Code for Information Interchange (ASCII). ASCII text was encoded using 95 printable characters and 33 nonprintable control characters (such as the carriage return). ASCII is strictly a 7-bit encoding useful for the English language.

The examples that converted the strings to a byte array and back to a string used ASCII encoding. When the conversion routines were converting the string buffers, the *ü* presented a problem. The problem is that *ü* does not exist in the standard ASCII table. Thus the conversion routines have a problem; the letter needs to be converted, and the answer is 63, the question mark. The example illustrates that when using ASCII as a standard conversion from a string to byte array, you are limiting your conversion capabilities.

What is puzzling is why a .NET string can represent a *ü* as a buffer, but ASCII can't. The answer is that .NET strings are stored in Unicode format, and each letter is stored using a 2-byte encoding. When text is converted into ASCII, the conversion is from 2 bytes per character to 1 byte per character, resulting in lost information. Specifically, .NET strings use the Unicode format that maps to UTF-16[2] and cannot be changed. When you generate text using the default .NET string encoding, string manipulations are always based in Unicode format. Note that conversions always happen, you don't notice because the conversions occur automatically.

The challenge of managing text is not in understanding the contents of the string buffers themselves, but in getting the data into and out of a string buffer. For example, when using `Console.WriteLine` what is the output format of the data? The default encoding can vary and depends on your computer configuration. The following code displays what default encodings are used:

Source: /Volume01/LibVolume01/StringToBufViceVersa.cs

```
Console.WriteLine( "Unicode codepage (" +
    System.Text.Encoding.Unicode.CodePage +
    ") name (" +
    System.Text.Encoding.Unicode.EncodingName + ")");
Console.WriteLine( "Default codepage (" +
    System.Text.Encoding.Default.CodePage +
    ") name (" +
    System.Text.Encoding.Default.EncodingName + ")");
Console.WriteLine( "Console codepage (" +
    Console.OutputEncoding.CodePage + ") name (" +
    Console.OutputEncoding.EncodingName + ")");
```

When the code is compiled and executed, the following output is generated:

```
Unicode codepage (1200)
    name (Unicode)
Default codepage (1252)
    name (Western European (Windows))
Console codepage (437)
    name (OEM United States)
```

The code is saying that when .NET stores data in Unicode, the code page 1200 is used. *Code page* is a term used to define a *character-translation table,* or what has been called a lookup table. The code page contains a translation between a numeric value and a visual representation. For example, the value 32 when encountered in a file means to create a space. When the data is read and written, the default code page is 1252, or Western European Windows. And when data is generated or read on the console, the code page used is 437, or OEM United States.

Essentially, the code sample says that all data is stored using code page 1200. When data is read and written, code page 1252 is being used. Code page 1252, in a nutshell, is ASCII text that supports the "funny" Western European characters. And when data is read or written to the console, code page 437 is used because the console is generally not as capable at generating characters as the rest of the Windows operating system is.

---

2. `http://en.wikipedia.org/wiki/UTF-16`

Knowing that there are different code pages, let's rewrite the German text example so that the conversion from string to byte array to string works. The following source code illustrates how to convert the text using Unicode:

Source: /Volume01/LibVolume01/StringToBufViceVersa.cs

```
[Test]
public void GermanUTF32() {
    String initialString = "für";
    byte[] myArray =
        System.Text.Encoding.Unicode.GetBytes(
        initialString);
    String myString =
        System.Text.Encoding.Unicode.GetString(
        myArray);
    Assert.AreEqual( initialString, myString);
}
```

The only change made in the example was to switch the identifier ASCII for Unicode; now the string-to-byte-array-to-string conversion works properly. I mentioned earlier that Unicode requires 2 bytes for every character. In myArray, there are 6 bytes total, which contain the values 102, 0, 252, 0, 114, 0. The length is not surprising, but the data is.

Each character is 2 bytes and it seems from the data only 1 byte is used for each character, as the other byte in the pair is zero. A programmer concerned with efficiency would think that storing a bunch of zeros is a bad idea. However, English and the Western European languages for the most part require only one of the two bytes. This does not mean the other byte is wasted, because other languages (such as the Eastern European and Asian languages) make extensive use of both bytes. By keeping to 2 bytes you are keeping your application flexible and useful for all languages.

In all of the examples, the type Encoding was used. In the declaration of Encoding, the class is declared as abstract and therefore cannot be instantiated. A number of predefined implementations (ASCII, Unicode, UTF32, UTF7, UTF8, ASCII, BigEndianUnicode) that subclass the Encoding abstract class are defined as static properties. To retrieve a particular encoding, or a specific code page, the method System.Text.Encoding.GetEncoding is called, where the parameter for the method is the code page. If you want to iterate the available encodings, then you'd call the method System.Text.Encoding.GetEncodings to return an array of EncodingInfo instances that identify the encoding implementation that can be used to perform buffer conversions.

If you find all of this talk of encoding types too complicated, you may be tempted to convert the characters into a byte array using code similar to the following:

```
String initialString = "für";
char[] charArray = initialString.ToCharArray();
byte val = (byte)charArray[ 0];
```

This is a bad idea! The code works, but you are force-fitting a 16-bit char value into an 8-bit byte value. The conversion will work sometimes, but not all the time. For example, this technique would work for English and most Western European languages.

When converting text to and from a byte array, remember the following points:

- When text is converted using a specific Encoding instance, the Encoding instance assumes that text being encoded can be. For example, you can convert the German *ü* using ASCII encoding, but the result is an incorrect translation without the Encoding instance. Avoid performing an encoding that will loose data.

- Strings are stored in code page 1200; it's the default Unicode page and that cannot be changed in .NET.

- Use *only* the .NET-provided routines to perform text-encoding conversions. .NET does a very good job supporting multiple code pages and languages, and there is no need for a programmer to implement his own functionality.

- Do not confuse the encoding of the text with the formatting of the text. Formatting involves defining how dates, times, currency, and larger numbers are processed, and that is directly related to the culture in which the software will be used.

Parsing Numbers from Buffers

Here is a riddle: what is the date 04.05.06? Is it April 5, 2006? Is it May 4, 2006? Is it May 6, 2004? It depends on which country you are in. Dates and numbers are as frustrating as traveling to another country and trying to plug in your laptop computer. It seems every country has its own way of defining dates, numbers, and electrical plugs. In regard to electrical plugs, I can only advise you to buy a universal converter and know whether the country uses 220V or 110V power. With respect to conquering dates and numbers, though, I can help you—or rather, .NET can.

Processing Plain-Vanilla Numbers in Different Cultures

Imagine retrieving a string buffer that contains a number and then attempting to perform an addition as illustrated by the following example:

```
string a = "1";
string b = "2";
string c = a + b;
```

In the example, buffers a and b reference two numbers. You'd think adding a and b would result in 3. But a and b are string buffers, and from the perspective of .NET adding two string buffers results in a concatenation, with c containing the value 12. Let's say you want to add the number 1.23, or 1,23 (depending on what country you're in), the result would be 2.46 or 2,46. Even something as trivial as adding numbers has complications. Add in the necessity of using different counting systems (such as hexadecimal), and things can become tricky.

Microsoft has come to the rescue and made it much easier to convert buffers and numbers that respect the individuality of a culture. For example, Germans use a comma to separate a decimal, whereas most English-speakers use a period.

Let's start with a very simple example of parsing a string into an integer, as the following example illustrates:

Source: /Volume01/LibVolume01/ParsingNumbersFromBuffers.cs

```
int value = int.Parse( "123");
```

The type int has a Parse method that can be used to turn a string into an integer. If there is a parse error, then an exception is generated, and it is advisable when using int.Parse to use exception blocks, shown here:

Source: /Volume01/LibVolume01/ParsingNumbersFromBuffers.cs

```
        try {
            int value = int.Parse( "sss123");
        }
        catch( FormatException ex) {
        }
```

In the example the Parse method will fail because there are three of the letter *s* and the buffer is not a number. When the method fails FormatException is thrown, and the catch block will catch the exception.

A failsafe way to parse a number without needing an exception block is to use TryParse, as the following example illustrates:

Source: /Volume01/LibVolume01/ParsingNumbersFromBuffers.cs

```
int value;
if( int.TryParse( "123", out value)) {
}
```

The method TryParse does not return an integer value, but returns a bool flag indicating whether the buffer could be parsed. If the return value is true, then the buffer could be parsed and the result is stored in the parameter value that is marked using the out identifier. The out identifier is used in .NET to indicate that the parameter contains a return value.

Either variation of parsing a number has its advantages and disadvantages. With both techniques you must write some extra code to check whether the number was parsed successfully.

Another solution to parsing numbers is to combine the parsing methods with *nullable types*. Nullable types make it possible to define a value type as a reference. Using a nullable type does not save you from doing a check for validity, but does make it possible to perform a check at some other point in the source code. The big idea of a nullable type is to verify whether a value type has been assigned. For example, if you define a method to parse a number that the method returns, how do you know if the value is incorrect without throwing an exception? With a reference type you can define null as a failed condition, but using zero for a value type is inconclusive since zero is a valid value. Nullable types make it possible to assign a value type a null value, which allows you to tell whether a parsing of data failed. Following is the source code that you could use to parse an integer that is converted into a nullable type:

Source: /Volume01/LibVolume01/ParsingNumbersFromBuffers.cs

```
public int? NullableParse( string buffer) {
    int retval;
    if( int.TryParse( buffer, out retval)) {
        return retval;
    }
    else {
        return null;
    }
}
```

In the implementation of NullableParse, the parsing routine used is TryParse (to avoid the exception). If TryParse is successful, then the parsed value stored in the parameter retval is returned. The return value for the method NullableParse is int?, which is a nullable int type. The nullable functionality is defined using a question appended to the int value type. If the TryParse method fails, then a null value is returned. If an int value or a null value is returned, either is converted into a nullable type that can be tested.

The example following example illustrates how a nullable type can be parsed in one part of the source code and verified in another part:

Source: /Volume01/LibVolume01/ParsingNumbersFromBuffers.cs

```
public void VerifyNullableParse( int? value) {
    if (value != null) {
        Assert.AreEqual(2345, value.Value);
    }
    else {
        Assert.Fail();
    }
}
[Test]
public void TestNullableParse() {
    int? value;
    value = NullableParse( "2345");
    VerifyNullableParse( value);
}
```

In the code example the test method TestNullableParse declares a variable value that is a nullable type. The variable value is assigned using the method NullableParse. After the variable has been assigned, the method VerifyNullableParse is called, where the method parameter is value.

The implementation of VerifyNullableParse tests whether the nullable variable value is equal to null. If the value contained a value of null, then it would mean that there is no associated parsed integer value. If value is not null then the property value.Value, which contains the parsed integer value, can be referenced,

You now know the basics of parsing an integer; it is also possible to parse other number types (such as `float` -> `float.Parse`, `float.TryParse`) using the same techniques. Besides number types, there are more variations in how a number could be parsed. For example, how would the number 100 be parsed, if it is hexadecimal? (*Hexadecimal* is when the numbers are counted in base-16 instead of the traditional base-10.) A sample hexadecimal conversion is as follows:

Source: /Volume01/LibVolume01/ParsingNumbersFromBuffers.cs

```
[Test]
public void ParseHexadecimal() {
    int value = int.Parse("10", NumberStyles.HexNumber);
    Assert.AreEqual(16, value);
}
```

There is an overloaded variant of the method `Parse`. The example illustrates the variant that has an additional second parameter that represents the number's format. In the example, the second parameter indicates that the format of the number is hexadecimal (`NumberStyles.HexNumber`); the buffer represents the decimal number 16, which is verified using `Assert.AreEqual`.

The enumeration `NumberStyles` has other values that can be used to parse numbers according to other rules, such as when brackets surround a number to indicate a negative value, which is illustrated as follows:

Source: /Volume01/LibVolume01/ParsingNumbersFromBuffers.cs

```
[Test]
public void TestParseNegativeValue(){
    int value = int.Parse( " (10) ",
        NumberStyles.AllowParentheses | NumberStyles.AllowLeadingWhite |
        NumberStyles.AllowTrailingWhite);
    Assert.AreEqual( -10, value);
}
```

The number " (10) " that is parsed is more complicated than a plain-vanilla number because it has whitespace and brackets. Attempting to parse the number using `Parse` without using any of the `NumberStyles` enumerated values will generate an exception. The enumeration `AllowParentheses` processes the brackets, `AllowLeadingWhite` indicates to ignore the leading spaces, and `AllowTrailingWhite` indicates to ignore the trailing spaces. When the buffer has been processed, a value of –10 will be stored in the variable `value`.

There are other `NumberStyles` identifiers, and the MSDN documentation does a very good job explaining what each identifier does. In short, it is possible to process decimal points for fractional numbers, positive or negative numbers, and so on. This raises the topic of processing numbers other than `int`. Each of the base data types, such as Boolean, Byte, and Double, have associated `Parse` and `TryParse` methods. Additionally, the method `TryParse` can use the `NumberStyles` enumeration.

Managing the Culture Information

Previously I mentioned that the German and English languages use a different character as a decimal separator. Different languages and countries represent dates differently too. If the parsing routines illustrated previously were used on a German floating-point number, they would have failed. For the remainder of this solution I will focus on parsing numbers and dates in different cultures.

Consider this example of parsing a buffer that contains decimal values:

Source: /Volume01/LibVolume01/ParsingNumbersFromBuffers.cs

```
[Test]
public void TestDoubleValue() {
    double value = Double.Parse("1234.56");
    Assert.AreEqual(1234.56, value);

    value = Double.Parse("1,234.56");
    Assert.AreEqual(1234.56, value);
}
```

Both examples of using the Parse method process the number 1234.56. The first Parse method is a simple parse example because it contains only a decimal point that separates the whole number from the decimal number. The second Parse-method example is more complicated in that a comma is used to separate the thousands of the whole number. In both examples the Parse routines did not fail.

However, when you test this code you might get some exceptions. That's because of the culture of the application. The numbers presented in the example are encoded using en-CA, which is English (Canada) notation.

To retrieve the current culture, use the following code:

Source: /Volume01/LibVolume01/ParsingNumbersFromBuffers.cs

```
CultureInfo info =
    Thread.CurrentThread.CurrentCulture;
Console.WriteLine(
    "Culture (" + info.EnglishName + ")");
```

The method Thread.CurrentThread.CurrentCulture retrieves the culture information associated with the currently executing thread. (It is possible to associate different threads with different cultural information.) The property EnglishName generates an English version of the culture information, which would appear similar to the following:

```
Culture (English (Canada))
```

There are two ways to change the culture. The first is to do it in the Windows operating system using the Regional and Language Options dialog box (Figure 3-1).

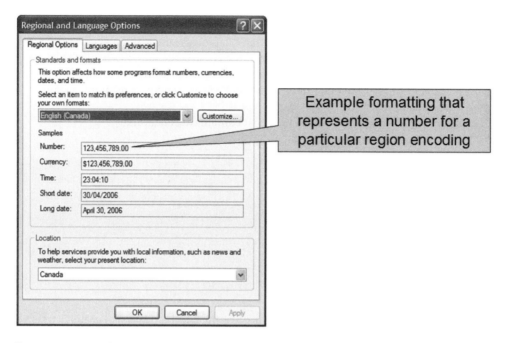

Figure 3-1. *Regional settings that influence number, date, and time format*

The Regional and Language Options dialog box lets you define how numbers, dates, and times are formatted. The user can change the default formats. In Figure 3-1 the selected regional option is for English (Canada). The preceding examples that parsed the numbers assumed the format from the dialog box. If you were to change the formatting to Swiss, then the function `TestDoubleValue` would fail.

If you don't want to change your settings in the Regional and Language Options box, you can instead change the culture code at a programmatic level, as in the following code:

```
Thread.CurrentThread.CurrentCulture =
    new CultureInfo("en-CA");
```

In the example a new instance of `CultureInfo` instantiated and passed to the parameter is the culture information `en-CA`. In .NET, culture information is made up using two identifiers: language and specialization. For example, in Switzerland there are four languages spoken: French, German, Italian, and Romansch. Accordingly, there are four different ways of expressing a date, time, or currency. The date format is identical for German speakers and French speakers, but the words for "March" (Marz in German or Mars in French) are different. Likewise, the German word for "dates" is the same in Austria, Switzerland, and Germany, but the format for those dates is different. This means software for multilanguage countries like Canada (French and English) and Luxembourg (French and German) must be able to process multiple encodings.

The following is an example that processes a `double` number encoded using German formatting rules (in which a comma is used as a decimal separator, and a period is used as a thousands separator).

Source: /Volume01/LibVolume01/ParsingNumbersFromBuffers.cs

```
[Test]
public void TestGermanParseNumber() {
    Thread.CurrentThread.CurrentCulture =
        new CultureInfo("de-DE");
    double value = Double.Parse( "1.234,56");
    Assert.AreEqual( 1234.56, value);
}
```

The source code assigns the de-DE culture info to the currently executing thread. Then whenever any of the parsing routines are used, the formatting rules of German from Germany are assumed. Changing the culture info does not affect the formatting rules of the programming language.

It is also possible to parse dates and times using the Parse and TryParse routines:

Source: /Volume01/LibVolume01/ParsingNumbersFromBuffers.cs

```
[Test]
public void TestGermanParseDate() {
    DateTime datetime = DateTime.Parse( "May 10, 2005");
    Assert.AreEqual( 5, datetime.Month);
    Thread.CurrentThread.CurrentCulture =
        new CultureInfo("de-DE");
    datetime = DateTime.Parse( "10 Mai, 2005");
    Assert.AreEqual( 5, datetime.Month);

}
```

In the example, notice how the first DateTime.Parse processed an English (Canadian)–formatted text and knew that the identifier May equaled the fifth month of the year. For the second DateTime.Parse method call, the culture was changed to German, and it was possible to process 10 Mai, 2005. In both cases, processing the buffer poses no major problems so long as you know whether the buffer is a German or an English (Canadian) date. Things can go awry if you have a German date paired with an English culture.

Converting a data type to a buffer is relatively easy in .NET 2.0 because the ToString methods have been implemented to generate the desired output. Consider the following example, which generates a buffer from an int value:

Source: /Volume01/LibVolume01/ParsingNumbersFromBuffers.cs

```
[Test]
public void TestGenerateString() {
    String buffer = 123.ToString();
    Assert.AreEqual( "123", buffer);
}
```

In the example the value 123 has been implicitly converted into a variable without our having to assign the value 123 to a variable. The same thing can be done to a double; the following example illustrates assigning a value to a variable.

```
double number = 123.5678;
String buffer = number.ToString( "0.00");
```

In the example the number 123.5678 is converted to a buffer using the method ToString, but the method ToString has a parameter. The parameter is a formatting instruction that indicates how the double number should be generated as a buffer. In the example we want a buffer with a maximum of two digits after the decimal point. Because the third digit after the decimal is a 7, the entire number is rounded up, resulting in the buffer 123.57.

You may be wondering if the culture information also applies to generating a buffer. Indeed it does, and when a double is generated the format for the selected culture is taken into account, as in the following example:

Source: /Volume01/LibVolume01/ParsingNumbersFromBuffers.cs

```
[Test]
public void TestGenerateGermanNumber() {
    double number = 123.5678;
    Thread.CurrentThread.CurrentCulture =
        new CultureInfo("de-DE");
    String buffer = number.ToString( "0.00");
    Assert.AreEqual( "123,57", buffer);
}
```

Like in previous examples, the CurrentCulture property is assigned the desired culture. Then when the double variable number has its ToString method called, the buffer "123,57" is generated.

Finally, if you need to convert a number into a buffer of a different number system (for example, convert a decimal number in a hexadecimal), you could use the following code:

```
String buffer = Convert.ToString( 10, 16).ToUpper();
Assert.AreEqual( "A", buffer);
```

The class Convert has a number of methods that allow you to test and convert numbers and buffers into other numbers and buffers. In the example the number 10 is converted into base-16, which is hexadecimal, and assigned to the variable buffer. The Assert.AreEqual method tests to make sure that the buffer contains the letter *A* that represents a 10 in hexadecimal.

When parsing or converting numbers, times, dates, and currencies, consider the following:

- Do not hard-code and assume specific formats; there is nothing more frustrating than applications that make assumptions about formatting.

- Be consistent when managing numbers, dates, times, and currencies in your application.

- Use *only* the .NET-provided routines to perform the number, date, time, or currency conversions.

When to Use StringBuilder

One of the most commonly used classes within .NET (or any programming environment) is a string type. The string is popular because humans communicate using text, and therefore it has a special function. In .NET a string is a collection of characters in Unicode format, and it has some special properties; a string is immutable, which means that once it's assigned it cannot be changed.

The big idea behind immutability is that if you want to append a string to an already existing string, a new string is created. The existing string is not expanded. The ramification is that a new string buffer is allocated; the data from the original string and the string to append are copied into the new string buffer.

Imagine an application that builds a string by appending a string 100 times. The result is the allocation of 100 buffers that is copied 100 times. Allocating so many times wastes resources, and the .NET Framework contains a class called StringBuilder. StringBuilder is not immutable and uses an expandable buffer to append a string. You would use StringBuilder when manipulating a buffer that is concatenated with many smaller buffers, thus saving the allocations.

You must ask if it is wise to use StringBuilder for all of your string manipulations; the C# compiler's behavior illustrates that StringBuilder is not always necessary. The following code shows common string-building operations:

Source: /Volume01/LibVolume01/WhenToUseStringBuilder.cs

```
class TestStrings {
    private static string _left = "On the left (";
    private static string _right = ") On the right";

    public static string Example1(string param1) {
        string buffer;
        buffer = _left;
        buffer += param1;
        buffer += _right;
        return buffer;
    }
    public static string Example2( string param1) {
        StringBuilder buffer = new StringBuilder();
        buffer.Length = 256;
        buffer = buffer.Append( _left);
        buffer = buffer.Append( param1);
        buffer = buffer.Append( _right);
        return buffer.ToString();
    }
    public static string Example3( string param1) {
        return _left + param1 + _right;
    }
}
```

In the class TestStrings there are three method declarations: Example1, Example2, and Example3. Each method's implementation generates the same result, but each uses a difference technique. We want to find out what the compiler does and which method has the best performance.

Example1 illustrates the building of the buffer using the = and += operators. When a buffer is built with this approach, new buffers are created for each operation. Each new buffer is concatenated with the old buffer to build another. The Example1 code is translated to the following IL code. For explanation purposes in Example1 the details of how the variable buffer is created are ignored.

```
IL_0001:  ldsfld string
    WhenToUseStringBuilder.TestStrings::_left
IL_0006:  stloc.0
IL_0007:  ldloc.0
IL_0008:  ldarg.0
IL_0009:  call string
    [mscorlib]System.String::Concat
    (string, string)
IL_000e:  stloc.0
IL_000f:  ldloc.0
IL_0010:  ldsfld string
    WhenToUseStringBuilder.TestStrings::_right
IL_0015:  call string
    [mscorlib]System.String::Concat
    (string, string)
```

In the IL there are two calls to String::Concat, which means two buffers are created. The function String::Concat takes two parameters, which are two strings. For the first call the two strings are the parameter param (ldarg.0), and the parameter _left (ldsfld). After ldsfld are the instructions stloc.0 and ldloc.0 that save the result in the variable buffer. The content of the variable buffer (stloc.0) is then pushed onto the stack again (ldloc.0), with the variable _right (ldsfld). A second String::Concat is executed, and the result is again pushed into the variable buffer.

In the IL of the method Example1, two string buffers are created. In the implementation of Example1 the cost of each += is an additional string instantiation. For very large strings the cost of performing an instantiation could be expensive in terms of performance and resources— it's better to use StringBuilder, as that manipulates a buffer as a single piece of memory.

In Example2 the class StringBuilder concatenates the strings. The purpose of the class StringBuilder is to build a buffer incrementally. The StringBuilder class contains memory manipulation routes that will manipulate text using a single buffer. When calling the Append method the data is appended to an already existing buffer. Assigning the property Length preallocates a buffer large enough to contain all of the text. It is not necessary to the assign the Length property, but it can optimize the program. Let's look at the generated IL of Example2.

```
IL_0001:  newobj    instance void [mscorlib]System.Text.StringBuilder::.ctor()
IL_0006:  stloc.0
IL_0007:  ldloc.0
IL_0008:  ldc.i4    0x100
IL_000d:  callvirt  instance void ➡
```

```
[mscorlib]System.Text.StringBuilder::set_Length(int32)
    IL_0012:  nop
    IL_0013:  ldloc.0
    IL_0014:  ldsfld      string WhenToUseStringBuilder.TestStrings::_left
    IL_0019:  callvirt    instance class [mscorlib]System.➡
Text.StringBuilder ➡
[mscorlib]System.Text.StringBuilder::Append(string)
    IL_001e:  stloc.0
    IL_001f:  ldloc.0
    IL_0020:  ldarg.0
    IL_0021:  callvirt    instance class [mscorlib]System.Text.StringBuilder ➡
[mscorlib]System.Text.StringBuilder::Append(string)
    IL_0026:  stloc.0
    IL_0027:  ldloc.0
    IL_0028:  ldsfld      string WhenToUseStringBuilder.TestStrings::_right
    IL_002d:  callvirt    instance class [mscorlib]System.Text.StringBuilder ➡
[mscorlib]System.Text.StringBuilder::Append(string)
    IL_0032:  stloc.0
    IL_0033:  ldloc.0
    IL_0034:  callvirt    instance string [mscorlib]System.Object::ToString()
```

It is not necessary to go through the individual details of the code, but it is necessary to understand the overall intent of the IL code. In the IL code there are multiple stloc.0 and ldloc.0 instructions. The contents of the string variables are pushed onto the stack, and then the stack is processed by the call to StringBuilder::Append, which pops the stack and appends the popped strings to its internal text buffer. The approach of Example2 has only two performance and resource costs: instantiation of StringBuffer and appending of the string buffers to the internal memory of StringBuffer.

I added the last approach, Example3 (which seems similar to Example1) to illustrate how the C# compiler will optimize the manipulation of buffers. In theory Example3 should be as inefficient as Example1, but Example3 results in the C# compiler doing a look ahead and allocates a single buffer. It is a clever technique implemented at the compiler level. The following IL code illustrates what does occur:

```
IL_0000:  nop
IL_0001:  ldsfld      string
    WhenToUseStringBuilder.TestStrings::_left
IL_0006:  ldarg.0
IL_0007:  ldsfld      string
    WhenToUseStringBuilder.TestStrings::_right
IL_000c:  call        string
    [mscorlib]System.String::Concat(
    string, string, string)
IL_0011:  stloc.0
```

In the disassembled code for Example3, only one buffer is instantiated and that is created by the method String::Concat. But unlike the previous examples of Concat, there are three parameters rather than two. The three parameters are needed because all of the concatenated

string buffers are pushed onto the stack and combined in one step. This is a clever optimization by the C# compiler, and if written out in C# it would resemble the following source code:

```
public static string Example4( string param1) {
    return String.Concat( _left, param1, _right);
}
```

Of course, the source code of Example4 is not what was originally written in the C# code.
But in logic terms the methods Example3 and Example4 are equal.

So which method is fastest: Example1, Example2, Example3, or Example4? The best way to
answer that question is to use a profiler. For the examples I used the profiler nprof.[3] The
profiler reveals the following runtimes:

```
Example1:   0.30%
Example2:   3.38%
Example3:   0.33%
Example4:   0.28%
```

The execution times are both surprising and seemingly illogical. The surprising fact is that
the Example2 method, which uses the StringBuilder class, is 10 times slower than any of the
other methods. The problem is that the code illustrated a narrowly defined situation in which
the cost of setting up StringBuilder is relatively high. This does not mean that StringBuilder
is inappropriate; it is still the best option when building a larger string buffer that is the result
of many smaller string operations.

The illogical part is that Example3 and Example4 have different times, even though both are
implemented using the same IL. That's because when the profiler is run multiple times, the
garbage collector is not entirely consistent about when memory is freed; the runtimes give you
only a general idea of what the application is doing.

When using string buffers, remember the following:

- The .NET memory allocator is particularly clever and knows how to optimize memory
  usage. Memory is divided into predefined segments that can be allocated on a
  moment's notice. This means you should not be afraid to work with individual strings
  that are concatenated using the + and += operators.

- When manipulating small blocks like the ones shown in the examples, the technique
  illustrated in Example3 is best.

- When manipulating blocks of 4K or greater, it is best to use StringBuilder because
  larger blocks may be harder to allocate and de-allocate on a moment's notice.

- Know when to optimize for performance and resources and when not to. In the example the difference between the two techniques seems large, but in a big-picture sense it
  is as if one method took 3 milliseconds, and the other took 30 milliseconds. That is not
  much of a difference, and hence either technique is adequate.

- Sometimes the best approach is a combination of techniques. For example, the
  StringBuilder of the method Example2 can be combined with the all-in-one
  concatenation of Example3 when iterating loops.

---

3.   Available at http://nprof.sourceforge.net/Site/SiteHomeNews.html

Finding a Piece of Text Within a Text Buffer

Any programmer will need to find text within a buffer at some point. There are multiple ways to find text in .NET, but some methods are simple and others are more complicated. The simplest way is to use the IndexOf method of the String type, as the following example illustrates:

Source: /Volume01/LibVolume01/FindingTextWithinBuffer.cs

```
String buffer = "Find the text in the buffer";
            //   01234567890
int index = buffer.IndexOf( "the");
```

In the example the variable buffer references some text. All String types have an associated method IndexOf, which has a single parameter. The single parameter is the text to find in the variable. When IndexOf finds the text in the buffer, it returns the index of where the text was found. If the text cannot be found, then IndexOf returns a value of –1.

In the example, the line below the buffer declaration contains a comment that counts up. Executing IndexOf with the parameter "the" will cause the search routines to start at index 0 and continue until they find the substring "the". Using the numbers in the comment, the letter *t* of "the" is above the number 5. Calling the method IndexOf would return the number 5, (assuming that the first letter is the zeroth index). In C#, indices start at zero rather than at one.

In the text "Find the text in the buffer" there are two instances of the text "the". If the method IndexOf were used repeatedly, the same offset would be found. That's because the way that the method IndexOf is called in the example means the text search will always start at the zeroth index. A different variation of IndexOf allows you to indicate at which index the search for the buffer should begin. The following source code would find all instances of the text "the":

Source: /Volume01/LibVolume01/FindingTextWithinBuffer.cs

```
String buffer = "Find the text in the buffer";
int startIndex = 0;
int foundIndex = -1;
do {
    foundIndex = buffer.IndexOf( "the", startIndex);
    Console.WriteLine( "Index (" + foundIndex + ")");
    startIndex = foundIndex + 1;
} while( foundIndex != -1);
```

The source code has two variables: startIndex and foundIndex. The variable startIndex indicates where the method IndexOf should start its search. The variable foundIndex indicates where the "the" text was found. The variable buffer contains the text that is to be searched.

After the variables have been declared, a loop is started with the do keyword. Within the loop the method IndexOf is called with two parameters. The first parameter is like the preceding example and represents the text to find in the buffer. The second parameter is the index of where the search should start. Again, the method returns an index of the found buffer.

On the line where the startIndex variable is assigned, it is important to notice the addition of the number 1. Without it, the same index would be returned in an infinite loop. When no more instances of the text are found, the variable `foundIndex` returns a –1 value, which stops the looping.

Another variation of the `IndexOf` function searches for a single character, as in the following source code:

Source: /Volume01/LibVolume01/FindingTextWithinBuffer.cs

```
String buffer = "Find the text in the buffer";
int foundIndex = buffer.IndexOf( ' ' );
```

Notice the use of single quotes instead of double quotes in the second line of code. Single quotes are used to define a single character that is to be found in a text buffer. In this example, we're looking for the space character.

One of the downsides of searching using a character that employs `IndexOf` is that you can specify only one character to find. What if you wanted to search for two characters in a buffer? Using the method `IndexOfAny` you can pass an array of characters to find, as in the following example:

Source: /Volume01/LibVolume01/FindingTextWithinBuffer.cs

```
String buffer = "Find the text in this buffer";
int foundIndex = buffer.IndexOfAny( new char[] { 'a', 'e', 'i', 'o', 'u'});
```

In this example, we're searching for any English-language vowel in the buffer. As with `IndexOf`, the first found match is returned. However, `IndexOfAny` can match multiple characters. If the example were executed, it would return the index value 1, which correlates to the letter *i*.

However, matching a character has limitations: In the preceding example, all of the vowels were lowercase letters. If in the text buffer to be searched there were capitalized vowels, they would not be found. One solution is to specify the characters to be searched as follows:

Source: /Volume01/LibVolume01/FindingTextWithinBuffer.cs

```
buffer.IndexOfAny( new char[] { 'a', 'A', 'e','E','i','I','o','O','u','U'});
```

In the example each letter was declared twice in the `char` array—once uppercase and once lowercase. The result is a case-insensitive search. Creating an array where each letter is repeated to enable a case-insensitive search is doable. However, creating an array of buffers to search for a piece of text is not efficient; it results in a permutations and combinations as illustrated by the following example:

```
foundIndex = buffer.IndexOf( "to");
foundIndex = buffer.IndexOf( "To");
foundIndex = buffer.IndexOf( "tO");
foundIndex = buffer.IndexOf( "TO");
```

The text to be found is "to," and when doing a case-insensitive search, four combinations of the text exist. Doing four searches for a two-character text buffer is inefficient and tedious. Imagine if the text buffer had nine characters—such a scenario would be a permutations and combinations nightmare.

When doing case-insensitive searches the common solution has been to convert the text to be searched into either lowercase or uppercase. Having the text to be searched be of a single case makes it easier to find specific pieces of text.

Converting the text to be searched to either uppercase or lowercase is not an ideal solution, as it means altering the text to be searched. .NET 2.0 offers a new option: the StringComparison enumeration allows you to perform a string case-insensitive search. The following example illustrates it:

Source: /Volume01/LibVolume01/FindingTextWithinBuffer.cs

```
String buffer = "find the text in this buffer";
int foundIndex = buffer.IndexOf( "THE",
    StringComparison.OrdinalIgnoreCase);
```

In the rewritten example IndexOf has another overloaded version that accepts as its last parameter a StringComparison enumeration value. For the purposes of doing a string case-insensitive search, the enumeration value OrdinalIgnoreCase is passed as a parameter value. The foundIndex will not return a –1 value but, rather, the value 5. Of course, there is a variation of IndexOf that can start a search at a specific index. An example is as follows:

Source: /Volume01/LibVolume01/FindingTextWithinBuffer.cs

```
String buffer = "Find the text in this buffer";
int foundIndex = buffer.IndexOf( "TH", 6,
    StringComparison.OrdinalIgnoreCase);
```

In the example, IndexOf has three parameters, where the second parameter represents the location where the search is started. Executing the example will assign a value of 17 to the variable foundIndex.

The StringComparison enumeration does have other enumeration values, but by and large for the IndexOf method they are not useful. The main purpose of the StringComparison enumeration is to deal with the details and special rules of sorting and comparing Unicode text in languages other than English.

Thus far all of our text searches have involved searching for a piece of text from the beginning of a buffer. It is possible to search for a piece of text from the end of the buffer using the method LastIndexOf:

```
String buffer = "Find the text in this buffer";
int foundIndex = buffer.LastIndexOf( "the");
```

When the code is executed the variable foundIndex is assigned the value of 5. If the IndexOf method were used, it too would return the value of 5.

As with the IndexOf function, it is possible to find all instances in a text buffer using an overloaded version of LastIndexOf. However, when using LastIndexOf in a loop, the starting index is one less than the last found index. The following example illustrates how to find all instances of a piece of text in a buffer:

Source: /Volume01/LibVolume01/FindingTextWithinBuffer.cs

```
String buffer = "Find the text in the buffer";
int startIndex = buffer.Length;
int foundIndex = -1;
do {
     foundIndex = buffer.LastIndexOf( "the", startIndex);
     Console.WriteLine( "Index (" + foundIndex + ")");
     startIndex = foundIndex - 1;
} while( foundIndex != -1);
```

When using the method LastIndexOf you need to specify the buffer's last index as the first index used to start searching. You don't start searching at index 0 because 0 is the beginning of the buffer, not the end. To begin searching at the end, use the buffer.Length property—it is the buffer's last index. For each found index, the next start index is one less than the last found index; hence the use of foundIndex - 1.

When executing simple searches, remember the following points:

- The methods IndexOf, IndexOfAny, and LastIndexOf have various overloaded implementations. Familiarize yourself with the examples to get acquainted with the implementations.

- When searching for strings within a buffer in a case-insensitive manner, use the enumeration StringComparison.OrdinalIgnoreCase.

- IndexOf, IndexOfAny, and LastIndexOf are best suited to finding a complete buffer within another buffer.

Always Implement ToString

In the .NET platform, ToString is not implemented consistently. The definition of ToString is as follows:

> *Every object in C# inherits the* ToString *method, which returns a string representation of that object.*

—MSDN Overriding OnPaint and ToString

Consider this source code, which shows both a working implementation of ToString and a broken implementation of it:

Source: /Volume01/LibVolume01/AlwaysImplementToString.cs

```
List< string> elements = new List< string>();
string buffer1 = "buffer 1";
string buffer2 = "buffer 2";
```

```
Console.WriteLine( "buffer1.ToString( " + buffer1 + ")");
elements.Add( buffer1);
elements.Add( buffer2);
Console.WriteLine( "_elements.ToString( " +
    elements.ToString() + ")");
```

In the source code there are three variables: elements, buffer1, and buffer2. The variables buffer1 and buffer2 are string types, and the variable elements is a list of string types. Theoretically, calling ToString on buffer1 will return the contents of buffer1. And calling ToString on elements will return the contents of buffer1 and buffer2 in the context of a list.

To see if the theory matches the reality, look at the following generated output:

```
buffer1.ToString( buffer 1)
elements.ToString(
    System.Collections.Generic.List`1[System.String])
```

The ToString method worked properly for buffer1, but improperly for elements. The incorrect implementation for the list is baffling. Looking at the reverse engineered code from the .NET Reflector[4] utility, it appears that ToString has not been implemented for any of the collection classes. The information returned by ToString could have been found just as easily using the GetType method.

Following is the source code for implementing the ToString method for a List class.

Source: /Volume01/LibVolume01/AlwaysImplementToString.cs

```
public class ToStringList< type> : List< type> {
    public override string ToString() {
        string buffer = base.ToString() + " \n";
        foreach( type element in this) {
            buffer += "Element (" + element.ToString() + ")\n";
        }
        return buffer;
    }
}
```

A new type, ToStringList<>, is defined. It subclasses the List<> type to enable the implementation of the ToString method without having to create a helper function. The new type implements only a single method call—ToString. Within the ToString implementation the variable buffer is initially assigned the contents of the base ToString variable. Calling the base ToString method is good practice because then you are assured of capturing all vital information related to the state of the object. The foreach keyword iterates the list and adds content incrementally. Once the content adding is complete, the value of the variable buffer is returned.

Executing the ToString function generates the following output:

```
AlwaysImplementToString.ToStringList`1[System.String]
Element (buffer 1)
Element (buffer 2)
```

---

4. http://www.aisto.com/roeder/dotnet/

The generated buffer contains the type information and the contents of the list, making it easy to identify the state of the object.

Consider the following when implementing ToString:

- Implementing ToString is not required, but doing so makes it more useful to know the object's state. This is important when you are doing post-mortem analysis, or tracing and logging.

- When you are using test-driven development it is necessary to implement ToString because otherwise you will have problems finding out why tests failed.

- When generating the ToString string buffer, attempt to enforce some type of output convention—otherwise you will struggle to figure out the meaning of the generated content.

- When creating the ToString string buffer, consider only the state that is relevant to the object. For example, don't generate the contents of a database connection. Instead, generate the attributes about the database connection, such as SQL string, number of records found, etc.

Using a Disposable Type to Find Multiple Text Pieces and Iterate the Results

In this solution the focus will be on taking the techniques presented in "Finding a Piece of Text Within a Text Buffer" section and wrapping them in an enumerator. Wrapping the code in an enumerator allows us to use the more code-friendly foreach keyword instead of having to track an index and then add 1 to the index. The enumerator code is more compact and easier to understand. This section will teach you how to create general reusable infrastructure to find consumer-friendly text.

To implement the new solution, I'll illustrate two new concepts: using the yield keyword and using a disposable type. The yield keyword was introduced in .NET 2.0 and is meant to simplify creating an iterable collection. A *disposable type* is a type that you use instantiate once in a context, and not again. That means you would instantiate the type, most likely not assign it to a variable, and call a method directly on the instantiated type. A disposable type encapsulates some functionality you could write as a function, but would prefer as a separate type.

We'll use the following code from the "Finding a Piece of Text Within a Text Buffer" section:

Source: /Volume01/LibVolume01/FindingTextWithinBuffer.cs

```
String buffer = "Find the text in the buffer";
int startIndex = 0;
int foundIndex = -1;
do {
    foundIndex = buffer.IndexOf( "the", startIndex);
    Console.WriteLine( "Index (" + foundIndex + ")");
    startIndex = foundIndex + 1;
} while( foundIndex != -1);
```

The bolded code in the example marks the infrastructure code, which you would need to write over and over again for each time that you wanted to find a piece of text within a buffer. The nonbolded code is custom to the search, and not reusable.

One way to rewrite this code would be to use a method and a delegate, as in the following code:

Source: /Volume01/LibVolume01/DisposableTypeIterateText.cs

```
delegate void FoundIndex( int offset);

[TestFixture]
public class Tests {
    void FindAndIterate( String buffer, String textToFind,
        FoundIndex delegateFoundIndex) {
        int startIndex = 0;
        int foundIndex = -1;
        do {
            foundIndex = buffer.IndexOf( textToFind, startIndex);
            delegateFoundIndex( foundIndex);
            startIndex = foundIndex + 1;
        } while( foundIndex != -1);

    }
    void ProcessMethod( int foundIndex) {
        Console.WriteLine( "Index (" + foundIndex + ")");
    }
    [Test]
    public void TestDelegateIterate() {
        String buffer = "Find the text in the buffer";
        String textToFind = "the";
        FindAndIterate( buffer, textToFind, new FoundIndex( ProcessMethod));
    }
}
```

The modified code has three methods where before there was one. The method FindAndIterate is the infrastructure code used to find and iterate the found pieces of text. Reference to the delegate that is called whenever a piece of text is found appears in boldface. The parameters of FindAndIterate are the buffer to search (buffer), the text to find in the buffer (textToFind), and the delegate instance (delegateFoundIndex) that is called whenever a piece of text is found.

The delegate instance that is called is based on the defined delegate FoundIndex, which has a single parameter representing the index of the found text. Notice that in the declaration of the delegate there is a single parameter that serves as the index to the found text.

The method TestDelegateIterate ties everything together and calls the method FindAndIterate. Note that buffer and textToFind are variables declared at the method-scope level.

The method ProcessMethod is the function that is assigned to the delegate FoundIndex and called by the function FindAndIterate. Notice how the function is called with an index, but has no idea what the index is for. From the function's perspective, the index could be next week's lottery numbers. You know the index represents an offset in a buffer, but only because you wrote the code.

The implementation of ProcessMethod has to establish a meaning for the parameter foundIndex. Establishing a meaning is difficult because the original meaning of the variable foundIndex is based on variables declared at the method level but not related to ProcessMethod. To allow two methods to know each other's data-class level, we must use data members. But is it appropriate that FindAndIterate is a class-level method? Its functionality seems only indirectly related to the class's purpose. It would seem that FindAndIterate is a need-once functionality that can be discarded when it's not needed.

Think about this problem at the abstract level. You are creating an object-oriented hierarchy that needs some non–object-oriented functionality—a function. Should you add the function to the object hierarchy, or create a new type with a single function? From an object-oriented perspective it is very lame to create a type with a single method. But it is just as lame to add the method if you use it once only. You are caught in a bind.

Assuming that FindAndIterate did belong in the class, how would you give a contextual meaning to the variable foundIndex? You could use data members, or you could expand the declaration of the delegate FoundIndex to include the text to which the variable foundIndex associated. The next question is, what did the index find? ProcessMethod had no idea if the search text was one letter or fifty letters. Again, a solution would be to expand the declaration of the delegate to include the text that was searched.

Let's put all of the information together: A delegate was defined that did not provide enough contextual information to the information that was discovered. Thus to figure out what the found information represents, all of the data passed to the method FindAndIterate has to be passed to ProcessMethod. This is an example of *passing through* data.

One way to solve the pass-through data problem is to not expand the delegate declaration, but to instead use anonymous delegates, as in the following source code:

Source: /Volume01/LibVolume01/DisposableTypeIterateText.cs

```
[Test]
public void TestAnonymousDelegateIterate() {
    String buffer = "Find the text in the buffer";
    String textToFind = "the";
    FindAndIterate(buffer, textToFind,
                new FoundIndex(delegate(int foundIndex) {
                                Console.WriteLine("In text (" + buffer +➡
                                    ") found ("
                                        + textToFind + ➡
") at index ("                          + foundIndex + ")");

                })) ;
}
```

In this modified example, FindAndIterate calls the anonymous delegate implementation and can reference the variables declared at the method level. The anonymous delegate implementation is an improvement over using a delegate implementation that's not part of the method, albeit some may critique the code's readability.

The best solution is to use a disposable type and the yield keyword. The method TestDelegateIterate would be rewritten as follows:

Source: /Volume01/LibVolume01/DisposableTypeIterateText.cs

```
[Test]
public void TestIterate() {
    String buffer = "Find the text in the buffer";
    String textToFind = "the";
    foreach (int index in new IterateIndices(buffer, textToFind)) {
        Console.WriteLine("Found index (" + index + ")");
    }
}
```

Without thinking about what the classes mean, look at the elegance of the TestIterate method. It is simple, does what is expected, and the implementation has the contextual data because no methods are called. This is the solution we want. The elegance is due to the class IterateIndices, which is a disposable type.

In the source code, IterateIndices is not assigned to a variable, nor is it referenced anywhere else. The class IterateIndices serves one purpose: to implement the functionality to find a piece of text within a buffer. In a classical object-oriented sense, IterateIndices does not fulfill the requirements of being an object-oriented type, but that is OK because it is not meant to be an object-oriented class, but rather a helper class. You might be tempted to associate a static function to a helper class. However, static helper functions force you to embed all logic in the state of variables declared at the method level, and if you call other static methods all states must be carried to the other static methods. Using a disposable type, there can be multiple methods, and data can be assigned to the data members. In short, using disposable types is object-oriented programming, but using static functions is not.

A disposable type has all of its required states passed to it using the constructor. In the case of IterateIndices, the required states consist of the buffer and the text to find in the buffer. IterateIndices seems to offer no functionality, as no methods are called. But in fact there is quite a bit of hidden functionality that the foreach statement uses. IterateIndices must implement IEnumerable and must use the yield keyword. A full implementation of IterateIndices is as follows:

Source: /Volume01/LibVolume01/FindingTextWithinBuffer.cs

```
public class IterateIndices : IEnumerable {
    private String _toSearchBuffer;
    private string _toFind;

    public IterateIndices(string toSearchBuffer, string toFind) {
        _toSearchBuffer = toSearchBuffer;
        _toFind = toFind;
    }
    public IEnumerator GetEnumerator() {
        int temp;
        int startIndex = 0;
        int foundIndex = -1;
        do {
            foundIndex = _toSearchBuffer.IndexOf(_toFind,
```

```
                startIndex,
                 StringComparison.OrdinalIgnoreCase);
            if (foundIndex != -1) {
                yield return foundIndex;
            }
            startIndex = foundIndex + 1;
        } while( foundIndex != -1);
    }
}
```

In the rewritten code the bulk of the looping code is put into the method GetEnumerator. I won't detail why the code is structured the way it is. What is important about this class is that the bulk of the logic is embedded in a single function and that the code can be used in a general context.

In summary, when creating loops and disposable types, consider the following:

- The yield keyword is an effective way to create a collection of iterable data because the yield keyword can be used in conjunction with a standard loop.

- Disposable types are focused—they do one task very well.

- All operational data for a disposable type is passed via constructor parameters.

- Disposable types are rarely assigned to variables.

- Using a disposable type avoids having to declare a static function.

Making ToString Generate Structured Output

I mentioned earlier that you should always implement ToString, and I illustrated how to implement it using simple means. What I did not illustrate is the format of the data that ToString should generate. If you are coding using Java or .NET, there is no single defined format for generating a buffer or the ToString. As a result, there are many, many combinations and permutations possible.

Why should you care about the format of the text generated by ToString? Because when you generate the text from a complex structure using ToString, not having the text formatted makes it darn near impossible to figure out what you are looking at. Only with a structure and format can you present the data in an organized manner that makes it possible to figure out where the object states might be incorrect.

In generating the buffer, the bigger-picture question is which format to use. Should you use plain-vanilla text, or should you use XML? Or should you use some other format? The answer is to generate the text into a "neutral" format that is then converted into other formats. The approach could be simple, where everything is hand-tuned, or more sophisticated, where (for instance) XML is generated and converted using Extensible Stylesheet Language Transformations (XSLT).

Why generate an intermediate format when you can save work by generating in a single format? Because you will want different output formats. For example, when an error occurs you might want to send the generated output using email or a text message to a cellular phone. Each approach has a format that works best for it.

No matter which approach you take, the way you generate the buffer should be simple. The following is an example ToString implementation that uses a disposable class to generate the neutral data format:

Source: /Volume01/LibVolume01/MakingToStringGenerateStructuredOutput.cs

```
class Base {
    public override string ToString() {
        return new ToStringTracer()
            .Start( "Base")
            .Variable( "WhatAmI", "I am a base class")
            .End();
    }
}
```

In the example the class Base overrides the method ToString to provide a custom implementation. In the implementation of ToString, the disposable class is used to generate a buffer. The disposal type has multiple methods that return the current object instance, making it possible to chain together a number of method calls without ever having to assign the instance to a variable. The chained method calls make it possible to create an indented buffer like the one in the following generated output:

```
Type: Base
    Variable: WhatAmI (I am a base class)]
```

In the generated buffer the top-level item is the type, Base. The top-level item is defined using the Start method call, which generates the type text and is used to identify an indentation. The method Variable outputs the value of a variable. Since Base does not have any variables to output, an example variable is created by passing two buffers. Then to finish the chained-together methods and return a buffer, the method End is called without any parameters.

It is possible to chain together types; some class could subclass Base as illustrated in the following source code:

Source: /Volume01/LibVolume01/MakingToStringGenerateStructuredOutput.cs

```
class Derived : Base {
    public override string ToString() {
        return new ToStringTracer()
            .Start("Derived")
            .Variable("WhatAmI", "I am a derived class")
            .Base(base.ToString())
            .End();
    }
}
```

The class Derived subclasses Base and defines its own ToString implementation. The implementation of Derived.ToString and Base.ToString are fairly similar. The difference is that in the Derived.ToString implementation there is an additional method call, Base. The method Base calls base.ToString, and that generates a buffer. The generated buffer from Base is added to the generated buffer from Derived.

Executing the code generates the following indented buffer:

```
Type: Derived
    Variable: WhatAmI (I am a derived class)
    Base
        Type: Base
            Variable: WhatAmI (I am a base class)
```

In the generated buffer the top-level type is Derived, and one indent level in is a variable that belongs to Derived. At the same indent level is the text Base to indicate that Derived subclasses the type Base. After the text Base is another indent level, and the state associated with the Base type.

Looking at the generated text, you should see why you want to implement ToString properly: the generated text makes it simple to inspect and understand the state of an object instance.

■**Note** The indented buffer is not generated directly; it is the result of converting a neutral format into an indented buffer format. An intermediary format is defined so that various structures could be generated. For example, instead of an indented buffer, XML could have been generated.

The neutral format for the Derived class is as follows:

```
{Type: Derived{Variable: WhatAmI (I am a derived class)}}{Base {Type: ➡
Base{Variable: WhatAmI (I am a base class)}}}}
```

In the neutral format there are no line breaks and there is one line of text. The curly brackets are delimiters used to indicate subelements. The neutral format is not intended for human consumption.

Notice that the ToString implementations did not reference any format—that is on purpose. The ToString implementations should not have to care about how to format the buffer. In most ToString implementations the buffer's format is hard-coded. Hard coding makes it more complicated to integrate the ToString value into other frameworks. An example would be when an exception handler uses the ToString method to output the state of an object that caused an error. In the previous example the neutral format is illustrated for the ToString implementation, but could just as easily be extended to an exception framework.

ToStringTracer implements the neutral format as follows:

Source: /jaxson.commons.dotnet/Tracer/ToStringTracer.cs

```
class ToStringTracer {
    private string _buffer;

    public ToStringTracer() {
    }
    public ToStringTracer Start(string name) {
        _buffer += "{Type: " + name + "";
```

```
            return this;
        }
        public string End() {
            _buffer += "}";
            return _buffer;
        }
        public ToStringTracer Variable(string identifier, int value) {
            _buffer +=  "{Variable: " + identifier + " (" + value + ")}";
            return this;
        }
        public ToStringTracer Variable(string identifier, string value) {
            _buffer +=  "{Variable: " + identifier + " (" + value + ")}";
            return this;
        }
        public ToStringTracer Base(string value) {
            _buffer += "{Base " + value + "}";
            return this;
        }
}
```

The implementation of the ToStringTracer class is by no means complete. In a full implementation, methods such as Variable would be overloaded for the different types, and there
would be a host of other methods that would include the ability to generate the state for arrays.

The source code contains a data member _buffer, which contains the generated buffer.
The implementation of the Start method adds a type; notice the use of an opening curly
bracket. To close a ToString implementation the End method is called, which adds to the
buffer a closing curly bracket. In the implementation of Variable and Base the buffers are generated with appropriate use of curly brackets to indicate new definition blocks that are
separate from the parents or other elements.

In the implementation of the ToString methods the various methods (Start, Variable,
Base) were chained together. In those methods the return type is ToStringTracer, and the current object instance is returned. It is as if we are referencing a variable, except the variable is
the return value of a method. As all of the methods except End return ToStringTracer, you can
ensure that the End method is the last method called. If we forgot to call End, then the compiler
would complain because the ToString method expects a string return value.

To convert the neutral format into a specific format, the challenge is to create an infrastructure in which the generated format can be plugged into the application at runtime rather
than be in the code. Consider the context: You are creating an application and have defined a
general exception format. The ToString-generated buffers need to adhere to the same format.
The solution involves using the State pattern to define the type that is used to convert the neutral format into a specific format.

The State pattern is useful in this context because the pattern uses an embedded logic to
determine which formatter is used. The consumer then uses only the State pattern and is
assured of formatting the generated buffers correctly. Following is the implementation of the
State pattern:

Source: / jaxson.commons.dotnet/Tracer/ToStringTracer.cs

```
class ToStringFormatState {
    private class DefaultFormatter : IToStringFormat {
        public String FormatBuffer(String input) {
            return input;
        }
    }
    private static IToStringFormat _defaultFormat = new DefaultFormatter();
    private static IToStringFormat _spacesFormat = new FormatToSpaces();
    private static IToStringFormat _defaultState = _defaultFormat;
    public static IToStringFormat DefaultFormat {
        get {
            return _defaultState;
        }
    }
    public static void ToggleToDefault() {
        _defaultState = _defaultFormat;
    }
    public static void ToggleToSpaces() {
        _defaultState = _spacesFormat;
    }
}
```

The class ToStringFormatState contains an embedded class DefaultFormatter, which implements the general interface IToStringFormat. I have not defined the interface IToStringFormat, but by looking at the implementation of the embedded class you can guess that the interface has a single method. The single method has a single parameter of type string, and returns a buffer of type string. The parameter represents the neutral-formatted buffer, and the return buffer represents the specific-formatted buffer. In the case of the embedded class the implementation does nothing and returns as a formatted buffer the formatted buffer given to it. The purpose of the embedded class is not to provide an implementation, but to provide a facility where it is possible to inspect the neutral format without having to modify the code that generates the specific format.

The purpose of the State pattern is to carry out a default action, where the action was determined by some other action. For example, the methods ToggleToDefault and ToggleToSpaces define what the default action should be. The default action is stored in the data member _defaultState, and referenced using the property DefaultFormat. The data member _defaultState is assigned a default value so that if none of the state definition methods have been called there is a valid state. This little aspect is extremely important for the State pattern because the state of the object must be consistent, and initial defaults cannot be null. The exception to having a null default is when null represents a valid state.

You could write the following code to use the State pattern:

Source: /Volume01/LibVolume01/MakingToStringGenerateStructuredOutput.cs

```
ToStringFormatState.ToggleToSpaces();
Console.WriteLine("ToString[ \n" +
    ToStringFormatState.DefaultFormat.FormatBuffer(new Base().ToString()) + "]");
```

In the example source code the first step is to call `ToggleToSpaces` to indicate that the chosen specific format is indented spaces. The second step is to convert the neutral format to an indented format using the method `FormatBuffer`. Notice in the reference to `FormatBuffer` that the property `DefaultFormat` is used. Providing a default implementation in the form of a data member makes it simpler to use the same formatting throughout an application.

Now you know how the State pattern is applied, but there is still one small detail to iron out. The State pattern exposes the methods `ToggleToSpaces` and `ToggleToDefault`, which can be construed as hard-coded methods that determine a specific format, and little can be done to change it. For example, the following code seems to be more abstract because an enumeration is used instead of a specific method. Yet you still need to reference the method and associate a specific format:

```
ToStringFormatState.ToggleToFormat( enumBufferToSpaces);
```

The State pattern object is enhanced to include a method called `ToggleToFormat`, which accepts as a parameter an enumeration value of the specific format. The enumeration could have been replaced with a string buffer, or even an object instance. Whatever the parameter is, hard coding still occurs. The hard coding has been delegated from the method name to the enumeration value. Both methods are hard-coded because a specific format has been indicated.

The State pattern deals with the hard-coding problem by explicitly requiring the existence of the property `DefaultFormat`. Hard coding is not bad, but you don't want hard coding that is tweaked along the way. If you want to hard-code, do it consistently so that when you change the hard coding it is a simple find-and-replace operation. Whenever functionality managed by the State pattern is required, the generic property `DefaultFormat` is referenced.

The last piece of functionality is the implementation of the converter that reads the neutral data format and generates a specific format. Following is that source code:

Source: / jaxson.commons.dotnet/Tracer/ToStringTracer.cs

```
class FormatToSpaces : IToStringFormat {
    string _inputBuffer;
    private int _spaceCounter;
    bool _needSpaces;
    private StringBuilder _builder = new StringBuilder();

    public FormatToSpaces() {
    }
    private void GenerateSpaces() {
        for (int c1 = 0; c1 < _spaceCounter; c1 ++) {
            _builder.Append("   ");
        }
    }
    public string FormatBuffer(string inputBuffer) {
        _inputBuffer = inputBuffer;
        _needSpaces = false;
        foreach (char character in _inputBuffer) {
            switch (character) {
                case '{':
                    _spaceCounter ++;
```

```
                        _needSpaces = true;
                        break;
                case '}':
                        _spaceCounter -;
                        _needSpaces = true;
                        break;
                default:
                        if (_needSpaces) {
                            _builder.Append('\n');
                            GenerateSpaces();
                            _needSpaces = false;
                        }
                        _builder.Append(character);
                        break;
            }
        }
        return _builder.ToString();
    }
}
```

The class FormatToSpaces implements the IToString interface and the method
FormatBuffer. In the implementation of FormatBuffer each character of the buffer is iterated
using a foreach. Each character is inspected to see if it is an opening or closing curly bracket.
If the character is an opening curly bracket, then the data member _spaceCounter is incremented and the data member _needSpaces is assigned a value of true. The curly bracket is
an indentation indicator and the data member _spaceCounter counts indentation levels.
The spaces representing an indentation are first generated when a character other than a
curly bracket is encountered in the text. When a closing curly bracket is encountered the data
member _spaceCounter is decremented, indicating removal of an indentation level. With a
change of indentation level, the _needSpaces data is assigned a value of true to write a new
indentation level when text is generated.

In the switch statement the default case is to copy the buffer contents from the source to
the destination. Before an individual character is copied the data member _needSpaces is
tested. If the _needSpaces data member is true, then a line feed and spaces are appended
to the buffer using the method GenerateSpaces. The next step is to copy the character from
the source buffer to the destination buffer using the StringBuilder instance _builder. A
StringBuilder instance is used because that is more efficient than copying a buffer using
String operations. Once the details have been copied, the method _builder.ToString is
called to return the specifically formatted buffer.

Remember the following points when formatting the ToString implementation:

- A structured ToString implementation can be used for a multitude of things, including
  post-mortem analysis in test-driven development or structured exception handling.

- Chaining methods that a disposable type uses is a good way of calling methods without
  having to assign the disposable type instance to a variable.

- In the ToString implementation there is no reference to specific formatting rules.

- The ToString implementation generates a buffer using a neutral formatting structure that
  is then converted into a specific structure, enabling multiple uses of the formatted data.

CHAPTER 4

■■■

C# Coding Solutions

In the previous chapters, the focus was on how to use the .NET API. All of the examples were illustrated using C#, but the examples did not use any particular feature of C#. The examples could have been implemented with VB.NET or any other .NET language. That changes in this chapter, as the focus is on the C# programming language. Specific features of the language will be dissected and analyzed. Sometimes patterns will be used, and other times not. In the overall scheme of this chapter, the idea is to give you a better understanding of what C# is capable of and not capable of.

What Does the Yield Keyword Really Generate?

The yield keyword was added to C# 2.0 and is used to simplify the implementation of enumeration in custom classes. Before the yield keyword, we had to implement a number of interfaces to have a class support enumeration. Implementation of enumeration was a pain, yet we did it so that we could take advantage of the foreach looping mechanism. The foreach looping mechanism makes it easy to iterate a collection.

The yield keyword simplifies the implementation of iterable collections, but it also allows us to move beyond collections and into result sets. Using the yield keyword, we can convert calculated sequences into collections. Let me give an example. Let's say that I am calculating the sequence of square roots for all numbers. Saying that you will calculate a sequence of numbers for all numbers should already indicate to you that a giant array would be calculated, as numbers are infinite.

Assuming for the moment that we do create an infinite array, let's look at how those numbers would be generated without using the yield keyword. There would be a piece of code that would call the algorithm to generate the sequence of numbers. The sequence of numbers would be added to an array, which is returned to the calling code when the algorithm has completed. Yet we are calculating an infinite sequence of numbers, meaning that the algorithm will never end and the array will never be complete.

Of course, in reality, algorithms do end, and arrays do become complete. But the example illustrates that if you were to generate a collection that could be iterated, you must first generate the collection and then iterate the collection. This would mean you first allocate the space for an array and then fill the array, resulting in a not-as-efficient solution. The yield keyword is more efficient, because it allows a calculation to generate numbers on the fly, making it appear like there is a collection of precalculated numbers.

Consider the following example, which is an iterable collection of one item:

Source: /Volume01/LibVolume01/WhatDoesYieldGenerate.cs

```
public class ExampleIterator : IEnumerable {
    public IEnumerator GetEnumerator() {
        yield return 1;
    }
}
```

The class `ExampleIterator` implements the `IEnumerable` interface, which requires the `GetEnumerator` method to be implemented. The `GetEnumerator` method returns an `IEnumerator` instance. In the implementation of `GetEnumerator`, the value 1 is returned rather than an `IEnumerator` interface instance. This is odd, because how can a value type be returned when a reference type is expected? The magic is the `yield` keyword, which provides the missing code in the form of generated IL.

The `yield` keyword is a compiler directive that generates a very large chunk of IL code. Using ILDASM.exe it is possible to reverse engineer what the compiler generated; Figure 4-1 shows an outline of the generated code.

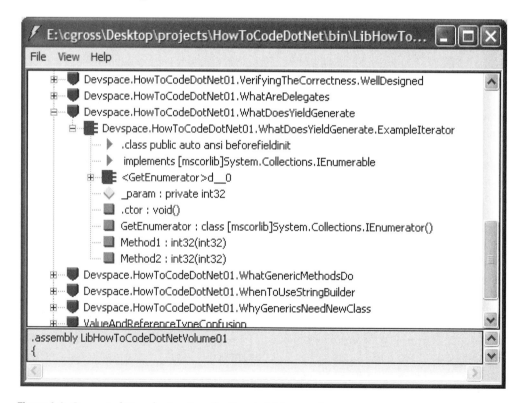

Figure 4-1. *Generated IL code structure for the* `yield` *keyword*

In Figure 4-1 the class `ExampleIterator` has an embedded class called `<GetEnumerator>d__0`. The naming of the embedded class is peculiar; it seems to indicate that the actual class name is d__0 and the <GetEnumerator> references a .NET Generics type. This is not the case, and the <GetEnumerator> identifier is indeed part of the class identifier. If you had tried using such an identifier in C# or VB.NET, there would have been a compiler error.

The oddly named class ensures that a programmer that uses the yield keyword will never define a class that conflicts with the generated class, and it does the heavy lifting of implementing the IEnumerator interface. Additionally, the class <GetEnumerator>d__0 has the associated attributes CompilerGenerated and sealed, making it impossible to subclass the type in the code. The yield keyword does not introduce a new feature in the .NET runtime, but generates all of the plumbing necessary to implement iterable sets.

The generated class contains the logic that was coded in the implementation of GetEnumerator and replaces it with the following:

```
public IEnumerator GetEnumerator() {
    ExampleIterator.<GetEnumerator > d__0 d
        __1 = new ExampleIterator.< GetEnumerator > d__0(0);
    d__1.<>4__this = this;
    return d__1;
}
```

The replaced code illustrates that when an IEnumerator instance is asked, it is returned, and the magic generated by the C# compiler is returned. The logic (yield return 1) is moved to the IEnumerator.MoveNext method, which is used to iterate the generated sequence of numbers. We are wondering how the magic code converts the yield into a sequence of numbers. The answer is that the magic code creates a sequence of numbers by using a state engine to mimic a collection of numbers.

To see how the statement yield return 1 is converted into something that foreach can use, look at the implementation of generated MoveNext. The generated method <GetEnumerator>d_0.MoveNext is implemented[1] as follows:

```
private bool MoveNext() {
    switch (this.<>1__state) {
    case 0:
        this.<>1__state = -1;
        this.<>2__current = 1;
        this.<>1__state = 1;
        return true;

    case 1:
        this.<>1__state = -1;
        break;
    }
    return false;
}
```

A stable table is generated, and when it's called multiple times it will change state and do the appropriate action. Let's go through the sequence of events: The foreach starts and calls the

---

1. The generated code has been converted from IL into C# using Lutz Roeder's .NET Reflector.

method MoveNext for the first time. The value of the data member this.<>1__state is 0, and is the state position. The switch statement will execute the case statement with the value 0.

The statement with the value 0 reassigns the state position to –1 to put the state position into an undetermined state in case the assignment of the state member causes an exception. If an exception occurs, you do not want the foreach loop constantly repeating itself and generating the same content or same error.

If the assignment of the state member (this.<>2__current) is successful, then the state position (this.<>1__state) is assigned a value of 1 indicating the value of the next state. With the state member assigned and the state position incremented, a true value can be returned. A true value indicates that the foreach loop can use the state member to assign the variable. The client code processes the variable and loops again.

The next loop causes a call to MoveNext again. This time the switch statement causes a branch to the state position of 1, which reassigns the state position to –1 and returns false. When MoveNext returns false, foreach will break out of its loop.

The yield statement has created a state table that mimics collection behavior. At a glance, the yield statement has ceased to be a simple programming construct, and has become an instruction used by a code generator. The yield statement is a code generator, because the generated IL could have been written using C# code. Lower-level type programming languages, such as Java, C#, C++, and C, have in the past taken the approach that the language is not extended, but that the libraries are extended to enhance the language.

Getting back to the yield statement, the following example illustrates how to use ExampleIterator to iterate the collection of one item:

Source: /Volume01/LibVolume01/WhatDoesYieldGenerate.cs

```
[Test]
public void ExampleIterator() {
    foreach (int number in new ExampleIterator()) {
        Console.WriteLine("Found number (" + number + ")");
    }
}
```

In the example, foreach will loop once and display to the console the number 1.

Knowing that a state engine is created, we can look at a more complicated yield example that calls methods and other .NET API. Following is a more complicated yield example:

```
public class ExampleIterator : IEnumerable {
    int _param;
    private int Method1( int param) {
        return param + param;
    }
    private int Method2( int param) {
        return param * param;
    }
    public IEnumerator GetEnumerator() {
        Console.WriteLine("before");
        for (int c1 = 0; c1 < 10; c1 ++) {
            _param = 10 + c1;
```

```
        yield return Method1(_param);
        yield return Method2(_param);
    }
    Console.WriteLine("after");
  }
}
```

In this example, the yield example the GetEnumerator implementation calls the Console.WriteLine function at the beginning and the end of the method. The purpose of the two lines of code is to provide code boundaries that can be easily found in the MSIL. In the implementation of ExampleIterator, the variable _param is declared, and passed to Method1 and Method2, which return modified values of the variable param. These variable declarations and method calls, while trivial, mimic how you would write code that uses the yield statement.

The sequence of events from the perspective of written C# code would be as follows:

1. Call GetEnumerator.

2. Console.WriteLine generates text before.

3. Start a loop that counts from 0 to 10.

4. Assign the data member _param with a value of 10 plus the loop counter c1.

5. Call Method1 with the _param value that will add the number to itself and return the number's value.

6. Return the number generated by Method1 to the foreach loop.

7. The foreach loop calls GetEnumerator again.

8. Call Method2 with the _param value that will multiply the number to itself and return the value of the number.

9. Return the number generated by Method2 to the foreach loop.

10. The foreach loop calls GetEnumerator again.

11. The end of for loop is reached, c1 is incremented, and the loop performs another iteration. Local iteration continues until c1 has reached the value of 10.

12. Console.WriteLine generates text after.

The foreach loop will iterate 20 times, because for each GetEnumerator two foreach iterations are generated. The logic presented is fairly sophisticated because the generated state table has to be aware of a loop that contains two yield statements that include method calls.

The generated MSIL IEnumerator.MoveNext method is as follows:

```
private bool MoveNext() {
    switch (this.<>1__state)
    {
    case 0:
        this.<>1__state = -1;
        Console.WriteLine("before");
        this.<c1 > 5__1 = 0;
```

```
        while (this.<c1 > 5__1 < 10)
        {
            this.<>4__this._param = 10 + this.<c1 > 5__1;
            this.<>2__current = this.<>4__this.Method1(<>4__this._param);
            this.<>1__state = 1;
            return true;
            Label_0089:
            this.<>1__state = -1;
            this.<>2__current = this.<>4__this.Method2(<>4__this._param);
            this.<>1__state = 2;
            return true;
            Label_00BC:
            this.<>1__state = -1;
            this.<c1 > 5__1++;
        }
        Console.WriteLine("after");
        break;

    case 1:
        goto Label_0089;

    case 2:
        goto Label_00BC;
    }
    return false;
}
```

The bolded code cross-references the logic from the original GetEnumerator method implementation that used the yield statement. The generated code looks simple, but its behavior is fairly complex. For example, look in the while loop for the code this.<>1__state = 1. Right after that is a return true statement, and right after that is Label_0089. This code, which is rare, is the implementation of the yield statement that causes an exit and entry in the context of a loop.

The state table (switch(this.<>1__state)) has three labels: 0, 1, and 2. The state position 0 is called the first time when the loop is started. Like previously illustrated, the state position is assigned to –1 in case errors occur. After the repositioning, the method Console.WriteLine is called, and the data member this.<c1>5__1 is assigned to 0. The naming of the data member is not coincidental—it is the loop counter. But what is curious is that the loop counter (c1) that was originally declared as a method scope variable has been converted into a class data member.

In the original implementation the challenge was to exit and enter back into a loop using the yield statement. The solution in the generated code is to move method-level declarations to the class level. This means that the state is based at the level, and thus if a loop is exited and entered again, the loop will see the correct state. It is not common to store the loop counter as a data member, but in this case it helps overcome the exit and entry of the loop.

Continuing with the loop analysis, the for loop is converted into a while loop. The counter c1 is assigned in the line before the while loop. After the while loop line, the data member _param is assigned and the method Method1 is called. How can a generated class access the data members and methods of another class instance? The magic lies in the fact that the generated class is a private class, enabling access to all data members and methods of the parent class. To access the parent instance, the data member <>4__this is used.

Once the method Method1 has been called, the state position is changed to 1 and the while loop is exited, with a return value of true.

When the foreach loop has done its iteration, the MoveNext method is called again, and the code jumps back into the loop with the state that the loop had as the loop was exited. The loop is started again by using the state table value of 1, which is a goto[2] to the Label_0089 that is located in the middle of the while loop. That jump makes the method implementation behave as if nothing happened, so processing continues where the method last left off.

Remember the following about the yield statement:

- In the C# programming language, the yield keyword enhances the language to simplify the implementation of certain pieces of code.

- You do not *have* to use the yield keyword; the old way of implementing an iterable collection still applies. If you want to, you could create your own state engine and table that would mimic the behavior of yield 100 percent.

- The yield statement creates a state table that remembers where the code was last executed.

- The yield statement generates code that is like spaghetti code, and it leaves me wondering if it works in all instances. I have tried various scenarios using foreach and everything worked. I wonder if there are .NET tools that would act and behave like a foreach statement that could generate some esoteric language constructs and cause a failure. I cannot help but wonder if there are hidden bugs waiting to bite you in the butt at the wrong moment.

- If I had one feature request, it would be to formalize the state engine into something that all .NET developers could take advantage of.

Using Inheritance Effectively

Now we'll focus on how to use inheritance in .NET. Many people consider inheritance an idea past its prime. .NET, though, has improved inheritance and solved many of its associated problems by using an explicit inheritance model.

One of the problems usually associated with inheritance is the *fragile base class*: Due to inheritance, changes in a base class may affect derived classes. This behavior should not happen, and indicates that inheritance implicitly creates a tightly coupled situation. The following Java-language example illustrates the fragile-base-class problem. (I am not picking on Java—other languages also have this problem. I am using Java because Java and C# syntax is almost identical.)

```
class BaseClass {
    public void display(String buffer) {
        System.out.println("My string (" + buffer + ")");
    }
}
```

2. Goto statements and data members manage the state of the state table.

```
    public void callMultipleTimes(String[] buffers) {
        for (int c1 = 0; c1 < buffers.length; c1++) {
            display(buffers[c1]);
        }
    }
}
```

BaseClass has two methods: display and callMultipleTimes. The method display is used to generate some text to the console. The method callMultipleTimes accepts an array of string buffers. In the implementation of callMultipleTimes the array is iterated, and every foreach iteration of an element of the array is displayed.

Functionally, BaseClass provides a method to generate output (display) and a helper method (callMultipleTimes) to generate output for an array of strings. In abstract terms, BaseClass defines a method display that is called multiple times by callMultipleTimes.

The following code illustrates how to use BaseClass:

```
public void doCall(BaseClass cls) {
    cls.callMultipleTimes(new String[]
        { "buffer1", "buffer2", "buffer3" });
}
public void initial() {
    doCall( new BaseClass());
}
```

The method initial instantiates the type BaseClass and then calls the method doCall. In the implementation of doCall the method callMultipleTimes is called with an array of three buffers. Calling callMultipleTimes will end up calling display three times.

Suppose the code is called version 1.0 and is released. Some time later the developer would like to use the same code elsewhere, and realizes that the functionality of display needs to be modified. Instead of changing BaseClass, the developer creates a new class and overrides the base functionality. The new class, Derived, is illustrated here:

```
class Derived extends BaseClass {
    public void display(String buffer) {
        super.display("{" + buffer + "}");
    }
}
```

The new class Derived subclasses BaseClass and overrides the method display. The new implementation of display calls the base version of display while modifying the parameter buffer. To have the client call the new code, the method initial is changed as follows:

```
public void initial() {
    doCall( new DerivedClass());
}
```

The doCall method is kept as is, and when the client code is executed the following output is generated:

```
My string ({buffer1})
My string ({buffer2})
My string ({buffer3})
```

Calling the method `callMultipleTimes` calls `display`, and because of the way inheritance works, the new `display` method is called. For sake of argument, this behavior is desired and fulfills our needs.

However, problems arise if the developer decides to change the behavior of the method `BaseClass.callMultipleMethods` to the following:

```
class BaseClass {
    public void display(String buffer) {
        System.out.println("My string (" + buffer + ")");
    }
    public void callMultipleTimes(String[] buffers) {
        for (int c1 = 0; c1 < buffers.length; c1++) {
            System.out.println("My string (" + buffers[ c1 ] + ")");
        }
    }
}
```

In the modified version of `callMultipleTimes`, the method `display` is not called. Instead, the code from `display` has been copied and pasted into `callMultipleTimes`. Let's not argue about the intelligence of the code change. The reality is that the code has been changed and the change results in a major change of functionality. The result is disastrous because if the client code is executed, where `Derived` is instantiated, a call to `Derived.display` is expected by the client code, but `BaseClass.display` is called and not `Derived.display` as was expected. That's because the base class changed its implementation, causing a problem in the subclass. This is the fragile-base-class problem.

A programmer will look at the code and quickly point to the fact that `callMultipleTimes` has broken a contract in that it does not call `display`. But this is not correct, as there is no contract that says `callMultipleTimes` must call `display`. The problem is in the Java language, because it is not possible to know what defines a contract when inheritance is involved. In contrast, if you were to use interfaces, the contract is the interface, and if you were not to implement the complete interface, a compiler error would result indicating a breaking of a contract. Again, I am not picking on Java, as other programming languages have the same problem.

What makes .NET powerful is its ability to enforce a contract at the interface level and in an inheritance hierarchy. In .NET, the fragile-base-class problem does still exist, but it is brought to the developer's attention in the form of compiler warnings.

Following is a simple port of the original working application before the modification of `callMultipleTimes` that changed the behavior of the base class:

Source: `/Volume01/LibVolume01/InheritanceCanBeUsedEffectively.cs`

```
class BaseClass {
    public void Display(String buffer) {
        Console.WriteLine( "My string (" + buffer + ")");
    }
    public void CallMultipleTimes(String[] buffers) {
        for (int c1 = 0; c1 < buffers.Length; c1++) {
            Display(buffers[c1]);
        }
```

```
        }
    }
    class Derived : BaseClass {
        public new void Display(String buffer) {
            base.Method("{" + buffer + "}");
        }
    }
    [TestFixture]
    public class Tests {
        void DoCall(BaseClass cls) {
            cls.CallMultipleTimes(new String[]
                { "buffer1", "buffer2", "buffer3" });
        }
        void Initial() {
            DoCall(new BaseClass());
        }
        void Second() {
            DoCall(new Derived());
        }
        [Test]
        public void RunTests() {
            Initial();
            Second();
        }
    }
```

The ported code has one technical modification: the new modifier on the method Derived.Display. The one little change has a very big ramification—the .NET-generated output is very different from the output generated by Java:

```
My string (buffer1)
My string (buffer2)
My string (buffer3)
My string (buffer1)
My string (buffer2)
My string (buffer3)
```

The difference is because the new keyword has changed how the classes Derived and BaseClass behave. The new keyword in the example says that when calling the method Display, use the version from Derived if the type being called is Derived. If, however, the type doing the calling is BaseClass, then use the functionality from BaseClass. This means that when the method DoCall is executed, the type is BaseClass, and that results in the method BaseClass.Display being called.

Using the new keyword does not cause a fragile-base-class problem because the inheritance chain does not come into play. The idea of the new keyword is that whatever functionality was defined at a base class level is explicitly overwritten. The new keyword is a contract that forces a separation of base class and derived class functionality. By having to use the new keyword, the developer is explicitly making up his mind as to how the inheritance hierarchy will work. This is good for the fragile-base-class problem, but bad for inheritance in general. The reason why this is bad for inheritance is because the developer of Derived wanted to override the functionality in BaseClass, but is not allowed to do so by the original developer of BaseClass.

The original developer of BaseClass explicitly said none of his methods could be overwritten because he might change the functionality of BaseClass. The other option that the original developer could use is to declare the methods to be overwritten, thus generating the same output as in the Java example. Following is that source code:

Source: /Volume01/LibVolume01/InheritanceCanBeUsedEffectively.cs

```
class BaseClass {
    public virtual void Display(String buffer) {
        Console.WriteLine("My string (" + buffer + ")");
    }
    public void CallMultipleTimes(String[] buffers) {
        for (int c1 = 0; c1 < buffers.Length; c1++) {
            Display(buffers[c1]);
        }
    }
}
class Derived : BaseClass {
    public override void Display(String buffer) {
        base.Display("{" + buffer + "}");
    }
}
```

The modified source code has two new keywords: virtual and override. The virtual keyword indicates that the class is exposing a method that can be overridden. The override keyword implements a method that overrides a base method. In this modified example, the original developer of BaseClass is telling that whoever subclasses BaseClass can override the functionality of Display. The original developer who implemented CallMultipleTimes to call Display will knowingly create a contract where CallMultipleTimes calls Display, which may be overwritten. Thus, the original developer will not come to the crazy idea of breaking the implied contract of CallMultipleTimes.

Of course, it doesn't mean that the original developer cannot change and break the contract, thus creating a fragile-base-class problem. What you need to remember is that .NET does not stop you from shooting yourself in the foot. .NET has the facilities to indicate to you and say, "Dude, you are about to shoot yourself in the foot."

When using inheritance in .NET, remember the following:

- The inheritance model in .NET is contract-driven and geared toward making inheritance predictable and robust. The advantage of the .NET inheritance model is its ability to indicate what to do when two methods in a hierarchy conflict.

- The new keyword can be used in an inheritance chain to indicate new functionality. It is possible to use the new keyword on a base-class method that was declared to be virtual.

- Use the virtual and override keywords when the implementation of a derived class method overrides the implementation of the base class method.

Implementing Interfaces

The Bridge pattern is used to decouple a class that consumes and a class that implements logic. The purpose of the Bridge pattern is to be able to separate intention from implementation. Technically the Bridge pattern is implemented using interfaces and classes that implement interfaces. A class that consumes manipulates the interface, which results in the consuming class not knowing what the implementation is. Changing the implementation has no ramifications on the consuming class because the consumer is using an interface that has not changed. If we call the consumer a client, and the class implementing an interface the server, the Bridge pattern has decoupled the client from the server.

Using .NET the Bridge pattern can be implemented in multiple variations. What makes each variation different is how a type is declared using details like scope. The following source code illustrates the simplest example of a server that is implementing an interface:

Source: /Volume01/LibVolume01/EverythingImplementInterfaces.cs

```
public interface ISimple {
    void Method();
}

class SimpleImplement : ISimple {
    public void Method() {
    }
}
```

In the example the interface ISimple exposes a single method Method. The class SimpleImplement implements ISimple and exposes the method Method. The code is simple, and does what is expected of it. In a nutshell, this is the proverbial Hello World implementation of the Bridge pattern.

Looking at the code example, notice the following details:

- The interface ISimple is declared as public, which means it is accessible from an external assembly.

- The class SimpleImplement is not public, and thus it is not accessible from an external assembly.

- The method SimpleImplement.Method is declared as public and has no scope modifiers such as virtual, new, or override.

The ramifications of the details are that ISimple can be exposed in an assembly and publicly accessed, but SimpleImplement cannot. This behavior is desired because we want external clients knowing the implementation details of SimpleImplement. The client only needs to call some functionality that will instantiate SimpleImplement and return an interface reference. However, in the context of an assembly, SimpleImplement could be directly instantiated and all methods could be called.

What if SimpleImplement did not want to expose Method publicly? Let's say that SimpleImplement wanted to expose Method only through the interface ISimple. You may want this behavior so that no client within an assembly or external to the assembly had direct references to the class methods. To avoid exposing a method publicly the public keyword is removed. Removing the `public` keyword generates a compiler error because `ISimple.Method` has not been defined and implemented breaking the contract of the interface. Another solution is to explicitly associate `Method` with the implementation of `ISimple.Method`, as in the following example:

```
class SimpleImplement : ISimple {
    void ISimple.Method() {
    }
}
```

With the new declaration `Method` has been associated with `ISimple` and can be referenced using only an interface reference as illustrated by the following code:

```
ISimple simple = new SimpleImplement();
simple.Method();
```

The new declaration of `Method` is so foolproof that even `SimpleImplement` cannot access `Method` without a typecast to `ISimple`, as illustrated in the following source code:

Source: /Volume01/LibVolume01/EverythingImplementInterfaces.cs

```
class SimpleImplement : ISimple {
    void ISimple.Method() {
    }
    public void AnotherMethod() {
        ((ISimple)this).Method(); // <-- This is ok
        Method(); // <--Causes a compiler method not found error
    }
}
```

In `AnotherMethod` the `this` reference is typecast to `ISimple`, enabling the calling of the method `ISimple.Method`.

It would seem silly to force `SimpleImplement` to perform a typecast of itself so that it can call `Method`. But there is another reason why you would want to use interface-based addressing on an interface; it relates to the situation when you want a class to implement two interfaces that happen to have identical method names, as in the following source code:

Source: /Volume01/LibVolume01/EverythingImplementInterfaces.cs

```
public interface ISimple {
    void Method();
}
public interface IAnother {
    void Method();
}

class SimpleImplement : ISimple, IAnother {
    void ISimple.Method() {
    }
    void IAnother.Method() {
    }
}
```

In the example there are two interface declarations (ISimple and IAnother). Both interface declarations expose the same method, Method. When SimpleImplement implements the interfaces ISimple and IAnother, the default declaration of using a single public method Method will wire Method for both interfaces. To distinguish which implementation of Method is called for which interface, the interface identifier is prefixed to the method name, and the method is made private.

When interfaces have numerous methods or properties, they are tedious to implement for classes that only completely implement a fraction of the interface. The other methods and properties are either default implementations or empty declarations. For example, when implementing the Decorator, State, or Strategy pattern there is functionality that you don't want to reimplement for each class. The object-oriented approach is to create a default base class that is then subclassed. The default base class implements the interface, and your class implements only the methods that you need it to. Following is an interface declaration that has two methods where one method requires a default implementation and the other not:

```
public interface IFunctionality {
    void Method();
    string GetIdentifier();
}
```

The interface IFunctionality has defined two methods: Method and GetIdentifier. The purpose of Method is to represent a method that all derived classes implement. The purpose of GetIdentifier is to retrieve the name of the class that implements IFunctionality and is identified as the method that could have a default implementation for all classes that implement the interface. You can use the following code to implement GetIdentifier:

```
this.GetType().FullName;
```

If 15 classes will be implementing the IFunctionality interface, then 15 classes have to implement GetIdentifier using this line of code. But that is excessive coding, and you can optimize it by using an abstract base class that is subclassed by the classes that want to implement IFunctionality. The following is a sample implementation:

```
abstract class DefaultFunctionality : IFunctionality {
    public void Method() {
        throw new NotImplementedException();
    }
    public string GetIdentifier() {
        return this.GetType().FullName;
    }
}
class MyFunctionality : DefaultFunctionality {
    public void Method() {
        Console.WriteLine( "My own stuff");
    }
}
```

In the example the class DefaultFunctionality is declared as an abstract base class that implements IFunctionality. The base class is declared as abstract so that it can never be instantiated, because it is a partial implementation of the interface IFunctionality. A rule of thumb is that whenever class implementations are incomplete, mark them as abstract. Any class that subclasses DefaultFunctionality decides what should be implemented. Though the base class is declared as abstract, technically it is necessary to completely implement IFunctionality including the unknown Method; otherwise, the compiler generates an error. The base class method implements Method by throwing an exception, indicating that some subclass must implement the method. Of course, the proper way would have declared the method as abstract, but we did not for a reason that will become apparent shortly. The derived class MyFunctionality inherits the Method and GetIdentifier functionalities, and defines a custom implementation of Method.

Having our hierarchy, let's use the individual classes and see what happens:

Source: /Volume01/LibVolume01/EverythingImplementInterfaces.cs

```
MyFunctionality instDerived = new MyFunctionality();
DefaultFunctionality instBase = instDerived;
IFunctionality instInterface = instDerived;
Console.WriteLine("Type is (" + instInterface.GetIdentifier() + ")");
Console.WriteLine("Calling the interface");
instInterface.Method();
Console.WriteLine("Calling the derived");
instDerived.Method();
Console.WriteLine("Calling the base class");
instBase.Method();
```

The idea behind the illustrated code is to explicitly call each method associated with each type and see what response is generated. In particular, there are two responses: "My own stuff" or an exception. The instantiated type MyFunctionality is assigned to instDerived. Then instDerived is downcast to base class DefaultFunctionality (instBase) and interface IFunctionality (instInterface). Then Method is called for each variable. Compiling the classes, interfaces, and calling code generates the following warning:

```
ImplementingInterfaces.cs(32,17): warning CS0108:
MyFunctionality.Method()' hides inherited member DefaultFunctionality.Method()'.
Use the new keyword if hiding was intended.
```

This is a very common warning message, and it says that MyFunctionality.Method hides the method DefaultFunctionality.Method. From an interface perspective, that seems acceptable because we are not interested in having the method DefaultFunctionality.Method called. Based on this warning it seems that generated output from the calling sequence should be similar to the following:

```
Type is (MyFunctionality)
Calling the interface
My own stuff
Calling the derived
My own stuff
Calling the base class
<<Exception>>
```

Yet when we run the code the generated output is as follows:

```
Type is (MyFunctionality)
Calling the interface
System.NotImplementedException: The method or operation is not implemented.
```

The output is particularly interesting because when IFunctionality.Method is called, DefaultFunctionality.Method is called—not MyFunctionality.Method as we expected. The interface binds its methods and properties to the class that implements the interface. If a class subclasses a class that implements an interface, the hierarchy rules apply to the class and not the interface. This is confusing because in other programming languages, implementing an interface in a class and then subclassing that class should have automatically overridden methods in the class that was subclassed. To be able to overload implemented interface methods, you need to use the following declaration:

```
abstract class DefaultFunctionality : IFunctionality {
    public virtual void Method() {
        throw new NotImplementedException();
    }
    public string GetIdentifier() {
        return this.GetType().FullName;
    }
}
class MyFunctionality : DefaultFunctionality {
    public override void Method() {
        Console.WriteLine( "My own stuff");
    }
}
```

In the modified declaration DefaultFunctionality.Method is declared as virtual, meaning that DefaultFunctionality implements the interface method IFunctionality.Method and exposes the method as a candidate for being overloaded. The declaration of MyFunctionality.Method also changes and needs to include the override keyword to indicate that the method should overload the base class method. When you run the code, you get the following correctly generated output:

```
Type is (MyFunctionality)
Calling the interface
My own stuff
Calling the derived
My own stuff
Calling the base class
My own stuff
```

Of course, we could have avoided all of these problems by applying the abstract keyword to the method, as in the following source code:

Source: /Volume01/LibVolume01/EverythingImplementInterfaces.cs

```
abstract class DefaultFunctionality : IFunctionality {
    public abstract void Method();
```

```
public string GetIdentifier() {
    return this.GetType().FullName;
}
}
```

Applying the `abstract` keyword to `Method` allows the class to implement an interface method without providing a method implementation. The `abstract` keyword delegates the implementation to any class that subclasses `DefaultFunctionality`. The class that implements `Method` uses the `override` keyword, creating the same inheritance behavior as using the `virtual` keyword in the abstract base class.

Using both an interface and an abstract base class is a very common technique. It allows functionality to be shared among multiple class types, and the derived class needs to implement only what concerns it. In the example some methods were not implemented or generated exceptions, but often classes will create default actions that can be overridden.

You now know how to use `virtual`, `override`, and `abstract` keywords, but there is another solution for calling the appropriate method—you can implement the interface when required.

The strategy is to define an abstract base class with the required default functionality. But this time the abstract base class does not implement the interface. The modified definition of `DefaultFunctionality` would be as follows:

```
abstract class DefaultFunctionality {
    public void Method() {
        Console.WriteLine( "Default Functionality");
    }
    public string GetIdentifier() {
        return this.GetType().FullName;
    }
}
```

The class `DefaultFunctionality` has implemented two methods with some functionality. In this declaration of the abstract base class there are no constraints. The constraints are added by the derived class that implements the interface, as the following code example illustrates:

Source: `/Volume01/LibVolume01/EverythingImplementInterfaces.cs`

```
class MyFunctionality : DefaultFunctionality, IFunctionality {
    public void Method() {
        Console.WriteLine("My own stuff");
    }
}
```

The class `MyFunctionality` subclasses `DefaultFunctionality` and implements the interface `IFunctionality`. Notice though in the declaration of `MyFunctionality` the implementation of the method `GetIdentifier` is missing. When the compiler assembles the code it will look at `MyFunctionality` and attempt to associate the interface with methods. Missing in `MyFunctionality` is the method `GetIdentifier`. The compiler will also look at `DefaultFunctionality`, find `GetIdentifier`, and consider the implementation of `IFunctionality` as complete.

In the example, there was no use of the new, virtual, or override identifiers. In this case, because the interface is associated with MyFunctionality, the priority of finding a method to call is first MyFunctionality, and then DefaultFunctionality. The correct output is generated using the following calls:

```
IFunctionality instInterface = new MyFunctionality ();
Console.WriteLine("Type is (" + instInterface.GetIdentifier() + ")");
instInterface.Method();
```

With the latest version of our inheritance hierarchy, we can have our cake and eat it too. An abstract base class provides default implementations when necessary, and we don't have to use a virtual keyword.

Let's go back to an original declaration that is illustrated again:

```
class MyFunctionality : DefaultFunctionality, IFunctionality {
    public void Method() {
        Console.WriteLine("My own stuff");
    }
}
class DerivedMyFunctionality : MyFunctionality {
    public new void Method() {
        Console.WriteLine("Derived Functionality");
    }
}
```

The way that DerivedMyFunctionality is declared is identical how MyFunctionality originally subclassed DefaultFunctionality. And in our earlier example the generated output generated an exception. Therefore, by instantiating DerivedMyFunctionality, casting to IFunctionality will still call MyFunctionality.Method. However, you can get around that by making DerivedMyFunctionality implement IFunctionality like the following code:

```
class DerivedMyFunctionality : MyFunctionality, IFunctionality {
    public void Method() {
        Console.WriteLine("Derived Functionality");
    }
}
```

In this modified class declaration, instantiating DerivedMyFunctionality then casting to IFunctionality and finally calling IFunctionality.Method will call DerivedMyFunctionality.Method. It might seem odd to have multiple classes implement the same interface over and over again. The advantage of this approach is due to the way that .NET resolves methods at runtime. If you were to create an object hierarchy and an interface reference associated with each object, you could pick and choose the appropriate object at which certain methods are being called. The compiler very cleverly will pick and choose the methods when exposing the interface.

When implementing interfaces, consider these rules of thumb:

- When functionality dictated by an interface needs to be implemented over and over again, use an abstract base class.

- Do not implement interfaces on abstract base classes, but rather in the derived classes.

- When creating an inheritance hierarchy, don't be afraid of implementing the identical interface at different places in the inheritance hierarchy. So long as you instantiate the appropriate object in the inheritance hierarchy, the appropriate methods will be called.

- Use the `virtual`, `abstract`, and `override` keywords to define default implementations that some derived class can or should override.

Naming Conventions for a Namespace, a Class, and an Interface

There are two main elements of understanding code: coding style and naming convention. Coding style involves how your code is structured. Naming convention involves how types, methods, and so on are named. I will not go into detail about coding style because there are so many permutations and combinations. For the basics, read the naming-convention guidelines from Microsoft.[3] I will fine-tune or tweak the Microsoft guidelines.

Namespaces

Millions of lines of source code have been written using .NET. Therefore it is important to choose identifiers well to avoid using an identifier that somebody has already used for another functionality.

Consider the following namespace:

```
namespace Devspace.Commons.Cache { }
```

The namespace can be split into three pieces that are defined as follows:

Devspace. This is the entity that creates the application, assembly, source code, etc. This could be a corporation or an organization. In most cases you should use the unique Internet domain identifier associated with your company. Be careful when using corporate identifiers that are not Internet-based, as multiple companies in multiple countries may have the same identifier.

Commons. This is a project's main identifier. Typically it is either the overall project name or an important part of a project.

Cache. This is the subsystem project identifier. Multiple identifiers can all relate to the subsystem.

Using three unique identification chunks creates a unique namespace. Don't worry if a namespace becomes long; a well-named namespace makes the code consistent and easy to identify. Naming the subsections underneath a project is fuzzier. Here is how the examples for this book are laid out:

- `Devspace.HowToCodeDotNet01`: This defines the root namespace for the examples in this book. There are two pieces to the root namespace because the book is called *How to Code .NET*, and this is Volume 1.

---

3. Read "Designing .NET Class Libraries" at http://msdn.microsoft.com/netframework/programming/classlibraries/.

- Devspace. HowToCodeDotNet01.MakingToStringGenerateStructuredOutput: The identifier MakingToStringGenerateStructuredOutput references the concepts of a solution that is explained in this book. The solution identifier is very long so that the reader of the namespace does not have to guess what the short forms mean. In general, avoid using short forms because they lead to guessing, and often incorrect guessing.

- Devspace. HowToCodeDotNet01.VersioningAssemblies.Assembly: This is an embedded namespace (Assembly) within the solution namespace identifier (VersioningAssemblies). The embedded namespace identifies a piece of functionality that belongs to the solution. The solution is an assembly used to illustrate how versioning works in .NET.

■**Note** Microsoft does not follow exact naming conventions for many packages (such as System.Windows, which could have been written as Microsoft.Windows because after all, there are multiple GUI packages on .NET), and you should not follow suit. Microsoft created the .NET Framework and has identified the common namespaces that most .NET applications will use.

In all three examples the namespace is relatively long so that there is no conflict with other namespaces. I could have dropped the Devspace. HowToCodeDotNet01 identifiers because my examples likely will not be used anywhere but in my examples. However, if I were to write another .NET coding book a conflict could arise. Additionally, I often end up using one-time sample code in production, and vice versa.

Class and Interface Identifiers

Using the class identifier in conjunction with the namespace identifier is an easy way to quickly identify the class's purpose. In general a class identifier should represent the functionality that it is implementing. A class identifier should be a noun, except in the case of helper and disposal classes, which can be verbs. The name of the class should not be abbreviated unless the abbreviation is common (such as HTTP).

Sometimes the name of the class is related to a general programming terminology. Typically you identify such classes by appending the general programming term to the name of the class. So if the general programming term were *interface implementation*, and the class name were FileReader, then the new name would be FileReaderImplementation. The following is a list of general programming terms and how they are used. (A text identifier within square brackets represents the class identifier, such as FileReader.)

Exception—[identifier]Exception

This is used to throw an exception, which signals that something went wrong. There are two types of exceptions: fatal and nonfatal. A fatal exception occurs when the application does something that forces it to exit. A nonfatal exception happens when something goes wrong and processing stops, but the application can continue executing. In the following example, ConfigurationDoesNotExistException is a fatal exception, and FileIsCorruptException is a nonfatal exception:

```
public class ConfigurationDoesNotExistException : Exception { }
public class FileIsCorruptException : ApplicationException { }
```

Test—[identifier]Test | [identifier]TestSuite | [identifier]TestClass | [identifier]TestCase

The multiple identifiers here used to identify classes that implement testing functionality. You can use Test, TestClass, or TestCase to identify a single set of tests for a unit test. The identifier TestSuite can identify a suite of tests that is composed of tests, test cases, or test classes.

Default—Default[identifier]

Typically a class uses the Default identifier when the class is defined to be a default implementation of an interface. The Default identifier is prefixed to the class identifier, and does not have a prefix. A default implementation is necessary when defining an interface, because you should not use null values in code that uses interfaces.

Delegate—[identifier]Delegate

This identifies a type that represents a .NET delegate. When you use the delegate keyword, you append the identifier with Delegate.

Algorithm—[identifier]Builder | [identifier]Compiler | [identifier]Parser, etc.

A class or interface with the keyword Builder, Compiler, Parser or any word that is a verb and has an "er" ending processes data in a fairly sophisticated algorithm. Routines move data from one object to another. These types of routines involve only the assigning of data. But the more-complex routines used here consume a larger amount of data, perform some analysis, and then spit out an answer. Typically such routines will parse data looking for certain tokens or assemble a more complex tree structure.

Handler—[identifier]Handler

The Handler class type is a specific type of class that deserves its own class-type identification. The Handler class types serves as a callback mechanism when a piece of code is making asynchronous requests.

Source—[identifier]Provider

A Provider class type is very special because it is a class or interface that provides a bridge to another resource. It is a source of data that the provider's user consumes. Database access classes are common providers.

Navigation—[identifier]Child | [identifier]Parent, [identifier]Manager, Etc.

Navigation identifiers are very common in component structures. The Navigation identifier is not limited to Child, Parent, or Manager, but could include Sibling, Descendent, and so on.

Additionally, Navigation does not need to be restricted to class or interface identifiers. With Navigation identifiers, methods can be used as identifiers. Navigation identifiers let you construct a complex data structure that encompasses many different objects. Typically a class or interface of Navigation type is a bridge that combines several references into a useful structure. Navigation identifiers let you move from one part of the data structure to another.

Data—[identifier]Data

A data type contains data members only. The type is typically defined as structure, but can be class type. A data type usually focuses on storing data, and any methods or properties are meant to aid data manipulations. A data type does not have methods or properties that implement business logic.

Utility—[identifier]Utils

The Utility class type is common, and provides basic runtime support. A Utility class is often called a helper class because it provides a single piece of functionality. The class itself is not complete, but it implements some complete business logic.

A Utility class attempts to encapsulate some common programmatic steps into a simple easy-to-use class. The following source code illustrates the Utility class:

```
public class FactoryUtils {
    public FactoryUtils() {
    }
    public static Factory ExceptionFactory() {
    }
    public static Factory NullFactory() {
    }
    public static Factory ConstantFactory(
        Object constantToReturn) {
    }
    public static Factory reflectionFactory(
        Class classToInstantiate) {
    }
}
```

In the code example the class FactoryUtils provides four functions to instantiate the interface Factory based on the choice of instantiation process. The methods encapsulate complexity that would have to be written over and over again. A Utility class is typically an implementation of the Façade pattern. The implementation of the class FactoryUtils contains quite a bit of source code to perform the operation. However, the class FactoryUtils hides the complexity.

Structural—[identifier]Support | [identifier]Base

The Structural class type is a base class or support class that provides functionality so that a developer does not have to implement the same functionality over and over. In .NET terms, a structural class is typically an abstract class that implements an interface. The structural class is defined as an abstract class because a subset of interface functionality is implemented.

A structural class typically cannot execute on its own; it comes into play when the Template pattern is implemented.

Collection—[identifier]List | [identifier]Map | [identifier]Bag | [identifier]Set | [identifier]Collection

The Collection class type is a class that is used to manage a collection of objects. The objects can be associated or arranged using different techniques, and therefore various identifiers are used for various collection types.

Constants—[identifier]Constant(s)

The Constants type defines a class that contains a number of constants used throughout a piece of source code. The type being named might also be a data member.

Type: Interface—I[identifier]

In .NET, interfaces are usually prefixed with a capital *I*. I am a bit uneasy with this because it breaks all of the other naming conventions, and could easily be replaced with [identifier]Interface. Be that as it may, you should follow the accepted convention and prefix an *I*.

Remember the following points when writing code that uses a naming convention.

- A good namespace is indispensable when code needs to be maintained, extended, and shared with other developers.

- A well-thought-out namespace is crucial if your code will reside in an assembly that is subject to strong naming conventions.

- Namespaces have a parent-child relationship, where a child namespace contains specializations or implementations defined in the parent namespace.

- Devote some time to naming classes, interfaces, and so on—doing so makes it easier for you and others to find and understand a piece of code.

Understanding the Overloaded Return Type and Property

Recently someone came to me wanting to define two classes that related to each other. The relation between the two classes would be defined as a common architecture, and based on those two classes two specialized classes would be defined that would have the same relation. The problem is that the person wanted to use the exact same access code to access the new specialized types. In .NET you cannot define two methods with the same parameter signature but different return types. In this section I'll show you how to solve the problem by using the overloaded return type and property.

The following code is disallowed because the two variations of GetValue have the same signature but different return values:

Source: /Volume01/LibVolume01/UnderstandingOverloadedReturnTypeProblem.cs

```
class Illegal {
    public int GetValue() {
    }
    public double GetValue() {
    }
}
// …
Illegal cls = new Illegal();
cls.GetValue(); // Which variation is called?
```

At the bottom of the code example the class Illegal is instantiated and the method GetValue is called. Because GetValue's return value is not assigned, the compiler has no idea which variation of GetValue to call. The solution is the following code:

```
class Legal {
    public int GetValueInt() {
    }
    public double GetValueDouble() {
    }
}
```

The methods have been relabeled to be unique, and thus each can return whatever it wants. However, the client needs to know that the two methods exist, and it needs to call the correct version. Going back to the original variation where the method names were identical, if the return value were assigned to a variable, then the compiler could figure out which variation of the method is called. The compiler does not allow such decision-making. However, the compiler does allow some things that boggle the mind. For example, the following code is completely legal:

Source: /Volume01/LibVolume01/UnderstandingOverloadedReturnTypeProblem.cs

```
class BaseIntType {
    public int GetValue() {
        Console.WriteLine( "BaseIntType.GetValue int");
        return 0;
    }
}
class DerivedDoubleType : BaseIntType {
    public double GetValue() {
        Console.WriteLine( "DerivedDoubleType.GetValue double");
        return 0.0;
    }
}
// Client code
```

```
new BaseIntType().GetValue();
new DerivedDoubleType().GetValue();
((BaseIntType)new DerivedDoubleType()).GetValue();
```

Using inheritance and having two methods return different types is legal, yet putting those definitions in the same class is not. You can understand the reasoning by looking at the IL used to call the types:

```
.method public hidebysig instance void  Test() cil managed
{
  .custom instance void [nunit.framework]NUnit.Framework.
TestAttribute::.ctor() = ( 01 00 00 00 )
  // Code size       34 (0x22)
  .maxstack  8
  IL_0000:  newobj       instance void BaseIntType::.ctor()
  IL_0005:  call         instance int32 BaseIntType::GetValue()
  IL_000a:  pop
  IL_000b:  newobj       instance void DerivedDoubleType::.ctor()
  IL_0010:  call         instance float64 DerivedDoubleType::GetValue()
  IL_0015:  pop
  IL_0016:  newobj       instance void DerivedDoubleType::.ctor()
  IL_001b:  call         instance int32 BaseIntType::GetValue()
  IL_0020:  pop
  IL_0021:  ret
} // end of method Tests::Test
```

The compiler used the contract rules defined by the object hierarchy and associated the method with the type that calls the GetValue method. This works so long as the virtual and override keywords are not used with the method GetValue. The compiler treats this inheritance situation as unique. For example, the following declaration for DerivedDoubleType would be illegal:

```
class DerivedDoubleType : BaseIntType {
    public new int GetValue() { return 0;}
    public double GetValue() {
        return 0.0;
    }
}
```

The compiler allows the definition of return types at different levels of the inheritance. But you cannot use that information because the code is bound to a particular implementation defined at the same level as the class that is instantiated. The compiler is incapable of going up the inheritance hierarchy and figuring out the available return-value variations.

We can use parameter declarations to get around this return-value problem; for example, GetValue with int has one parameter, and GetValue for double has two parameters. The compiler knows which method to call when dealing with an overloaded method. However, that solution is silly in that you still need to know whether to call GetValue with one parameter or two.

Another attempt is the following source code, which illustrates the same situation as the method examples, except it uses properties:

Source: /Volume01/LibVolume01/UnderstandingOverloadedReturnTypeProblem.cs

```
class User {
    public void Method() {
        Console.WriteLine( "User.Method");
    }
}

class Session {
    protected User _myUser = new User();
    public User MyUser {
        get {
            return _myUser;
        }
    }
}
class UserSpecialized : User {
    public new void Method() {
        Console.WriteLine( "UserSpecialized.Method");
    }
}
class SessionSpecialized : Session {
    public SessionSpecialized() {
        _myUser = new UserSpecialized();
    }
    public UserSpecialized MyUser {
        get {
            return _myUser as UserSpecialized;
        }
    }
}
```

There are two base classes: Session and User. Session exposes the MyUser property, which is of type User. The class SessionSpecialized derives from the class Session, and the class UserSpecialized derives from User. The class SessionSpecialized also exposes a MyUser property, but it is of type UserSpecialized.

We have two properties of different types in a hierarchy. To illustrate which methods are called, the classes could be called as follows:

```
new Session().MyUser.Method();
new SessionSpecialized().MyUser.Method();
((Session)new SessionSpecialized()).MyUser.Method();
```

The first line should call User.Method because a type Session is instantiated where Session exposes MyUser as type User. For the second line, the generated output should be UserSpecialized.Method because SessionSpecialized instantiates the type UserSpecialized.

The third line poses a more serious challenge because SessionSpecialized is instantiated and downcast to Session. Because no virtual or override keywords were used, downcasting to Session means referencing a User instance, and it causes User.Method to be called when generating output. The generated output is as follows:

```
User.Method
UserSpecialized.Method
User.Method
```

The generated output is what we expected. This means that unlike with methods, it is possible to overload properties and then reference them arbitrarily. This works as long as you respect the rules of not overwriting the properties. The .NET compiler returns the property associated with the type being queried.

So far everything seems to work, but there is still a nagging problem. Inheritance is an interesting way to create methods or properties that return different types, but it can create a conflict with respect to a value type. For example, the following code would generate a compiler failure:

```
int value = new DerivedDoubleType().GetValue();
```

To make the code work, a downcast to BaseIntType would be necessary before assigning value. Not ideal, but possible. Another solution is a bit more complicated and involves the use of .NET Generics.

The complete solution is illustrated as follows, minus the definitions for User and UserSpecialized, as they do not change from the previous declarations:

Source: /Volume01/LibVolume01/UnderstandingOverloadedReturnTypeProblem.cs

```
class Session {
    protected User _myUser = new User();
    public virtual type MyUser< type>() where type: class {
        if (typeof( User).IsAssignableFrom(typeof( type))) {
            Console.WriteLine( "Is User");
            return _myUser as type;
        }
        else {
            Console.WriteLine( "Could not process");
            return null;
        }
    }
}
class SessionSpecialized : Session {
    UserSpecialized _myUserSpecialized = new UserSpecialized();
    public SessionSpecialized() {
        _myUser = _myUserSpecialized;
    }
    public override type MyUser< type>() {
        if (typeof( UserSpecialized).IsAssignableFrom(typeof( type))) {
            Console.WriteLine( "Is UserSpecialized");
```

```
            return _myUserSpecialized as type;
        }
        else {
            Console.WriteLine( "Delegated");
            return base.MyUser< type>();
        }
    }
}
```

The new code uses method declared .NET Generics and converts the properties into a method. Sadly, it is not possible to declare properties that use .NET Generics. Using .NET Generics at the method level enables a very flexible mechanism to determine the parameter type at runtime.

The idea behind using .NET Generics at the method level is to enable the implementation of the method to decide whether or not a certain type could be returned. For example, if in the derived class a requested type cannot be returned, then the derived class will call the base class. And then the base class will determine if the certain type can be returned. In the source code, the MyUser method has no parameters and uses .NET Generics to define the return type. The method is declared using the virtual keyword, which enables a derived class to overload the method. In the case of SessionSpecialized the MyUser method is overloaded.

Going through a scenario, when the virtual and override keywords are used, calling either Session.MyUser or SessionSpecialized.MyUser when SessionSpecialized has been instantiated results in SessionSpecialized.MyUser being called first. Calling SessionSpecialized.MyUser results in the IsAssignableFrom method being called. The method IsAssignableFrom is used to test if one type can be assigned to another type. In the case of SessionSpecialized.MyUser, the implementation is tested if the type can be cast to UserSpecialized, and if so, then it returns the instance _myUserSpecialized. If not, then you call the base class Session. In the implementation of Session.MyUser the method IsAssignableFrom is used again, but this time the type User is tested. If the test is successful, then the instance _myUser is returned. Otherwise, a null value is generated indicating that something went wrong. Another option to indicate that something went wrong is to use an exception.

Using virtual methods and calling the base class ensures that if a conversion is possible it will be made:

```
Session session = new SessionSpecialized();
User user = session.MyUser< User>();
UserSpecialized userSpecialized =
        session.MyUser< UserSpecialized>();
```

In the example source code the type SessionSpecialized is instantiated. The instantiated instance is assigned to the variable session, which is a downcast. Then the method MyUser is called twice with different types for the .NET Generics parameter (User and UserSpecialized). Calling the method MyUser will first call SessionSpecialized.MyUser because of the virtual method hierarchy. If SessionSpecialized.MyUser cannot fulfill the needs of the .NET Generics type, then SessionSpecialized.MyUser calls the base class method Session.MyUser.

Using .NET Generics, we can write methods that overload the return parameter using a .NET inheritance hierarchy that we are used to. Remember the following points when using overloaded return types:

- The compiler cannot cope with two methods that have the same signature but different return types being declared in a single type.

- The compiler can cope with two methods having the same signature and different return types so long as they are declared in different places in the hierarchy chain. The compiler uses type-to-method or type-to-property cross-referencing. When declaring these types of methods, you cannot use keywords such as `virtual` and `override`.

- The safest and most flexible technique is to use .NET Generics and declare the return type as a .NET Generics parameter. It is not possible to declare properties using this technique.

- Using .NET Generics at the method level allows a piece of code to determine the type at runtime and make decisions based on the runtime.

Nullable Types: A Null Is Not Always a Null

In .NET `null` means no value, and we all understand what it represents, right? For example, the following code illustrates a null:

```
Object value = null;

if( value == null) {
    Console.WriteLine( "Yupe a null");
}
```

The example is obvious, and does nothing useful. If I attempted to call the method `Object.ToString()` an exception would be generated. So I have created is a variable value that references nothing and is nothing. This works because I am using a .NET reference type. Let's write the same code, except we'll use the value type `int`:

```
int value = 0;

if( value == 0) {
    Console.WriteLine( "Yupe a null?");
}
```

This time `value` is not of the type `Object`, but of the type `int`. And `value` is assigned a value of 0 to indicate a null value. In C++, and C, null and 0 have the same contextual meaning, so why not apply the same meaning to C#?

In .NET 2.0, and C# there is a new programming construct called nullable types. A nullable type in C# defines a variable that has a null state. For example, in the previous example the `int` value was assigned a value of 0, but a value of `null` would have been more appropriate. Yet we cannot assign a value `null` because the compiler will not let us. The compiler expects some valid value, and 0 is that valid value. The following example uses a `struct` to illustrate the restrictions of a value type even more clearly:

```
struct ExampleStructure {
    int value;
}
ExampleStructure ex = null;
```

The structure ExampleStructure is defined using the struct keyword, which means that ExampleStructure is a value type. The next line, in which the variable ex is assigned a value of null, will again result in a compilation error. It is not possible to assign a null value to a struct type because it is value type.

Assigning an int value to 0 resulted in code that compiled, but is logically incorrect. .NET considers a null a null, and a 0 as a valid value. .NET is not like C or C++ where null and 0 are interchangeable. This brings us back to square one and the inability to define a null for a value type. We would like to assign null values when situations occur where the algorithm has to indicate to the caller that no value for the parameter could be determined.

Nullable types make it possible for value types (such as structs) to behave like reference types and give value types the ability to indicate a null value. Nullable types are geared for usage by value types; they are not intended to be used in conjunction with reference types. There is no other reason to use a nullable type.

You don't have to use nullable types; you could use the solution Java took. Java's solution was to declare a reference type for each and every value type. It sounds good in theory, but in reality, it's a real pain in the butt.

In C# the notation to declare a value type as a nullable type for the ExampleStructure type is as follows:

```
ExampleStructure? ex = null;
```

You define a nullable type by attaching a question mark after the type declaration. As the preceding example illustrates, you can use nullable types to assign a null value to a value type. However, the C# compiler works some magic, illustrated in the generated IL of the example nullable type:

```
initobj valuetype [mscorlib]System.'Nullable`1'<
    valuetype ExampleStructure>
```

The C# compiler has converted the nullable type declaration into a type declaration that uses the .NET base class System.Nullable<>. The System.Nullable<> type is a .NET Generics class that has a single generic parameter that wraps the value type. It is not necessary to use the nullable type notation, and you could use the System.Nullable<> type directly, as follows:

```
System.Nullable< ExampleStructure> ex = null;
```

Compiling the example, which uses System.Nullable<>, generates the exact same IL as if you had used the C# nullable-type notation. The System.Nullable<> class allows you to perform operations on nullable values.

To understand nullable types, let's go through an example that would perform a calculation using value types:

```
int unknown1 = 0;
int known1 = 10;
int result1 = unknown1 + known1;

ExampleStructure unknown2 = new ExampleStructure( 0);
ExampleStructure known2 = new ExampleStructure( 10);
int result2 = unknown2.value + known2.value;
```

In the example the int variable unknown1 represents an unknown value, and the ExampleStructure variable unknown2 represents an unknown struct value. The variables are unknown because in our pretend application, no value has been assigned to the variables. Yet technically, have been assigned in the source code values. Values have to be assigned because the compiler will complain about adding types without having them assigned.

So to satisfy the demands of the compiler, you assign the value types with zero values, but from an abstract logic perspective they are considered as null values. Now the compiler sees the variables assigned and compiles the sources. The problem is that the assignment was arbitrary and meaningless. If the variables were reference types, then doing a plain-vanilla assignment would have meant assigning the variables to null. Null is a valid reference value, and if a variable with a null value is manipulated, a null value exception error will result. Not so with the value types, as value types contain values and hence all manipulations, and in this case additions are syntactically correct.

This example illustrates how nullable types solve the problem of operating on an unknown value:

```
int? unknown1 = null;
int known1 = 10;
int result1 = (int)unknown1 + known1;

ExampleStructure? unknown2 = null;
ExampleStructure known2 = new ExampleStructure( 10);
int result2 = ((ExampleStructure)unknown2).value +
    known2.value;
```

In this modified example unknown1 and unknown2 are nullable types and assigned a value of null to indicate an unknown state. To be able to add the numbers, you need a typecast to convert the nullable type from a reference to a value. The code using nullable types functions identically to the code that uses only value types. However, with nullable types if the additions are attempted an exception (System.InvalidOperation) is generated. System.InvalidOperation indicates that the values are not consistent, and hence the operation cannot be carried out. This is the correct behavior, as we don't want to add unknown values, and this clearly illustrates the need for nullable types.

Now let's look deeper into the System.Nullable<> type. Following is the System.Nullable<> class declaration, abbreviated for illustration purposes:

```
namespace System {
    public struct Nullable<T> :
        System.IComparable, System.INullableValue  {
        public Nullable(T value) {}

        public static implicit operator
            System.Nullable<T > (T value) {}
        public static explicit operator T
            (System.Nullable<T > value) {}
        public static bool operator
            ==(System.Nullable<T > left,
            System.Nullable<T > right) {}
        public static bool operator
            !=(System.Nullable<T > left,
```

```
            System.Nullable<T > right) {}

        object INullableValue.Value {
            get {}
        }
        public virtual bool HasValue {
            get {}
        }
        public T Value {
            get {}
        }
    }
}
```

Notice that the declaration of `System.Nullable<>` is a structure, not a class. This is consistent with value type behavior because when you assign one value type with another value type, you are exchanging complete state and not references. The declaration of `System.Nullable` contains an implicit conversion to the `System.Nullable<>` type, but an explicit conversion to the .NET Generics' type T. The implicit cast means you can assign one nullable type to another nullable type. The explicit cast means a typecast is needed to access the managed nullable type (such as `int` or `ExampleStructure`). The equals and does-not-equal operators are also implemented so that the managed type instance is compared rather than the nullable types. Finally, the properties `INullableValue.Value`, `HasValue`, and `Value` are read-only, making an instance of `System.Nullable<>` immutable.

The `Nullable` type is used in the following contexts:

- When using value types to represent a `null` value state

- When writing database applications to define record values that have null value states

Abstract-Class Bridge-Pattern Variation

The classic Bridge pattern implementation defines a class that implements an interface. Some extra code is associated with the formal definition of the Bridge pattern. For this section I'll focus on one variation of the Bridge pattern and why you would use it.

One variation of the Bridge pattern has no interface definition and only a defined abstract class. Decoupling the interface from the implementation is a good idea, but often the implementation of the interfaces becomes very tedious. A classic example is the XML DOM—when using interfaces extensively, implementing them can be tedious because you must implement the details for all classes.

To illustrate the tedious work I am going to implement the Composite pattern that is used to build a hierarchy of objects. Each object in the hierarchy has to implement the following interface:

Source: /Volume01/LibVolume01/AbstractClassBridgePatternVariation.cs

```
interface INode {
    void Add(INode node);
    void PrintContents();
}
```

The interface INode has two methods: Add and Print. The method Add is structural and Print is an application method. Structural methods are used in a utilitarian context. The method Add adds another Node to the instance associated with the node. Based on the implementation of Add we have no idea what the associated application logic is.

The PrintContents node, on the other hand, is related to the application logic. The implementation of the method could be to write the contents to the database or the screen, or even to translate the contents of the node. PrintContents will have some structural aspects, but the method's primary function is to do something that the application requires. I differentiated between the two so that you understand that interfaces have methods that serve different purposes.

Continuing with the example, a class called Collection is defined and represents the implementation of a class that contains other nodes:

Source: /Volume01/LibVolume01/AbstractClassBridgePatternVariation.cs

```
class Collection : INode {
    protected string _name;
    protected List< INode> _nodes = new List< INode>();
    public void Add(INode node) {
        _nodes.Add(node);
    }
    public Collection(string name) {
        _name = name;

    }
    public void PrintContents() {
        Console.WriteLine("Is Collection");
        foreach (INode node in _nodes) {
            node.PrintContents();
        }
    }
}
```

The implementation details are not particularly important, but they illustrate a thought process of implementing an interface's tedious details. Imagine if you had 15 different implementations of the same interface. If each one had to be uniquely implemented, that would take quite a bit of your time. So for coding optimization you decide to reuse code and use inheritance. You define an interface, a default abstract base class, and then the specific implementations. However, you do have to ask yourself, if the interface is only relevant to a local assembly or application, why put yourself through the pain of defining an interface and abstract base class combination for each and every interface?

You use the abstract class variation on the Bridge pattern when you want the advantages of interface-based development, but do not want the overhead of having to write all of the plumbing related to interface-based development. You should use this variation of the Bridge pattern *only* in the context of a single assembly or a single application.

This Bridge pattern variation lets you decouple, but because the interface and implementation are used in the context of one assembly, you can relax the strict separation rules. The reason why you would use interfaces is that a change to the implementation has no ramifications to the interface. If the interface is an abstract base class, then changes to the abstract base class could have potentially huge ramifications. But because we are limiting this solution to a single assembly or application, it is easy to trace where the problems lie.

The following code shows INode and Collection rewritten to use an abstract class:

Source: /Volume01/LibVolume01/AbstractClassBridgePatternVariation.cs

```
public abstract class Node {
    protected string _name;
    protected List< Node> _nodes = new List< Node>();
    public Node(string name) {
        _name = name;
    }
    public virtual void Add(Node node) {
        _nodes.Add(node);
    }
    public abstract void PrintContents();
}
class Collection : Node {
    public Collection(string name) : base( name) {

    }
    public override void PrintContents() {
        Console.WriteLine("Is Collection");
        foreach (Node node in _nodes) {
            node.PrintContents();
        }
    }
}
```

When using abstract classes you are still using interface-driven development techniques except that the abstract class serves as interface and the default implementation for structural methods. In the example, the abstract class Node has two data members: _name and _nodes. Both data members have protected data access, allowing derived classes to access them directly. Normally, the internal state of classes is managed delicately, but considering the context it is acceptable to use protected scope.

Node has two methods: Add and PrintContents. Both methods are considered virtual in the abstract logic sense, but Add is marked as explicitly virtual and PrintContents is marked as abstract. By marking the methods as virtual Node is expecting the derived classes to provide their own functionality. In the case of Add the derived classes can define their own functionality, whereas with PrintContents a derived class must define its own functionality.

The class Collection subclasses the interface Node and represents the implementation of the interface. Collection uses the default functionality provided by Node for the method Add, and implements PrintContents.

When using an abstract class instead of an explicit interface definition, remember the following points:

- When using abstract classes in the context of the Bridge pattern, the abstract class is architectural; the derived class is the implementation.

- Using abstract classes as a combination interface and default class is simpler and quicker than implementing interfaces with their associated plumbing.

- You should use abstract classes as a Bridge-pattern variation only in the context of a single assembly or single application so that when dramatic changes are made the ramifications are easy to spot.

- Abstract classes implement the default functionality that all implementations share.

- Abstract classes can evolve as the application evolves, which is contrary to how interfaces are defined. Interfaces are defined ahead of time, and they define a contract that is implemented.

Nested Private-Class Bridge-Pattern Variation

Another variation of the Bridge pattern is to make the implementations of the Bridge pattern a nested private class. There can be multiple private classes and private abstract classes. You are moving code that would normally be in a separate namespace into a class. The class controls all access to the embedded classes. Usually the class that contains the implementations is the Factory pattern implementation itself. The big idea behind this pattern is to implement the Adapter pattern in a focused context.

Imagine writing an application that has the task to manage sources of data. The application is an evolution and there is an already existing source code base. In this existing source code base there are interfaces and implementations. Your task is to rewrite the code to use the new interfaces. The Adapter pattern provides an excellent way of fitting an old functionality into a new interface. The problem is that fitting new functionality on old functionality is a messy business. Typically you will implement a host of tricks to make a square peg fit into a round hole. Those tricks result in working code, but that code may require reworking and refactoring. You don't rewrite the base because it is still needed, and more importantly it works. At some later point in time you will rewrite, but not today.

The problem that you have with the new Adapter pattern code is that it works, but you would not be keen to have anybody else use the code. It is temporary code that will change at some later point in time. Using the private class variation of the Bridge pattern, all of the messy details stay in the context of the Factory used to instantiate the class. When implementing classes using this type of Factory, it is important to not write thousands of lines of code. The idea is to provide an adapter from an interface to another subsystem that has the already-working implementation.

The following example is a data source utility that reads a single byte from two data sources: file and ZIP file. The code used to implement the example is straightforward, but has some subtle details:

Source: /Volume01/LibVolume01/PrivateClassBridgePatternVariation.cs

```
public interface IDataSource {
    char ReadByte();
}
public interface IDataSourceFactory {
    IDataSource CreateZipDataSource();
    IDataSource CreateFileDataSource();
}
```

```csharp
class DataSourceAdapterFactory : IDataSourceFactory {
    #region ZIP Implementation (ZipDataSourceImplementation)
    private class ZipDataSourceImplementation : IDataSource {
        public char ReadByte() {
            // Call external assembly
            return 0;
        }
    }
    #endregion
    public IDataSource CreateZipDataSource() {
        return new ZipDataSourceImplementation();
    }

    #region File Implementation (FileDataSourceImplementation)
    private class FileDataSourceImplementation : IDataSource {
        public char ReadByte() {
            // Call external assembly
            return 0;
        }
    }
    #endregion
    public IDataSource CreateFileDataSource() {
        return new FileDataSourceImplementation();
    }
}
public class DataSourceFactoryImplementation {
    public static IDataSourceFactory CreateFactory() {
        return new DataSourceAdapterFactory();
    }
}
```

The interface IDataSource represents a core definition that is used throughout the application. The interface IDataSourceFactory can be specific to the implementation of the private class Bridge pattern variation. I say *can be specific* because in some situations you would use an interface to implement a factory. For the context of the private class implementation, defining an interface for the factory is the most appropriate because the private class implementation is an Adapter pattern implementation that will eventually be reworked and replaced with another factory. The class DataSourceFactory implementation will not change method signatures, but the implementation of DataSourceFactoryImplementation. CreateFactory will change.

The class DataSourceAdapterFactory implements the IDataSourceFactory interface and instantiates the private class implementations of the interface IDataSource. The method CreateFileDataSource instantiates the type FileDataSourceImplementation, and the method CreateZipDataSource instantiates ZipDataSourceImplementation.

The class implementations FileDataSourceImplementation and ZipDataSourceImplementation contain comments to the calling of an external assembly. The class implementations are lightweight classes that provide enough code to wire a new interface to an old subsystem. Extensive logic should not be implemented in the private classes. If extensive logic is required, then consider that logic as a half step toward reworking the legacy code, and create an intermediary layer that will eventually replace the DataSourceAdapterFactory class.

One last detail when implementing the methods and private classes is that they are wrapped in #region and #endregion directives. Using the directives and Microsoft Visual Studio makes it possible to fold large regions of code, making it simpler to understand the overall perspective of the class implementation.

When working with the private class variation of the Bridge pattern, remember the following:

- Nested private classes allow the implementation of interfaces without exposing the classes to external manipulations such as instantiation or subclassing.

- When using nested private classes, typically you will be implementing the Adapter pattern that converts an old system to a new system.

- Generally nested private classes are temporary and subject to reworking and refactoring. The classes are defined as nested and private so that all code can be isolated to a single class.

- Use a nested private class for long-term class implementation if you want to combine many disparate systems and expose those systems using a single interface.

Dealing with Marker Interfaces or Base Classes

When implementing the Command pattern or Chain of Responsibility pattern the objective is to execute a set of interface instances and make them do something useful. "Do something useful" is extremely vague, but that is what the patterns expect.

The idea behind the Command pattern is to be able to string together a set of interface implementations and have them execute a series of commands. The vagueness is the result of having to string together commands that may or may not be related, and thus you are looking for the lowest common denominator. For example, as the user is using an application, a record of each command executed would be added to a list. Then if the user wanted to undo or redo some actions, he would have only to inspect the list of recorded Command interfaces for the interfaces to be replayed or undone.

In the case of the Chain of Command pattern implementation, the idea is to present an object instance to a set of interface instances and expect the interface instances to process the data. For example, imagine writing a translation program and wishing to have some text translated. Using the Chain of Command pattern would find the appropriate translation.

These pattern implementations are very effective in dealing with vague intentions and converting them into specific actions. The following two interfaces are a classical definition of the Command pattern interfaces:

Source: /Volume01/LibVolume01/UsingPlaceholderClassesInterfaces.cs

```
public interface ICommand {
    void Execute();
}
public interface ICommandVariation {
    void Execute();
```

```
    void Undo();
}
```

And the following interface and delegate definition could be considered the classical definition of the Chain of Responsibility interfaces:

Source: /Volume01/LibVolume01/UsingPlaceholderClassesInterfaces.cs

```
public interface ICommand<contexttype> {
    bool Execute(contexttype context);
}
public delegate bool Handler<contexttype>(contexttype context);
```

In all three example definitions there is a common theme: the definition of a minimalist or marker interface, which defines only what is required. Under no circumstances can an implementation of the marker interface function on its own.

Editing Text Using the Command Pattern

To illustrate the minimalism of the ICommand interface, consider the following implementation of a Command pattern that saves a file to the disk:

Source: /Volume01/LibVolume01/UsingPlaceholderClassesInterfaces.cs

```
public class FileSaveImplementation : ICommand {
    private string _filename;
    private string _buffer;
    public void Execute() {
        StreamWriter writer = new StreamWriter( _filename);
        writer.Write( _buffer);
        writer.Close();
    }
}
```

The class FileSaveImplementation implements the method ICommand.Execute to save the string contents _buffer to the file with the identifier _filename. The method implementation of execute is an example action and says that one of the application actions is to save the text at a specific location. Notice that the ICommand interface is completely implemented, but the class is not completely implemented. Not shown is how the data referenced by _buffer, and _filename is created.

The FileSaveImplementation in conjunction with other ICommand interface instances could be used in the following application context:

1. The application is started and a class that manages the ICommand interface instances is emptied and reset to contain no actions.

2. The user enables a log that enables the application's ability to rollback commands.

3. The user performs some text operations that involve adding, removing, and formatting text.

4. Each text operation is saved as an ICommand interface instance.

5. The user decides to save the document, thus creating an instance of FileSaveImplementation that contains the state of the document. The state of the document is the result of applying all of the previous text operations.

6. The user decides to exit the application.

7. Another user loads the document and looks at the log information generated by the ICommand interface instances.

8. The user decides that some text edits executed before saving the file need to be deleted; this creates a chain effect of updating every ICommand interface instance stored after the affected ICommand interface instances.

9. The other user saves the document again.

10. The users exit the application.

From a high level that does not include the nice GUI code, steps 1 through 5 could be implemented as follows:

```
CommandImplementationsManager cmdMgr = NewDocument();
// Other code
cmdMgr.Add(new TextAddImplementation().Execute());
// Other code
cmdMgr.Add(new TextDeleteImplementation().Execute());
// Other code
cmdMgr.Add(new TextAddImplementation().Execute());
// Other code
cmdMgr.Add(new FileSaveImplementation().Execute());
```

The class CommandImplementationsManager manages all ICommand interface instances that are created during the application's execution. Calling the method NewDocument creates a new CommandImplementationsManager instance representing an empty document. As the user adds and deletes text to the document, TextAddImplementation and TextDeleteImplementation interface instances are added to the CommandImplementationsManager instance. For the context of the program the application logic exists in the implementation of the ICommand interface instances. What is not shown is what text to add or delete because it is not the responsibility of CommandImplementationsManager. CommandImplementationsManager expects the ICommand interface instances to figure out where to add or delete text. CommandImplementationsManager is only responsible for putting everything together in a robust, repeatable sequential manner. After the command FileSaveImplementation is executed and added to CommandImplementationsManager, the document is considered saved and the application can be exited.

The following source illustrates steps 6 through 10 carried out by the other user:

```
CommandImplementationsManager cmdMgr = LoadDocument();
// Other code
cmdMgr.Remove(
    IterateAndFindCommand( cmdMgr.GetEnumerator()));
// Other code
cmdMgr.Execute();
```

When a document is loaded, so is the list of ICommand interface instances. The document content loads when the ICommand instances do. To delete a command from the list, the method Remove is used. Changing the contents of the list will require the list of ICommand interface instances to be executed again, as there are changes in the state of the individual object instances. The ICommand instances are executed using the command Execute, which that will iterate the individual ICommand interface instances and execute them.

Marker Interfaces and Their Dependencies

There has been one missing piece of information in all of the discussion thus far: How does the ICommand interface implementation know what to manipulate? How are the data members _buffer and _filename of FileSaveImplementation assigned? The values of the data members do not come from thin air. This is a problem with minimalist or marker interfaces; they do not provide the mechanism to define the state of the class instance. The minimalist or placeholder interfaces delegate the task to the class and tell the class, "figure it out yourself!" That's a challenge for the class no matter how it is structured.

The challenge of the minimalist marker interface is to properly manage dependencies. The minimalist marker interfaces imply that the types that implement the interfaces have as few dependencies as possible. Ideally you would have no dependencies, but that is impossible. Figure 4-2 illustrates the types of dependencies that a marker interface might require.

In Figure 4-2 there are four potential dependencies: the Application Object Reference, IMarker Object Reference, IMarker State, and IMarker State Exchange. The arrows in the diagram represent the directions of the dependencies. The dependencies are defined as follows:

- Application Object Reference: A reference from an IMarker interface instance to the Application itself. This reference is necessary so that the IMarker interface can save files, manipulate text, or delete items.

- IMarker Object Reference: A reference from the Application to the IMarker interface instance. This reference would be a collection reference held by a class like CommandImplementationsManager.

- IMarker State: A reference from the Application to an IMarker interface instance. This type of reference is not common and should be avoided. However, it can occur when state in the Application references state in the IMarker interface instances. The reason why this dependency exists in the first place is so that you do not have the same data in multiple places. If at all possible the state should be referenced dynamically by the Application using accessor methods.

- IMarker State Exchange: A reference that can occur when two IMarker interface instances reference state from each other. The reason this happens is the same reason the IMarker State reference happens. This reference should be avoided and ideally an accessor method that dynamically finds the appropriate IMarker interface instances should be used.

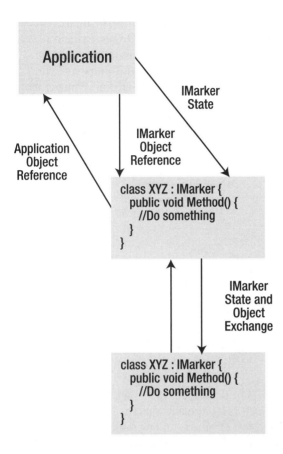

Figure 4-2. *Dependencies of a placeholder interface implementation*

How Marker Interfaces Dependencies Are Implemented

Having covered the dependencies let's look at how some of them could be implemented and their ramifications. When `Application` references `IMarker` like in the `IMarker Object Reference` what you want to be able to do is move from a general interface to a specific interface. The vague interface is used as the lowest common denominator interface, and the specific interface is used to perform some manipulation that only that instance supports. For every single general interface reference, there could be dozens of specific interfaces.

There are two solutions for implementing the `IMarker Object Reference` dependency: extending `IMarker` or using the Extension pattern. Extending the `IMarker` interface as in the following example adds methods and properties to it:

Source: /Volume01/LibVolume01/UsingPlaceholderClassesInterfaces.cs

```
interface IMarker {
    void Method();
    void ExtendedMethod();
}
```

This approach is very easy, but every class that implements IMarker has to implement the new method ExtendedMethod, whether it applies or not. Because of this disadvantage you should never use this method. Additionally adding methods or properties to an interface willy-nilly is asking for problems. This example, while silly, is meant to illustrate that if you ever feel the desire to extend a marker interface for one reason or another, don't. The point of the marker interface is to stick to a minimalist declaration.

The other solution is to use the Extension pattern, which means to do a typecast. There are two types of Extension pattern implementations: static and dynamic. The following is an implementation of the static Extension pattern:

Source: /Volume01/LibVolume01/UsingPlaceholderClassesInterfaces.cs

```
interface IMarker {
    void Method();
}
interface IExtension : IMarker {
    void ExtendedMethod();
}
class Implementation : IExtension {
    public void Method() {
    }
    public void ExtendedMethod() {
    }
}
```

In the example the IMarker interface is defined as it originally was. The interface declaration IExtension (which subclasses the interface IMarker) is new and represents the specific interface. There could be multiple specific interfaces all deriving from IMarker, and each specific interface can have as many methods or properties as need. Don't concern yourself with making the specific interface minimalist as that is not the role of the specific interface. Implementing IExtension means implementing IMarker, and that provides a complete and neatly defined interface package. The class Implementation implements IExtension, which implies implementing IMarker. This strategy could be used for multiple extension interfaces, while making it possible for CommandImplementationsManager to interact with the IMarker interface. The application accesses the IExtension interface from the IMarker, as the following condensed example illustrates:

```
IExtension extension =
    ((IMarker)new Implementation()) as IExtension;
```

In the example the instance of Implementation is cast to IMarker. Then using the as operator the IMarker instance is cast to IExtension. The as operator must be used because IExtension is an optional interface that may or may not be implemented. If the IExtension pattern is implemented, the cast assigns a reference to the variable extension. If a cast cannot be performed, then the variable extension contains a null value. If we used a cast that contains brackets, an exception would be generated if a cast could not be carried out. Generating an exception is wrong because IExtension is a specific interface that may or may not be implemented by the IMarker interface instance.

Another way to implement the same code is to use two separate interfaces, as in the following example:

Source: /Volume01/LibVolume01/UsingPlaceholderClassesInterfaces.cs

```
interface IMarker {
    void Method();
}
interface IExtension {
    void ExtendedMethod();
}
class Implementation : IExtension, IMarker {
    public void Method() {
    }
    public void ExtendedMethod() {
    }
}
// ...
IExtension extension =
        ((IMarker)new Implementation()) as IExtension;
```

The only real difference at a technical level is that IExtension does not subclass IMarker, and Implementation has to implement two interfaces. From the perspective of the application, the same code is used.

However, from an abstract logic perspective, implementing IExtension does not imply implement IMarker. The fact that the two interfaces are separate has the ramification that a specific interface does not have to be associated with the marker interface. The two interfaces can be used in other contexts. I tend to prefer this approach because not all specific interface implementations are required to be used in a marker context.

One advantage to this approach is that you may think having separate interfaces makes it simpler to implement abstract base classes. But as illustrated in the solution "Implementing Interfaces," abstract base classes do not have to implement interfaces.

In the context of the IMarker extension variation, there is another way to implement IMarker. In the preceding examples IMarker has a single method, which could have been replaced with a delegate defined as follows:

```
public delegate void MarkerDelegate();
```

To complete an implementation using a delegate, it is only required to implement IExtension. The modified Implementation class would appear similar to the following:

```
public class Implementation : IExtension {
    public void Method() { }
    public void ExtendedMethod() { }
}
```

The change in the Implementation is the missing IMarker interface implementation. The method declarations remain the same. The marker interface, more appropriately called marker delegate, is created and retrieved using the following source code:

```
MarkerDelegate delegates = new MarkerDelegate(
    new MarkerImplementation().Method);
IExtension extension =
    (delegates.GetInvocationList()[ 0].Target) as IExtension;
```

In the source code a delegate list is created and assigned to the delegates variable. The delegate list contains a single delegate that references the method MarkerImplementation.Method. Having a list of delegate method references is not the same as having a list of object references. Remember from Figure 4-2 it is necessary to convert the delegate into an object instance so that the IExtension interface can be manipulated. To be able to perform a typecast you need to iterate the individual delegates and then typecast the owner of the delegate method. The method GetInvocationList returns an array of delegates. From the example, we know that there is at least one delegate, and we can reference the delegate using the zeroth index. The zeroth index returns a delegate instance that references an object instance's method.

To move from the delegate instance and get at the object instance the property Delegate. Target is referenced. The value of Delegate.Target is an Object instance that can be typecast to the desired IExtension interface. It is important to perform the typecast using the as operator because Target might be a null value, and the object might not have implemented the optional interface. The property Target will be null when the delegate references a method that has been declared using the static keyword. This is logical because static methods are not associated with a class instance.

This is the only time that the IMarker interface is converted to a delegate and is meant to illustrate how delegates can be used in place of interfaces. For the remaining examples, illustrating every example using both the interface and delegate would be tedious. So the remaining examples will use the IMarker interface for explanation purposes. However, other variations could be implemented using a delegate. The only real different between an interface and a delegate is that you need to access a method and a property to get at the object that would be used in the interface explanation.

In Figure 4-2 another dependency is the IMarker State variation. This variation is typically used when a series of immutable objects are wired together. The application has a state that is transferable and is to be manipulated by the IMarker instances. The objects are considered immutable because the state is passed only once and the IMarker instance does not ask for more information and does not alter the state of the passed information. The application expects that once the state has been assigned, the IMarker instances are self-sufficient and know what to do with the state without any further intervention by the application.

The following is an example of implementing the IMarker State variation dependency:

```
interface IMarker {
    void Method();
}
class Implementation : IMarker {
    public Implementation( Object state) { }
    public void Method() { }
}
class Factory {
    public static IMarker Instantiate( Object state) {
        return new Implementation( state);
    }
}
```

The interface IMarker remains as is, and Implementation implements IMarker. The IMarker State variation is implemented by the constructor of Implementation. In the example the constructor is a single parameter of type Object. However, it does not *need* to be a single parameter, nor of the type Object, and the parameter could be multiple .NET Generics parameters. The type Object is used as an arbitrary example of how state can be transferred. The single parameter presents some state (defined by the application) that is manipulated by the constructor of the interface implementation.

Requiring parameters for the constructor puts us into a bind; any factory that is used to instantiate Implementation must have the means to provide the state. In the example the method Factory.Instantiate has a single parameter that is identical to the constructor parameters. This illustrates that the state is passed through, not manipulated by the factory.

Another of Figure 4-2's dependency variations between Application and IMarker implementation is the Application Object Reference. This variation occurs when the IMarker implementation requires information from the Application. This situation usually occurs when the IMarker implementation wants to carry out some logic but needs extra information from the application.

The Application Object Reference and IMarker State dependency variations are similar in that information is transferred from the application to the IMarker implementation. The difference is that Application Object Reference is a dynamic querying of application capabilities, and IMarker State is a static transfer of state. With IMarker State, the constructor provides all of the information that the IMarker needs. With Application Object Reference, the IMarker interface instance queries the information dynamically. The querying used is identical to the technique illustrated by IMarker Object Reference. For the IMarker interface instance to be able to query the application for supported interfaces, the application needs to provide an initial reference-object instance. The IMarker interface (or, more appropriately, an extension interface) could supply that reference-object instance.

The sequence of events would be for the Application to instantiate an IMarker instance. Then Application would typecast the IMarker for a special callback interface. If the special callback interface exists, then the parent assignment method is called. The parent assignment method provides an object that the IMarker instance can typecast for a particular interface. The interfaces used in the sequence of events are defined as follows:

Source: /Volume01/LibVolume01/UsingPlaceholderClassesInterfaces.cs

```
interface IMarker {
    void Method();
}
interface IApplicationCallback : IMarker {
    void AssignParent( IApplicationMarker parent);
}
interface IApplicationMarker {
}
```

The interface IApplicationCallback extends the IMarker interface and has a single method that Application uses to know whether a parent should be assigned to the IMarker instance. If the IMarker implementation supports IApplicationCallback then Application typecasts to IApplicationCallback and calls the method AssignParent. The interface IApplicationMarker is empty for illustration purposes, and is used as a reference for typecasting the Application object instance.

The code to make all of this work is as follows:

```
class Implementation : IApplicationCallback {
    public void Method() {

    }
    IApplicationMarker _parent;
    public void AssignParent( IApplicationMarker parent) {
        _parent = parent;
    }
}
class Application : IApplicationMarker {
    public void CallIndividualIMarkerImplementation(
        IMarker child) {
        IApplicationCallback callback = child as IApplicationCallback;
        if( callback != null) {
            callback.AssignParent( this);
        }
        callback.Method();
    }
}
```

The class `Implementation` implements the `IApplicationCallback` interface, which implies implementing `IMarker`. In the implementation of `AssignParent` the passed-in parent instance is assigned to the data member `_parent`. From the perspective of the `IPlaceholder` instance the type `IApplicationMarker` interface is a marker interface that needs to be typecast using the as operator. The typecast may or may not be supported by the application, and it is up to the `IMarker` implementation to deal with potential unsupported interfaces.

The class `Application` implements the `IApplicationMarker` interface. In the method `CallIndividualMarkerImplementation`, the `AssignParent` method (if supported) must be called before the `IMarker` method is called. This is so the `IMarker` instance can initialize its state and prepare to be called.

If a class implements the `IApplicationCallback` interface, then the class cannot make any assumptions about the parent. For example, it would be bad programming practice to keep application object references after `IMarker.Method` is called.

The final dependency variation in Figure 4-2 is between `IMarker` instances. Such dependencies happen when one `IMarker` instance relies on data generated by another `IMarker` instance. Typically, having `IMarker` instances depend on each other using direct referencing techniques is bad, as the following code illustrates:

```
interface IMarker {
    void Method();
}
class Implementation1 : IMarker {
    IMarker _sibling;
    public void Method() {
    }
}
class Implementation2 : IMarker {
```

```
    IMarker _sibling;
    public void Method() {
    }
}
```

The code illustrates two IMarker implementations: Implementation1 and Implementation2. Within each class is a single data member that references another IMarker instance. Even though the data members reference the sibling using the IMarker interface, the direct referencing is wrong.

Imagine using the CommandsImplementationManager class to remove an IMarker instance. If one of the implementations had a direct reference to the IMarker instance, from the perspective of IMarker instance the deleted instance would never seem deleted. This is a programmatic flaw that should never occur.

To avoid such problems, use the Mediator pattern. The implementation of the Mediator pattern is an extension of Application Object Reference. The application and the IMarker instances do everything expected when implementing the Application Object Reference, plus they add a sibling querying method. The complete code is similar to the following:

Source: /Volume01/LibVolume01/UsingPlaceholderClassesInterfaces.cs

```
interface IMarker {
    void Method();
}
interface IApplicationCallback : IMarker {
    void AssignParent(IApplicationMarker parent);
}
interface IApplicationMarker {
    IMarker GetSibling( object identifier);
}
interface IExtension {
    void AnotherMethod();
}
class Implementation1 : IApplicationCallback, IExtension  {
    IApplicationMarker _parent;
    public void AssignParent(IApplicationMarker parent) {
        _parent = parent;
    }
    public void AnotherMethod() { }
    public void Method() { }
}
class Implementation2 : IApplicationCallback {
    IApplicationMarker _parent;
    public void AssignParent(IApplicationMarker parent) {
        _parent = parent;
    }
    public void Method() {
        IExtension ext =
            _parent.GetSibling( "some-identifier") as IExtension;
```

```
        if( ext != null) {
            ext.AnotherMethod();
        }
    }
}
```

In the example code the new code with respect to `Application Object Reference` is bolded. In the interface `IApplicationMarker`, the `Application` implements the method `GetSibling`, which completes the implementation of the Mediator pattern. The `GetSibling` method acts like a gopher, retrieving information for an `IMarker` instance. If the information can be retrieved, then `GetSibling` returns an `IMarker` instance. Which sibling to retrieve is based on the value of the parameter identifier. In the example the parameter identifier is an object type, but you can use whatever you want to identify the data to be retrieved.

The preceding example shows a query for `Implementation2`'s sibling when `Implementations2`'s `IMarker` interface method is called; the sibling is the class `Implementation1`. If the sibling can be found, the result is typecast to `IExtension`, and that results in a call to the method `AnotherMethod`.

Using the Mediator pattern decouples the `IMarker` implementations from each other, thereby reducing the chance that an object reference will be inadvertently kept by the `IMarker` instances.

Remember the following when dealing with placeholder interfaces or base classes:

- Use minimal placeholder interfaces so that types are decoupled from each other. The result is that when type implementations change, the ramifications of those changes are kept to a minimum.

- Minimal or placeholder interfaces keep code decoupled, but also make it more complicated for implementations to exchange information outside of the placeholder interfaces.

- To exchange state information between `Application` or `IMarker` implementations, the best approach is to use the Extension pattern that will typecast for the interface that it is interested in.

- Optional interfaces must always be queried using the `as` operator so that if a typecast is not possible the code fails gracefully.

- Delegates can be typecast using extra method and property calls.

- When more-complicated interface or instance querying is required, the Mediator pattern (as illustrated by the `IMarker State`) or the `Object Exchange` dependency variation is used.

- If you use the techniques described in this section, there is absolutely no need for the `IMarker` implementations to reference any objects other than the parent. Everything can be passed as a state using the constructor the `IApplicationMarker` instance.

A Null Value Is Not Always a Null State

Developers attempt to write the best code they can, but they often make mistakes when complex objects are involved. Frequently a class will require a return value, and for ease of coding a null value is returned even though the state is inconsistent.

The following code illustrates how returning a `null` value is the wrong thing to do:

```
class ReferenceObject {
    public void GenerateOutput() {
        Console.WriteLine( "Generated");
    }
}
class InconsistentState {
    public ReferenceObject GetInstance() {
        return null;
    }
    public void CallMe() {
        GetInstance().GenerateOutput();
    }
}
```

In the example the class `InconsistentState` has two methods: `GetInstance` and `CallMe`. The method `CallMe` calls the method `GetInstance`. Though `GetInstance` always returns a null value, that is not checked for validity in the implementation of `CallMe`. That means an exception will be generated when it is not necessary. As a solution in most cases developers would add a decision to test whether `GetInstance` returns a valid instance.

You can fix the problem of a valid instance by saying that there is always a consistent state represented by a default object. This is where nullable types and the Null Object pattern come into play.

The following example shows how nullable types solve the problem of inconsistent state:

Source: /Volume01/LibVolume01/UsingPlaceholderClassesInterfaces.cs

```
class NullableReturn {
    public int ReturnValue() {
        int? returnvalue = null;
        return (int)returnvalue;
    }
}
```

The class `NullableReturn` has a single method `ReturnValue`, which returns a value type. The variable `returnvalue` is assigned a value of null indicating an inconsistent state. When the variable `returnvalue` is cast to an integer, the cast is saying, "Return an integer value." In the example, the nullable type `returnvalue` is assigned null, resulting in an exception. The exception is generated by the nullable type because the nullable type cannot extract any value. Of course, comparing this solution to the previous, which also generated an exception, you would be tempted to say that there is no advantage. There is a difference in that the nullable generated exception could be expected, whereas the null object reference is not expected.

Nullable types solve our value type problem, but what happens when reference types are used? Often programmers will return the wrong value. Consider the following source code, which offers three variations on a reference type that can be returned from a method without using a nullable type:

Source: /Volume01/LibVolume01/UsingPlaceholderClassesInterfaces.cs

```
class HowToReturn {
    public IList<string> Variation1() {
        return null;
    }
    public IList<string> Variation2() {
        return new List< string>();
    }
    public IList<string> Variation3() {
        throw new InvalidOperationException();
    }
}
```

When implementing your own application one of the three variations will have to be used; the question is, which one? Using the nullable-type example that generated an exception, Variation3 would be the best answer. However, that is not correct because the context has been properly defined—we don't know what is being attempted and why a valid value can't be returned. Adding a context reveals that each of the methods is appropriate. Variation1 is wrong in 95 percent of contexts. Variation2 is appropriate for most cases if there is no data to return. Variation3 is appropriate when there might be data to return but something went wrong in the execution of the method. So in most cases you will use Variation2; the following example illustrates why:

Source: /Volume01/LibVolume01/UsingPlaceholderClassesInterfaces.cs

```
HowToReturn cls = obj.getInstance();

foreach( string item in cls.Variation2()) {
    Console.WriteLine( "Item (" + item + ")");
}
```

The method obj.getInstance is called and instantiates the class HowToReturn that is assigned to the variable cls. Then a foreach loop is started. The code is living dangerously because there is no test to verify that cls is a valid object instance. If Variation1 were used to implement getInstance, an additional test would be required. That would complicate the solution and require additional coding of a test.

The proper solution is to implement getInstance using Variation2. Variation2 is the proper solution because the code can be expected to manipulate a valid instance at all times. The valid instance might be an empty collection, and that is OK because the foreach loop will not execute.

When a problem does arise, you'll use Variation3. This means if a problem due to an error arises in the execution of a method, an exception is thrown. Often developers are hesitant to throw exceptions because they are expensive. But an error is an error, and should be marked as an error. Returning a null value to indicate an error complicates things and requires a developer to figure out what went wrong.

As I mentioned, you'll rarely use Variation1, but the following source code illustrates when returning a null value is preferred action:

```
Hashtable table = new Hashtable();
Console.WriteLine( "Element (" + table[ "something"] + ")");
```

In the example, a Hashtable is instantiated and nothing is added. The next line retrieves from the hash table the object associated with the key "something". If the Hashtable returned a value based on the logic of Variation2 and Variation3, the consumer would be left wondering what to do. The logic of Variation1 is appropriate because querying a collection for a specific value, we can expect to be returned a null value indicating no value. In the case of Variation2 it is an incorrect implementation because returning an empty value implies that the Hashtable has some value. And Variation3 is incorrect because a null value is an appropriate response for an item that does not exist in the collection.

The Hashtable class has a solution that improves the reasoning for returning a null value. It has an additional method that you can use to query if a value exists; this takes the place of making a decision based on a null value:

```
if( table.Contains( "something")) {
    Console.WriteLine( "Element (" + table[ "something"] + ")");
}
else {
    Console.WriteLine( "Does not contain");
}
```

The method Contains will query the hash table to see if a valid value is available. If so, then the hash table indexer can be retrieved. The presented solution is correct, but there is a problem. The hash table is queried twice, which could mean wasting resources. The first query iterates the elements to see if the element exists, and the second iterates and retrieves the element. An application could provide some optimizations, but should the hash table do it instead? This is one of those 5-percent situations in which it is acceptable to return a null value.

Now that you're familiar with all three variations and you know that Variation2 is preferred, the Null Object pattern needs further explanation. It is an implementation of Variation2 and is used to define objects that are null values. The Null Object pattern solves null-value problems because you assign the variable a type instance that does nothing.

Illustrated will be how the Null Object pattern is exposed and implemented. The next set of declarations illustrates the Null Object pattern:

Source: /Volume01/LibVolume01/UsingPlaceholderClassesInterfaces.cs

```
public interface ILightState {
    bool IsLightOn {
        get;
    }
    void TouchButton();
}
```

A Null Object pattern always starts with a base class or an interface because you want the consumer of the interface or base class to think it is manipulating a valid instance. The Null Object pattern implementation is usually a distinct and minimalist implementation. You might be tempted to use an already existing implementation and modify it to support a default empty behavior, but that would be incorrect because a null value usually is an empty immutable object. In the case of the ILightState interface, a Null Object pattern implementation would be as follows:

```csharp
public class NullLightState : ILightState {
    public bool IsLightOn {
        get {
            throw new NotImplementedException();
        }
    }
}
```

Notice that instead of returning false for the property IsLightOn, an exception is thrown. That's because for the null object in this example, a state does not exist. The light is either on or off—there is no in-between. There is a default state, but that is not a null state. To understand the difference between null states and default states consider the following implementation of the State pattern, which acts like a light switch:

Source: /Volume01/LibVolume01/UsingPlaceholderClassesInterfaces.cs

```csharp
public class LightSwitch {
    private ILightState _onLight = new LightStateOn();
    private ILightState _offLight = new LightStateOff();
    private ILightState _current = _offLight;

    public ILightState LightState {
        get { return _current; }
    }
    public void TouchButton() {
        if(_current.IsLightOn) {
            _current = _offLight;
        }
        else {
            _current = _onLight;
        }
    }
}
```

The class LightSwitch manages a set of states, which are assigned by the method Touch-Button. The data member _current is assigned _offLight, meaning that when LightSwitch is instantiated the switch will be off.

Using the Null Object pattern would be appropriate if something went wrong while an instance of LightSwitch was being manipulated. For example, let's say that the light switch overloaded and blew a fuse. Then the light switch has neither an on nor an off state. The light switch blew a fuse and therefore _current must reference an instance of NullLightState.

In this example of the Null Object pattern, the implementation threw an exception. Is this the correct implementation for all situations? The answer is that the Null Object pattern implementation depends on what an appropriate object instance response is when manipulated. Following are some examples and the appropriate responses:

- **Collections**. An empty collection is an appropriate implementation because an empty collection indicates that everything is OK but that there is no data.

- **Proxy pattern**. A Null Object pattern implementation should generate an exception for the specified conditions. The idea behind the Proxy pattern is to provide a call-through mechanism. You would use the Null Object pattern if you want to indicate certain unsupported, unimplemented, or unusable functionality. For example, imagine having a read-write interface and writing to a read-only CD-ROM. Writing to the read-only CD-ROM is impossible and would require changing all the routines in the write modules to check if it is OK to write. Or you could use the Proxy pattern with a read-only Null Object pattern implementation. Then the write routines could be left as is, and the client would never call them because the read-only Null Object pattern would intercept the calls and generate an exception.

- **Decorator pattern**. A Null Object pattern implementation would act as a pass-through. The idea behind the Decorator pattern is to chain together some implementations and enhance the functionality of the decorated object. The Null Object pattern is a placeholder and thus should not interfere and should remain silent when queried.

Remember the following points when writing code that needs to return a null object instance because there is no valid object instance:

- There are three main ways of returning a null object instance: returning `null`, returning an empty value, and throwing an exception. Which one you should use depends on the context.

- The Null Object pattern can be used in conjunction with interfaces and base classes when returning an empty value.

- A Null Object pattern implementation cannot be generalized as being only one type of implementation. It is one of the few patterns that varies and has its implementation dependent on the context.

- Developers do not think enough about what the value `null` represents. It seems harmless, and it is easy to test for a `null`-value condition. However, `null` means an inconsistent state, and developers need to understand and define what a correct state is for their applications.

The Essentials of the Factory Pattern

The Factory pattern is an added complication no matter how you try to explain it. It is simpler to not use the Factory pattern, so why have it in the first place? The answers are flexibility, maintainability, and extensibility.

The Classical Factory Pattern

Consider the following source code that illustrates the code written without using a Factory pattern:

```
public class UseItDirectly {
    public void Method() {
        Console.WriteLine( "I will be called directly");
    }
}
// ...
UseItDirectly cls = new UseItDirectly();
cls.Method();
```

In the example the class UseItDirectly has a single method, Method. To call Method the class UseItDirectly is instantiated. The code works and is simple, but maintaining and extending the code is complicated. Imagine if UseItDirectly were a version 1.0 class, and that for the next version the class is used by other classes and methods, as illustrated in the following example:

Source: /Volume01/LibVolume01/UsingPlaceholderClassesInterfaces.cs

```
public class UseItDirectly {
    public void Method() {
        Console.WriteLine( "I will be called directly (with bugfix)");
    }
}

public class NewClassIntroduced {
    public void Method() {
        UseItDirectly cls = new UseItDirectly();
        cls.Method();
    }
}
// ...
UseItDirectly cls = new UseItDirectly();
cls.Method();

NewClassIntroduced cls2 = new NewClassIntroduced();
cls2.Method();
```

In the example NewClassIntroduced has a method Method that calls UseItDirectly. The old code that instantiates the class UseItDirectly still exists, but now additional code instantiates and calls UseItDirectly directly. During operations, NewClassIntroduced realizes that there is a bug in UseItDirectly. The bug causes NewClassIntroduced to work improperly, and the bug needs fixing. For illustration purposes the Console.WriteLine has been updated to reflect that UseItDirectly has been updated to fix a bug.

It seems everything is correct and the source code using the two classes should work properly. But in fact a new bug has been created, as illustrated by executing the code and looking at the generated output:

```
I will be called directly (with bugfix)
I will be called directly (with bugfix)
```

The two lines of generated output are identical, and that indicates a bug. You may think the output is identical because UseItDirectly has a fixed bug. The problem is that the old code that was working has the fixed bug as well. Maybe the old code did not want the bug fix, or maybe the coder assumed the bug was normal and compensated. The reality is that the system was buggy because of NewClassIntroduced, not because of version 1.0. This means that all of the old working code has to be retested and potentially fixed to adjust for the bug. When fixing bugs, be careful what you fix!

Using classes directly does not promote separation and modularization of code. You tend to write big lumps of code, which is one of the many reasons why you should not use classes directly. Instead you want to use component-driven development that involves using an interface and a class that implements an interface or a base class. The following example illustrates how to create a component:

Source: /Volume01/LibVolume01/UsingPlaceholderClassesInterfaces.cs

```
interface InterfaceToBeShared  { }
class ImplementsInterface : InterfaceToBeShared { }
// ...
InterfaceToBeShared inst = new ImplementsInterface();
```

The interface InterfaceToBeShared is a base type that all consumers use. In the example the interface has no methods, but that is only for illustration purposes. The interface defines your intent. The class ImplementsInterface implements InterfaceToBeShared and is called an *implementation of the intention*. A consumer could use the interface instance by instantiating the class ImplementsInterface. Instantiating the class and then assigning the instance to a variable referencing an interface is wrong. To instantiate the class ImplementsInterface you need to know about the class, and in .NET-speak that means having access to the type information. Yet that is what we want to avoid because we don't want instantiate a type directly. We would like to delegate the call to some other piece of functionality.

To be able to create an instance of an interface or abstract class using patterns, you use the Factory pattern. The Factory pattern says that instead of you instantiating an object directly, another class will do that for you. This lets the class that does the indirect instantiation figure out what type you want or need. In the simplest case the indirect instantiation would appear similar to the following:

Source: /Volume01/LibVolume01/UsingPlaceholderClassesInterfaces.cs

```
public interface InterfaceToBeShared  { }
class ImplementsInterface : InterfaceToBeShared { }
public class Factory {
    public static InterfaceToBeShared CreateObject() {
        return new ImplementsInterface ();
    }
}
```

In the example the class Factory has a static method CreateObject that instantiates the type ImplementsInterface but returns an InterfaceToBeShared interface instance. Notice the strategic use of the public keyword in the code example. The interface and factory were declared public, but the implementation was not. This means that anybody who uses the factory and interface does not need to know how the interface is implemented. The importance of this will become apparent shortly. To use the factory you could write the following code:

```
InterfaceToBeShared interf = Factory.CreateObject();
interf.SomeMethod();
```

The consumer of InterfaceToBeShared would call the method Factory.CreateObject that returns a manipulatable interface instance. The delegation of functionality has worked, and the implementation of Factory.CreateObject can decide how it wants to instantiate an interface instance. The consumer needs to know only about the factory and the interface.

The Factory pattern does enable a developer to write code that can be extended and maintained and is generally more flexible than writing code that accesses the classes directly. The downside is that the Factory pattern can complicate things, as illustrated by the following example that fixes the class that had one of its bugs fixed. The following solution shows that no matter how ugly things get underneath, the consumer is blissfully ignorant of the implementation:

Source: /Volume01/LibVolume01/UsingPlaceholderClassesInterfaces.cs

```
public interface IUseIt {
    void Method();
}
class UseItDirectly : IUseIt {
    public void Method() {
        Console.WriteLine("I will be called directly");
    }
}

class UseItDirectlyFixed : IUseIt {
    public void Method() {
        Console.WriteLine("I will be called directly (with bugfix)");
    }
}

class NewClassIntroduced : IUseIt {
    public void Method() {
        UseItDirectlyFixed cls = new UseItDirectlyFixed();
        cls.Method();
    }
}

public class Factory {
    public static IUseIt Version1() {
```

```
        return new UseItDirectly();
    }
    public static IUseIt Version2() {
        return new NewClassIntroduced();
    }
}
// ...
IUseIt cls = Factory.Version1();
cls.Method();

IUseIt cls2 = Factory.Version2();
cls2.Method();
```

In the solution, the class Factory has two methods: Version1 and Version2. Version1 instantiates the type UseItDirectly. Version2 instantiates the type NewClassIntroduced, which itself instantiates the type UseItDirectlyFixed. The type UseItDirectlyFixed is a copied-and-pasted version of UseItDirectly that contains the bug fixes needed for NewClassIntroduced.

In general, a copy and paste is extremely bad programming practice. But in this instance a developer pressed for time can say, "But the changes are contained in a single assembly and nobody will ever see the problems. We can fix the code later." The fact that no external assembly sees the problem is a not a carte blanche for bad programming practices. The example code illustrates that no matter the mess behind the Factory pattern and interface, the client is blissfully unaware. If at a later point the code is fixed and a refactoring were undertaken, then the consumer would still be blissfully unaware. This is the point of component-driven development and the reason why a factory is necessary. The code has been modularized and all that matters is the implementation of the interface contract.

At the beginning of this solution I said that the Factory pattern is technically more complex. I still stand by that assertion. But what I also want to point out is that because you only write a Factory once and modify it very rarely, your code becomes simpler because you don't have to do coding contortions when maintaining and bug-fixing code.

More Sophisticated Factory Implementations

There are multiple ways to define a factory's implementation. Classically speaking, with some frameworks, there is one factory for each implementation. But that can very quickly become tedious and it might be wrong in terms of decoupling the implementation from the interface. For example, imagine releasing version 1.0 and then releasing version 2.0. Will the Factory method be updated to instantiate the new type?

The correct approach is not to create a specific factory for each implementation, but to consider the types that the factory is instantiating. Consider the factory as a way of instantiating type groupings, as illustrated in the following improved factory:

Source: /Volume01/LibVolume01/UsingPlaceholderClassesInterfaces.cs

```
public sealed class MultiObjectSharedFactory {
    static const int INITIAL_VERSION = 1;
    static const int UPDATED_VERSION = 2;
```

```
    public static IUseIt AnImplementation(
        int version) {
        switch( version) {
            case MultiObjectSharedFactory.INITIAL_VERSION:
                return new UseItDirectly();
            case MultiObjectSharedFactory.UPDATED_VERSION:
                return new UseItDirectlyFixed();
        }
        return null;
    }
    public static IUseIt AnotherImplementation() {
        return new NewClassIntroduced();
    }
}
```

The class Factory has been renamed MultiObjectSharedFactory to indicate the factory's varying capabilities. The class MultiObjectSharedFactory has its declaration changed to sealed, indicating that nobody can subclass the factory. The class contains two methods that instantiate various implementations supporting the interface IUseIt.

The method AnImplementation is different from previous factory methods because it requires a parameter, which is an int value. The parameter represents a version number of the object to instantiate. The reason for using an int has to do with the previous example, where the Factory had methods Version1 and Version2. Imagine if a third version of the product became available. At that point another method would be added to the factory, causing a recompile of each client that uses the factory. This is neither the intent nor the desire. The int value is a solution, but other solutions (buffers, enumerations, interface instances, etc.) could be employed. Another way to solve the versioning problem at an application level is presented in the solution "Versioning Assemblies" in Chapter 2. When creating a factory you want to decouple, but also to avoid requiring the client to recompile its sources. What this example illustrates is that a factory does not need to be a single method with a single instantiation. The factory can contain logic that determines which object to instantiate and the instantiation conditions.

The other method, AnotherImplementation, instantiates another type that implements the IUseIt interface. AnotherImplementation belongs to the factory class because both methods are grouped together. A grouping would not belong together if the types they instantiate were not related. For example, if you are a producer of wheels, a factory that instantiates all sorts of wheel types (plane, car, etc.) would not be grouped together because they change independently of each other. A change in instantiating wheels for planes would result in a recompile for programs that require wheels for cars.

When defining factory groupings, usually you are defining abstractions, and that could involve abstracting the factory to an interface, as in the following example:

Source: /Volume01/LibVolume01/UsingPlaceholderClassesInterfaces.cs

```
public interface IWheel { }
public interface IWing { }
public interface IFactory {
```

```csharp
    IWheel CreateWheel();
    IWing CreateWing();
}
public class BoeingPartsFactory : IFactory {
    public IWheel CreateWheel() {
        return null;
    }
    public IWing CreateWing() {
        return null;
    }
}
public class AirBusPartsFactory : IFactory {
    public IWheel CreateWheel() {
        return null;
    }
    public IWing CreateWing() {
        return null;
    }
}
public class AirplanePartsFactory {
    public static IFactory CreateBoeing() {
        return null;
    }
    public static IFactory CreateAirBus() {
        return null;
    }
}
```

In the example some application manipulates the interfaces IWheel and IWing. Both interfaces represent parts of an airplane. And on this planet there are two major big airplane manufacturers: Boeing and Airbus. Imagine a service station at an airport. It needs to order parts from both manufacturers. However, the parts cannot be substituted, as it is not possible to put an Airbus wing on a Boeing plane. But from an abstraction perspective both Airbus and Boeing have wings, and therefore one abstraction (IWing) can be used to define both. We are caught in a bind where the abstraction is identical, but the technical implementation unique.

The solution is to define an interface that defines a common abstract theme (IFactory), where each unique manufacturer implements its own IFactory class. The interface IFactory has two methods: CreateWheel and CreateWing. The two methods are used as factory methods to instantiate types that have the same intention but unrelated implementations. The classes AirBusPartsFactory and BoeingPartsFactory implement IFactory and their appropriate IWheel and IWing implementations. Then to create the appropriate IFactory interface instance, another factory, AirplanePartsFactory, is defined.

The example is an abstraction of an abstraction, and is used to implement functionality where you want to instantiate types that are similar but not related. In the case of the airport that means the process of costing a wing is identical for both Boeing and Airbus. What is different between Boeing and Airbus are the details related to the costing.

In the airplane example, each factory allowed the creation of a single wheel or a single wing. But, a Boeing airplane might have two wheels whereas an Airbus has three. A dilemma is created because a consumer has an IFactory interface instance that can be used to create the wheels and wings, but not assemble them. The consumer does not have the assembly information, nor can it decide what the assembly information is.

Assembling the parts is not the responsibility of the factory that we have been discussing, but rather the responsibility of a pattern called Builder. You can think of the Builder pattern as a Factory pattern with a mission. A Builder pattern implementation exposes itself as a factory, but goes beyond the factory implementation in that various implementations are wired together. That would mean creating an airplane with wings and wheels. In code, the Builder pattern would be implemented as follows:

Source: /Volume01/LibVolume01/UsingPlaceholderClassesInterfaces.cs

```
public interface IPlane {
    IWheel[] Wheels { get; }
    IWing[] Wings { get; }
    IFactory CreateParts();
}
public interface IPlaneFactory {
    IPlane CreatePlane(  );
}
class Plane123Factory : IPlaneFactory {
    public IPlane CreatePlane() { return null;}
}
public class BoeingFactory {
    IPlaneFactory CreatePlane123Factory();
    IPlaneFactory CreatePlane234Factory();
}
```

The Builder pattern implementation does not create new factory implementations, but builds on top of the old ones. Therefore, the Builder pattern assumes that the previously defined factory interfaces and implementations (IWheel, IFactory, etc.) still exist. The new interfaces related to the Builder Pattern are IPlane and IPlaneFactory. When instantiated, the IPlane interface represents an assembled plane with wings and wheels. The IPlane interface exposes the wings and wheels as readonly properties for consistency. Had the properties been read-write, then in theory a developer could have added an Airbus wheel to a Boeing airplane. This is technically possible at an algorithm level, but in reality it is not possible to mix and match parts.

The Builder pattern also makes it possible to consistently assemble types such that their states cannot be violated. The Builder pattern implementation is responsible for putting the correct wheels and wings on the airplanes. This does not mean that all interfaces have read-only properties. If there is no problem with mixing and matching interface instances, then there is no problem with having read-write properties.

The interface IPlaneFactory is an implementation of the Builder pattern because it contains the method CreatePlane, which is used to create an instance of IPlane. The implementation of CreatePlane would add the right number of wheels and wings to an IPlane instance.

The method `IPlane.CreateParts` returns a factory that can be used to create wheels and wings. The method is associated with `IPlane` because from a logical sense any plane instance that needs parts should have an associated `IFactory` instance. The Builder pattern implementation manages the association of the `IPlane` implementation with the appropriate `IFactory` implementation.

The class `Plane123Factory` implements the `IPlaneFactory` interface and is responsible for instantiating and wiring together `IPlane`, `IWing`, `IWheel`, and `IFactory` interface instances. The class `BoeingFactory` is a general factory used to instantiate and return a Builder pattern implementation (`IPlaneFactory`) that can be used to instantiate planes and instantiate other interfaces. There is always a central factory that instantiates other implementations, which can be factories or classes that implement some business logic.

A factory can also instantiate an object based on another object. This is called *cloning an object* or implementing the Prototype pattern. The big-picture idea of the Prototype pattern is to be able to create a copy of an object that already exists.

In .NET the way to clone an object is to implement the `ICloneable` interface, as in the following example:

Source: /Volume01/LibVolume01/UsingPlaceholderClassesInterfaces.cs

```
class Boeing123Plane : IPlane, System.ICloneable {
    public Object Clone() {
        Boeing123Plane obj =
            (Boeing123Plane)this.MemberwiseClone();
        obj._factory = (IFactory)((System.ICloneable)_factory).Clone();
        return obj;
    }
}
```

The example method `Clone` implements both a *shallow clone* and *deep clone*. A shallow clone is when only the type's local data members are copied. The shallow clone is realized using the method call `MemberwiseClone`. Calling `MemberWiseClone` does not require an instantiation because the process of cloning will automatically instantiate the type. To implement a deep clone, the `clone` methods of each data member in a class are called.

One of the debates about cloning is whether to implement a deep clone. For example, if type A references type B, then a deep clone will copy both type instances. But imagine if type A references type B, and type B references another instance of type B, which references the original type-B instance. A cyclic reference scenario has been established, which when cloned using a deep clone could lead to a never-ending cloning scenario. To avoid such tricky situations, adding a `didClone` flag could be useful. However, even with a `didClone` flag problems will arise. The better solution is to rethink the cloning scenario and to clone each data member manually and rebuild the structure using manual object assignment. There is no silver-bullet solution when implementing a deep clone.

When implementing a factory, remember the following points:

- Using the Factory pattern means using component-oriented development, where there is an interface or a base class and some specific class is instantiated. The idea is to decouple the consumer from the implementation.

- There are multiple levels to creating a factory. In the lowest level a factory creates a specific implementation. In the next level factory methods are grouped into a single type to indicate a relation between the factories. In the higher level the Builder pattern is used to instantiate types that are wired together. Each level represents a type of factory functionality and is used when building applications.

- When grouping together factory methods, often interfaces are defined to indicate related factory operations. When converting a factory from a single class to an interface, you must manage additional considerations, such as interface relations.

- The Builder pattern is an abstraction that defines factory-like methods. The factory-like methods use other Factory classes to instantiate and wire together various instances.

- You can clone objects when you have an object instance but not the factory. Cloning requires more thought than a Factory or Builder pattern implementation to avoid cloning items that should have been referenced.

- In all of our examples the factory methods had no parameters. More often than not this will be the exception, not the rule.

Don't Expose a Class's Internal State

Classical object-oriented programming says that you should never expose the internal state of your class. Object-oriented programming dictates that the properties or methods exposed are based on application logic. A pragmatic reason for not to exposing the internal workings of a class is to decouple the class definition from the internal structure.

Let's consider oven temperature. A class exposes its internal state, and is progressively converted to not exposing the details. If we wanted to monitor an oven's temperature, we would create a property, as in the following source code:

Source: /Volume01/LibVolume01/DontExposeInternalState.cs

```
class Oven {
    private int _temperature;

    public int Temperature {
        get {
            return _temperature;
        }
        set {
            _temperature = value;
        }
    }
}
```

The type Oven exposes its temperature as a property, which is a direct reference to the variable _temperature. This means that the internal oven temperature implementation is tied directly to its external interface. The point of good object-oriented programming is to avoid this sort of programming.

To get to a better implementation, we should ask ourselves, what is the operation of an oven? An oven is used to bake something at a constant temperature. Hence an improved method and property interface would expose the oven as a device that bakes something. A better oven implementation would be as follows:

Source: /Volume01/LibVolume01/DontExposeInternalState.cs

```
class Oven {
    private int _temperature;

    public void SetTemperature( int temperature) {
        _temperature = temperature;
    }
    public bool AreYouPreHeated() {
        return false;
    }
}
```

In this implementation of Oven the internal variable _temperature is not tied to its external interface. The property Temperature is replaced with the methods SetTemperature used to assign the temperature, and AreYouPreHeated to indicate that the assigned temperature has been reached. This is a good object-oriented design, as you are telling the oven to take care of its own responsibilities and you are exposing only the logic of the oven.

The new oven implementation has stopped exposing its internal state. However, a client might want the internal information. For example, imagine an oven implementation that needs to poll the oven temperature for monitoring purposes. The new oven implementation could not deliver that information.

Nonetheless, we do not have to use the original implementation—the requested logic is to poll for the temperature at regular intervals. To implement this logic we can use a delegate and receive an asynchronous call whenever a new temperature has been polled. The advantage of this approach is that the oven is in charge of sending the information and could potentially send out alerts when there are dramatic changes in temperature. The following is the rewritten source code:

Source: /Volume01/LibVolume01/DontExposeInternalState.cs

```
delegate void OnTemperature( int temperature);

class Oven {
    private int _temperature;
    OnTemperature _listeners;

    public void BroadcastTemperature() {
        _listeners( _temperature);
    }
    public void AddTemperatureListener( OnTemperature listener) {
        _listeners += listener;
    }
```

```
}
class Controller {
    public Controller( Oven oven) {
        oven.AddTemperatureListener(
            new OnTemperature( this.OnTemperature));
    }
    public void OnTemperature( int temperature) {
        Console.WriteLine( "Temperature (" + temperature + ")");
    }
}
```

Using delegates, types external to the class Oven listen to the oven temperature. The object-oriented design rule where a type is responsible for its own data is not violated. The delegate OnTemperature is used to broadcast the oven's temperature to all listeners who want to know. The method AddTemperatureListener adds a delegate instance to the list of listeners. The method BroadcastTemperature broadcasts the temperature.

It is important to realize that the BroadcastTemperature method is optional and is an implementation detail. Maybe the class Oven executes using its own thread and broadcasts a temperature periodically. Maybe another class is responsible for polling the oven. In any case, the class Controller uses the Oven.AddTemperatureListener method to listen to the oven temperature.

The solution of using a delegate is elegant because the class Oven is loosely coupled with Controller and does not require the Controller to know about the implementation of the Oven class. In this example it was not necessary to use a property even though it would have been easier, as such use would violate good object-oriented design principles. However, the example ignores where the temperature came from in the first place. Think about where, when, and how Oven assigns the variable _temperature. Where does this temperature come from? It has not been defined, and without it our application will not work.

The Oven class has to get its temperature from somewhere, and most likely from a device driver that interfaces with the physical oven. In most cases that temperature is a property retrieved by the Oven class using a polling mechanism. In other words, the Oven class is hiding the fact that somewhere in the types used by Oven there exists a property called temperature. Even if the device driver used delegates, then in the implementation of the device driver a type has to be defined with a property called current temperature.

When writing types and exposing internal states, think about the following points:

- Expose properties only when the properties are fundamental types.

- Don't expose an internal state as a property, but expose application logic that represents the property.

- When properties are exposed they should be exposed as data types, not value types. For example, instead of exposing temperature as a double value, expose temperature as the class Temperature. That way you can avoid problems such as not knowing whether the temperature is in degrees Celsius, Fahrenheit, or Kelvin.

Designing Consistent Classes

There are many reasons bugs can appear in code. One reason could be because the algorithm was implemented incorrectly. Another reason, and the focus of this solution, is that the consistency of a class was violated due to an incorrect method or property call. Immutable classes are consistent because they avoid the problem of having their consistency corrupted by inappropriate manipulations. Classes that can have their properties read and written can be corrupted. To illustrate the problem, this solution outlines how to create an inheritance of shapes, and in particular the square and rectangle. The question whether a square subclasses a rectangle, or a rectangle subclasses a square.

Let's define a rectangle as a base class, as in the following example:

Source: /Volume01/LibVolume01/DesigningConsistentClasses.cs

```
class Rectangle {
    private long _length, _width;

    public Rectangle( long length, long width) {
        _length = length;
        _width = width;
    }
    public virtual long Length {
        get {
            return _length;
        }
        set {
            _length = value;
        }
    }
    public virtual long Width {
        get {
            return _width;
        }
        set {
            _width = value;
        }
    }
}
```

The class Rectangle has a constructor with two parameters that represent the length and width. There are two properties—Length and Width—that are the length and width of the rectangle, respectively. Like in a typical coding scenario, the properties can be retrieved and assigned, meaning that they are read-write.

Extending this theory, a square is a specialized form of rectangle, where the length and width happen to be equal. Using the previously defined Rectangle as a base class, the class Square could be defined as follows:

Source: /Volume01/LibVolume01/DesigningConsistentClasses.cs

```
class Square : Rectangle {
    public Square( long width) : base( width, width) {
    }
}
```

To define a square, the class Square only needs to redefine the base class Rectangle constructor to have a single parameter representing the dimensions. The constructor calls the base constructor and passes the same dimension to the length and width. When Square is instantiated, the type will have the correct dimensions. It seems all's well in our object-oriented design. However, all is not well—there is a major design flaw, which is illustrated in the following test code:

Source: /Volume01/LibVolume01/DesigningConsistentClasses.cs

```
[TestFixture]
public class TestShapes {
    [Test]
    public void TestConsistencyProblems() {
        Square square = newSquare( 10);
        Rectangle squarishRectangle = square;

        squarishRectangle.Length = 20;
        Assert.AreNotEqual( square.Length, square.Width);
    }
}
```

The variable square references a square with length and height of 10 units. The variable square is down cast to the variable squarishRectangle, which is of the type Rectangle. The consistency problem occurs when the squarishRectangle.Length property is assigned a value of 20. Even though it is legal to reassign the property, it is not consistent with the requirements of the type Square. A downcast square should not fail consistency tests. Changing one dimension of the rectangle should have changed the other dimension as well. Assert.AreNotEqual illustrates how the dimensions of the square are inconsistent and therefore we no longer have a square.

Polymorphism has caused consistency violations. One solution for making the Square consistent is the following source code:

Source: /Volume01/LibVolume01/DesigningConsistentClasses.cs

```
class Square : Rectangle {
    public Square( long width) : base( width, width) {

    }
    public override long Length {
        get {
            return base.Length;
        }
```

```
        set {
            base.Length = value;
            base.Width = value;
        }
    }
    public override long Width {
        get {
            return base.Width;
        }
        set {
            base.Length = value;
            base.Width = value;
        }
    }
}
```

In the new implementation, Square overrides the properties Length and Width. Changing the rectangle's length to 20 would have changed the width at the same time. This means that a square will always be a square, and the consistency is upheld. However, there is a price for this consistency, and that is complexity. The complexity is because both Rectangle and Square must implement all methods. So why use inheritance if a square and a rectangle are complete implementations?

Let's flip things around and define the Rectangle as a type that subclasses Square:

Source: /Volume01/LibVolume01/DesigningConsistentClasses.cs

```
class Square {
    private long _width;

    public Square( long width)  {
        _width = width;
    }
    public virtual long Width {
        get {
            return _width;
        }
        set {
            _width = value;
        }
    }
}

class Rectangle : Square {
    private long _length;

    public Rectangle( long length, long width) : base(width) {
        _length = length;
    }
```

```
    public virtual long Length {
        get {
            return _length;
        }
        set {
            _length = value;
        }
    }
}
```

The base class is Square and it defines the property Width, which represents the length and width of a square. Square does not define a Length property because it is not needed. Rectangle subclasses Square and adds its missing dimension, Length. Now, if a Rectangle is downcast to Square, the square will always have a consistent dimension, albeit the Length and Width of the Rectangle will change. Changing a single dimension does not violate the consistency of the Rectangle. Changing the one dimension does, however, change the state of the Rectangle.

The following test code illustrates how to use Square and Rectangle:

Source: /Volume01/LibVolume01/DesigningConsistentClasses.cs

```
[TestFixture]
public class TestShapes {
    void TestSquare( Square square) {
        square.Width = 10;
    }
    [Test]
    public void TestSubclass() {
        Rectangle rectangle = new Rectangle( 30, 30);
        long oldLength = rectangle.Length;
        TestSquare( rectangle);
        Assert.AreEqual( oldLength, rectangle.Length);
    }
}
```

In the test code the method TestSubclass instantiates Rectangle. Prior to calling the method TestSquare the length of Rectangle is stored. When the method TestSquare is called the property Width is modified. After the call to TestSquare, the following Assert.AreEqual call tests to ensure that the length of the rectangle equals oldLength. If, on the other hand, the Width property of the Rectangle is modified, then when a downcast to Square is made the dimensions of the Square will still be consistent.

This solution is correct from an object-oriented perspective because each type is responsible for its own data. Yet the solution feels strange because our thinking is that a square has a length and a width, and they happen to be equal. So from our thinking a Square subclasses Rectangle. But from an object-oriented perspective it should be the reverse. This is what makes object-oriented design so difficult sometimes—what is correct might be illogical, and vice versa.

Part of the reason why inheritance has not been working is that the solutions are wrong. The problem is neither object-oriented design nor inheritance, but rather the original assumption that a square is a shape with two dimensions: length and width. Instead of an inheritance structure, we need an object-oriented structure that dovetails into our thinking. That structure would indicate that have two shapes with a length and a width, and that the base class should not be a square or a rectangle, but an interface that is defined as in the following code. Using an interface, we can define our intention of defining a shape with a length and width:

Source: /Volume01/LibVolume01/DesigningConsistentClasses.cs

```
interface IShape {
    long Length {
        get; set;
    }
    long Width {
        get; set;
    }
}
```

The interface IShape does not indicate whether the shape is a rectangle or a square, but defines some implementation that has both a Length and Width. The implementation will determine if the shape is a square or rectangle using implemented constraints. An example implementation of both Square and Rectangle is as follows:

Source: /Volume01/LibVolume01/DesigningConsistentClasses.cs

```
class Rectangle : IShape {
    private long _width;
    private long _length;

    public Rectangle( long width)  {
        _width = width;
    }
    public virtual long Width {
        get {
            return _width;
        }
        set {
            _width = value;
        }
    }
    public virtual long Length {
        get {
            return _length;
        }
        set {
            _length = value;
```

```
            }
        }
    }

class Square : IShape {
    private long _width;

    public Square( long width) {
        _width = width;
    }
    public virtual long Length {
        get {
            return _width;
        }
        set {
            _width = value;
        }
    }
    public virtual long Width {
        get {
            return _width;
        }
        set {
            _width = value;
        }
    }
}
```

This time Square and Rectangle do the right things, and there are no consistency problems. Square exposes the properties Length and Width, but in the implementation there is only
one data member: _width. Neither Square nor Rectangle share any implementation details
and can be instantiated using a Factory pattern.

Finally we have a solution that is straightforward, maintainable, and extendable. So in a
sense we have found the right solution to our problem. Thinking about the Rectangle and
Square, let's take a step back. Would there ever be another shape that could be defined using a
length and width? Most likely not, because shapes are different from each other and contain
information unique to each shape. A circle is defined by its diameter; a triangle is defined by
the lengths of its the three sides; and a parallelogram (slanted rectangle) is defined by length,
width, and angle. But we can develop groupings using interfaces, and then use consistency
rules to make sure that the state of the implementation is correct.

Another approach does not use interfaces. Shapes are related (for instance, the square,
the rectangle, and the parallelogram), and using inheritance that has a common base class
would be useful for programming purposes. The solution is to make all shapes immutable so
that once the dimensions have been assigned, they cannot be modified. The following is an
example of the immutable Square and Rectangle implementation:

```
class Rectangle {
    private readonly long _length, _width;
```

```csharp
    public Rectangle( long length, long width) {
        _length = length;
        _width = width;
    }
    public virtual long Length {
        get {
            return _length;
        }
    }
    public virtual long Width {
        get {
            return _width;
        }
    }
}

class Square : Rectangle {
    public Square( long width) : base( width, width) {

    }
}
```

The properties Length and Width are missing the set keyword, meaning that neither Square nor Rectangle can be modified once the properties are assigned. The result is that consistency is not violated as it was when a Square was downcast to a Rectangle. When Square is downcast to Rectangle the dimensions reflect a shape that is a square. The result of making the inheritance hierarchy immutable is that all pieces of the hierarchy make sense. There is no missing information, and the hierarchy is always consistent. This is the best solution in terms of patterns, object-oriented design, and consistency. Overall this solution is not better or worse than the interface solution, however—it is simply different and uses a hierarchy.

When designing classes, always consider consistency and remember the following:

- Using inheritance is not a bad idea, but consistency is a concern. If a class is downcast to a base class, method calls on the base class do not violate the state in the derived classes.

- Interfaces are very useful means of introducing groupings of types that share the same characteristics but different implementations.

- Immutable types solve consistency problem by not allowing modifications that could break consistency.

Immutable Types Are Scalable Types

One of the most commonly used types is string, and string is an immutable class, meaning that once it's assigned the type cannot change. To change the state of an immutable class, a new class needs to be instantiated. Developers rarely consider using immutable classes because our logic says immutable classes are inefficient. Yet one of the most used types, string, is immutable.

Efficiency can be measured multiple ways, but for today's hardware efficiency is best measured as code that gets in the way of the processor very little. These days we have processors that can blow the socks off your feet. Yet we write code that accesses the disk too often, waits for other information, and worse, calls a network connection. During all of these operations the processor is idly twiddling its thumbs waiting for a response. And then where a response is generated the program uses threads and locks to control access to an object.

A scalable class uses the keyword lock as little as possible. The keyword lock blocks multiple threads from accessing the same piece of code concurrently. The following example uses the lock keyword:

Source: /Volume01/LibVolume01/ImmutableScalableTypes.cs

```
class ExampleSynchronized {
    public void OnlySingleThread() {
        lock( this) {
            Console.WriteLine( "Hello world");
            }
    }
}
```

In the example the method OnlySingleThread allows only one thread to output the text to the console. Allowing only one thread access is a bottleneck, and will cause a program to slow down. With the introduction of multicore CPUs the bottleneck problem will become worse as people adapt to writing multithreaded applications. An immutable class is the best type write in a multithread and multiprocess scenario.

In the section "Designing Consistent Classes" I designed an immutable class to illustrate a consistent class. Here is that source code again:

Source: /Volume01/LibVolume01/DesigningConsistentClasses.cs

```
class Rectangle {
    private readonly long _length, _width;

    public Rectangle( long length, long width) {
        _length = length;
        _width = width;
    }
    public virtual long Length {
        get {
            return _length;
        }
    }
    public virtual long Width {
        get {
            return _width;
        }
```

```
    }
}

class Square : Rectangle {
    public Square( long width) : base( width, width) {

    }
}
```

The example class is immutable because the `Length` and `Width` properties of `Rectangle` do not use the `set` keyword. Under most circumstances the immutable definition of `Rectangle` is faster than a read-write version of `Rectangle` and `Square` because memory managers have become smarter, and because there is no lock to slow down the code.

However, an immutable object requires more resources than other object types do. Our prevailing logic says that changing a variable requires less memory than copying and modifying a variable. The reality is quite a bit different, though, and depends on the context in which an immutable object is used.

One of reasons why immutable types can be faster is that they are optimized due to having dealt with memory management in years past. In C and C++, a buffer was allocated from the heap, which a memory manager managed. The memory manager split up the memory to mark used areas and unused areas. In the C and C++ memory model, whenever a piece of data is allocated, the memory manager searches the heap for an appropriate piece of memory to fit the need. This searching and slicing of the memory, however, costs many CPU cycles.

Memory management for immutable objects is more efficient because immutable object memory is of fixed dimensions and is either used or available. The memory manager does not have to split the memory, expand the memory, or do any of the expensive operations that most memory managers do currently. Memory managers in runtimes like .NET, Java, and Apache Portable Runtime (APR) make assumptions about memory use. These assumptions use linear mathematics and greatly speed up allocations and freeing. Of course, these assumptions work today because memory is plentiful. The old memory-manager model was geared toward computers that considered RAM scarce.

The other reason why immutable objects are faster is that there is no need for synchronization. When multiple threads access a piece of data, synchronization is needed so that each thread manipulates stable data. If the data is always stable, then synchronization is not necessary. Therefore, immutable objects have a definite speed advantage over objects that have synchronization requirements.

Ideally, an immutable class should be a data class, which stores and manipulates data but typically does not modify it. The `string` class is an excellent example of data class. It has data-member operations, but the operations do not operate on the local data. The operations copy the data and return new `string` instance. This separation of data and manipulations makes it possible to never need synchronization routines.

There is a downside to immutable classes: They can be resource-intensive. For example, performing too many string manipulations will result in memory thrashing as buffers are being constantly allocated and freed. Another problem is that if a class allocates 4MB with each instantiation, then that instantiation will become costly. In such a situation, the solution is to use *pooled objects*. Pooled objects are recycled immutable objects that are beyond the scope of this book.

To illustrate that immutable types are faster in most contexts, let's carry out a perform-ance test. The following source code illustrates three different class types that implement immutable and modifiable types:

Source: /Volume01/LibVolume01/ImmutableScalableTypes.cs

```
class Regular {
    private int _value;

    public Regular( int initial) {
        _value = initial;
    }
    public Regular Increment() {
        _value ++;
        return this;
    }
}

class Immutable {
    private readonly int _value;

    public Immutable( int initial) {
        _value = initial;
    }
    public Immutable Increment() {
        return new Immutable( _value + 1);
    }
}

struct structImmutable {
    private readonly int _value;
    public structImmutable( int initial) {
        _value = initial;
    }
    public structImmutable Increment() {
        return new structImmutable( _value + 1);
    }
}
```

The class Regular is a modifiable type that has the ability to manipulate its data members. The class Immutable is an example immutable class that has a data member that allocates a new class instance when the value is incremented. The structure structImmutable is like the class Immutable, except a structure is used. When a structure is defined, the data members are value types that are stored on the stack.

Let's put Regular, Immutable, and structImmutable side by side for performance analysis. The code will be executed in the context of one thread, running flat out without any type of synchronization. Intuitively, we'd think Regular should be the fastest, and following are the performance numbers, where the percentage times relate to how much was spent allocating and executing the Increment method:

```
Regular:            0.05%
Immutable:          0.25%
structImmutable:    0.10%
```

Our intuition was correct—the immutable types that were constantly allocating objects causes the routines to require five times more computing time than the read-write types. However, using a struct value type is only two times slower than using Regular. Right now the score is modifiable 1, and immutable 0.

The next performance test involves the use of code locks and synchronization techniques. Rerunning the performance tests generates the following data:

```
Regular:            0.46%
Immutable:          0.52%
structImmutable:    0.45%
```

This time the numbers indicate that it does not matter which type is used; they are all executing at roughly the same performance levels. The score now seems to be modifiable 2, and immutable 0. However, remember this code is running using code locks, but there are no concurrency situations. The modifiable code is running flat out with no waiting time. And this is where immutable gets bonus marks. The moment a modifiable object has to wait, the modifiable typetakes a massive performance hit. It could get worse; the code could deadlock. With immutable objects, there are no wait times and no deadlocks.

When creating immutable classes, remember the following:

- Immutable classes are often data classes. A data class holds data only, and does not provide many operations that relate to application logic. The class might have a large number of methods that relate to manipulating the data, such as the String class.

- An immutable class does not reference a read-write class. This means that an immutable class does not publicly expose a type that is read-write capable.

- Immutable classes typically do not implement interfaces. But a very useful technique is the implementation of an immutable interface by a read-write class. An immutable interface has read-only operations and allows a class implementation to optimize when synchronization is necessary.

- Immutable classes can be serialized and are typically transported across networks or AppDomains. Rarely will a type hold a remote reference to an immutable type.

Understanding and Using Functors

Here is a quick quiz question: Supposing you have a collection of int values and you want to find the total of the numbers, how would you find the total? Would your answer look similar to the following?

Source: /Volume01/LibVolume01/UnderstandingUsingFunctors.cs

```
public int AddAllElements( IList< int> list) {
    int runningTotal = 0;
    foreach( int value in list) {
        runningTotal += value;
    }
    return runningTotal;
}
```

This solution works, but is not extendable or modifiable. For example, how would you add only even numbers? Or how about adding a complete total, and then adding odd numbers and then even numbers to get three different totals? Of course, all of those solutions are possible, but they require modifying the proposed source code. There is a way to define an architecture where you can extend without having to constantly extend and maintain the code.

A functor is a mechanism where within the code you define a placeholder or functionality that acts as a pass-through filter before an actual functionality. The pass-through filter makes a client believe that they are using the real object without having to explicitly call a functor. For illustration purposes, I will quickly fix up the proposed code to use functors, but that is not how I would generally fix up the code. The illustration is meant to illustrate how a functor would be added to code that performs a specific task:

Source: /Volume01/LibVolume01/UnderstandingUsingFunctors.cs

```
delegate void FunctorDelegate(int value);
class Addition {
    FunctorDelegate _delegate;

    public Addition AddDelegate(FunctorDelegate deleg) {
        _delegate += deleg;
        return this;
    }
    public int AddAllElements(IList< int> list) {
        int runningTotal = 0;
        foreach( int value in list) {
            runningTotal += value;
            _delegate(value);
        }
        return runningTotal;
    }
}
```

The method AddAllElements has changed its implementation; the addition is still part of the method, but so is the calling of the delegate. For every iteration of the loop, the running total will be calculated and the delegates associated with _delegate will be called. Of course, it is silly to add the numbers and call the delegate at the same time. What is being illustrated is that you still need to loop at the appropriate time the delegate is called.

The following example illustrates how to make use of the delegate call, where client code calls the method AddAllElements and calculates the odd and even number totals:

Source: /Volume01/LibVolume01/UnderstandingUsingFunctors.cs

```
List< int> list = new List< int>();
list.Add(1);
list.Add(2);
list.Add(3);
list.Add(4);
int runningOddTotal = 0;
int runningEvenTotal = 0;
int runningTotal = new Addition()
    .AddDelegate(new FunctorDelegate(
                delegate(int value) {
                    if ((value % 2) == 1) {
                        runningOddTotal += value;
                    }
                }))
    .AddDelegate(new FunctorDelegate(
                delegate(int value) {
                    if ((value % 2) == 0) {
                        runningEvenTotal += value;
                    }
                }))
    .AddAllElements(list);
Console.WriteLine(
    "Running total is (" + runningTotal +
    ") Running even total is (" + runningEvenTotal +
    ") Running odd total is (" + runningOddTotal + ")");
```

The preceding code can be compiled only using .NET 2.0 because anonymous delegates are used. At the beginning of the code piece is the variable list, which contains all of the integers that will be added. Then variables runningOddTotal, runningEvenTotal, and runningTotal are declared. After that the disposal type Addition is instantiated, and the method AddDelegate is called twice. A FunctorDelegate delegate is passed to AddDelegate by using the delegate keyword.

The delegate keyword used in conjunction with a method defines an anonymous delegate. The anonymous delegate requires a single parameter value, and is declared right after the delegate keyword. The curly brackets thereafter indicate the body of the function. Notice how the implementation of the anonymous delegate references variables declared in the body of the method. This is a very powerful use of anonymous functions because it allows us to declare functionality that references local variables that will be called later. In the two anonymous function declarations, the mod (%) operator determines if the value is even or odd.

To finish the explanation for the type, the method AddAllElements is called, adding and calling the delegates. The Console.WriteLine method outputs the generated values.

What you should be able to see is that a functor allows the original functionality to be kept intact, and additional functionality to be attached dynamically. Abstracting the logic, the addition of all numbers would have been an anonymous delegate implementation. Though if we want to think ahead and promote a good design for functors, we should be thinking about using a Proxy pattern.

The Proxy pattern is useful when you want to modify a type's functionality without the blessing or cooperation of the type. Let's say that we want to add all elements of a list. So instead of iterating the list repeatedly, we use the Proxy pattern to intercept method calls that will add and subtract numbers as elements are added and subtracted from a list:

Source: /Volume01/LibVolume01/UnderstandingUsingFunctors.cs

```csharp
interface IRunningTotal {
    int RunningTotal {
        get;
    }
}
class TotalCalculator<type>: ICollection<type> , IRunningTotal {
    private ICollection<type> _parent;
    private int _runningTotal;

    public TotalCalculator(ICollection<type> parent) {
        _parent = parent;
        _runningTotal = 0;
    }

    public int RunningTotal {
        get {
            return _runningTotal;
        }
    }
    public void Add(type item) {
        _runningTotal += int.Parse( item.ToString());
        _parent.Add(item);
    }

    public bool Remove(type item) {
        bool retval = _parent.Remove( item);
        if( retval) {
            _runningTotal -= int.Parse( item.ToString());
        }
        return retval;
    }
    // Other methods have been removed for clarity
}
```

In the example code there are two types defined: IRunningTotal and TotalCalculator. TotalCalculator implements the ICollection<> interface and acts as a proxy to a list that implements ICollection<>. The interface IRunningTotal is implemented by TotalCalculator and used by the client to retrieve the running total of all the elements in the collection.

TotalCalculator implements the Proxy pattern because TotalCalculator contains a parent reference and delegates all method calls to the parent collection reference. In the example the TotalCalculator implements the ICollection interface, and the parent is an ICollection implementation. Then when the Add or Remove method is called the proxy will either add the amount to or subtract the amount from the running total, and call the parent. The client will not know the difference between the real ICollection implementation and the proxy, as the following example illustrates:

Source: /Volume01/LibVolume01/UnderstandingUsingFunctors.cs

```csharp
private void DoCollection( ICollection< int> list) {
    list.Add(1);
    list.Add(2);
    list.Add(3);
    list.Add(4);
    list.Remove( 4);
}
public void TestRunningTotalList() {
    ICollection< int> list =
        new TotalCalculator< int>( new List< int>());
    DoCollection( list);
    Console.WriteLine( "Total is (" +
        ((IRunningTotal)list).RunningTotal + ")");
}
```

In the client code the method DoCollection performs some actions on the collection. The operations add elements and remove elements. In the method TestRunningTotalList the class TotalCalculator<> is instantiated, and an instance of a collection type List is passed to the constructor. When the method DoCollection is called, the parameter references an instance of the proxy. The method DoCollection is not aware that it is manipulating a proxy. After the method DoCollection has been called, a typecast to IRunningTotal retrieves the sum of the collection.

The proxy code works, and illustrates how the Proxy pattern can be used to inject functionality that was not planned originally. The Proxy pattern is similar to a functor, but is not a functor. The example Proxy pattern implementation is too specific and cannot be abstracted easily. A proper functor architecture uses the proxy and provides some extra plumbing for the application-specific logic.

Functors make it possible to attach standard logic to another type using a predefined construct. For example, when collections use Generics, Generics validates the type but does not validate if the contents of the type is correct. A predicate functor can validate the contents of the type. Functors are little black boxes that carry out specific pieces of logic. When implementing functors, you must use interfaces or abstract base classes; otherwise it is not possible to make one type act like another.

The most common functor types are defined as follows:

Comparer. This accepts two objects and compares them. The return value is an int value, which represents whether the object is equal, less than, or greater than another value.

Closure. This accepts a single object and performs some logic, and there is no returned value.

Predicate. This accepts a single value and performs some logic. A `true` value indicates that the predicate logic triggered, and `false` means that the predicate logic did not trigger.

Transformer. This accepts a single value and performs a transformation, which could result in a new type being generated or the original type being transformed.

Functors are not specific to collection classes, but in most cases functors are used in conjunction with collections. For example, maybe you want to compare values and have the collection sorted whenever an element is added to the collection. Or maybe you want only to be able to filter objects that have certain properties constrained to certain values.

The Comparer Functor

`DelegateComparer` is not a static implementation and can compare different types according to different criteria. `DelegateComparer` could validate if the age of a person is greater than another person. These types of sorting, arranging, or filtering are typically implemented as unique collection types: `LinkedList Stack`, `Queue`, etc. A functor can offer more functionality, but uses standard collections types, as Figure 4-3 shows.

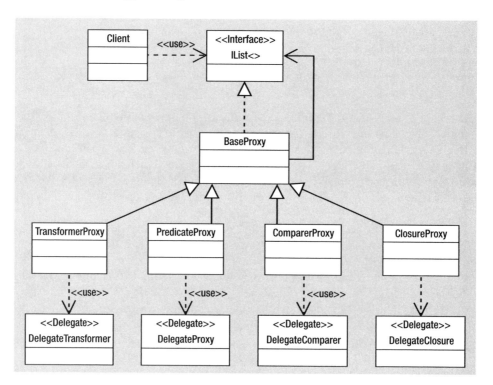

Figure 4-3. *UML functor architecture for collections*

The interface `IList<>` is the base interface for defining all functor proxies. `IList<>` extends the `ICollection<>`, `IEnumerable<>`, and `IEnumerable` interfaces. The class `BaseProxy<>` is an abstract base class that provides a default implementation for the `IList<>` interface.

The default action for BaseProxy<> is to proxy all requests to the parent ICollection<> implementation. The classes TransformerProxy<>, PredicateProxy<>, ComparerProxy<>, and
ClosureProxy<> represent the implementations of the various functors.

When defining a proxy that uses functors, the prime consideration is what functionality
the functor will override. A collection has many operations, such as adding, deleting, and
retrieving elements. A very popular use of functors is to execute a functor when adding
elements to a collection. However, nothing says that a functor cannot override the remove-
element operations. However, it is very important never to create proxies that will call a
functor when adding and removing elements. This is because the functors' default method
signature does not know what the operation is. The preferred approach is to create a proxy
for each grouping of operations, and then combine multiple proxies.

You may notice that combining a functor with Proxy pattern results in a Decorator
pattern. The architecture is very similar to a Decorator pattern. What is different is how the
interfaces are instantiated and manipulated. In the case of the functor and the Proxy pattern,
the client has no direct access to the underlying parent collection. The Proxy pattern controls
all access.

In the Decorator pattern a client can access any element in the chain of elements created
by the Decorator pattern. And more often than not, the Decorator pattern decorates a single
method or subset of the full functionality offered by the implementation. So in a nutshell the
difference between a Proxy and a Decorator pattern is that the Proxy pattern controls all
access to the underlying implementation, and the Decorator pattern does not.

The remainder of this section will illustrate the four functors and present a small example
to wrap everything together. You can use the predefined IComparable interface from the .NET
Framework to define a comparer functor; the definition is illustrated as follows:

Source: /Volume01/LibVolume01/UnderstandingUsingFunctors.cs

```
public interface IComparable {
    int CompareTo(object obj);
}
```

The IComparable interface has a single method, CompareTo, that represents the object
instance to compare to. The IComparable interface works if the object that performs the testing
implements the IComparable interface. The problem with this approach is if the objects to be
compared do not have IComparable implemented, then the comparable functor will not work.
As in the Decorator pattern, all implementations concerned have to cooperate.

From the .NET base classes you can use another interface to compare two objects;
IComparer is defined as follows:

```
public interface IComparer {
    int Compare(object x, object y);
}
```

IComparer has a single method that has two parameters representing the objects to be
compared. The advantage of the IComparer interface is that the objects to be tested do not
have to implement any additional functionality.

For illustration purposes I will use a delegate, not an interface. A delegate can be implemented using C# 2.0 anonymous methods, or any method of a class, whereas an interface
must be implemented and then instantiated. If necessary, the Adapter pattern can be applied

to convert the delegate into an interface. The IComparer interface, defined in terms of a delegate, is as follows:

```
public delegate int DelegateComparer< type1, type2>
    ( type1 obj1, type2 obj2);
```

The delegate DelegateComparer<> is defined using a template, making it type-safe, and returns an int value indicating the results of a comparison. The two parameters are the object instances to compare.

The definition of a flight ticket illustrates a use of the comparer delegate. The flight ticket will be defined in terms of flight legs that are wired together like a linked list. The individual flight legs will not be managed using a collection type. I've explicitly not used a collection to illustrate how functors can be used on types that do not include collections. The following interface definition defines one leg of a flight:

Source: /Volume01/LibVolume01/UnderstandingUsingFunctors.cs

```
interface IFlight {
    string Origin { get; set; }
    string Destination { get; set;}
    IFlight NextLeg { get; set; }
}
```

The interface IFlight has three properties, where two (Origin, Destination) are strings and one (NextLeg) is a reference to IFlight. To wire two flight legs together, one instance has its NextLeg property assigned to the other instance. The Comparer functor is important for stopping a consumer from assigning the same flight leg twice.

The following is an implementation of the FlightComparer class (note that the implementations of the Origin and String properties have been omitted for clarity):

Source: /Volume01/LibVolume01/UnderstandingUsingFunctors.cs

```
class FlightComparer : IFlight {
    IFlight _parent;
    DelegateComparer< IFlight, IFlight> _delegateComparer;

    public FlightComparer( IFlight parent,
        DelegateComparer< IFlight, IFlight> delg) {
        _delegateComparer = delg;
        _parent = parent;
    }

    public IFlight NextLeg {
        get {
            return _parent.NextLeg;
        }
        set {
            if( _delegateComper( _parent, value) != 0) {
                _parent.NextLeg = value;
```

```
        }
        else {
            throw new ComparerEvaluationException();
        }
    }
  }
}
```

The constructor of FlightComparer requires two parents: the parent IFlight implementation and a DelegateComparer delegate implementation. In the property NextLeg the get part calls the delegate _delegateComparer. If the delegate returns a nonzero value, the _parent.NextLeg data member can be assigned; otherwise an exception is generated.

This example illustrates how the logic of validation is not part of the original class. Validation has been removed from the Flight class, and if Flight is instantiated then an inconsistent hierarchy can be created since there is no validation. But this is very incorrect. Remember that Flight implements an interface, and that the interface is defined as public scope, whereas the implementation is internal scope. Therefore a factory is required to instantiate Flight. The factory can implement the Builder pattern that instantiates both classes, as illustrated by the following example:

```
IFlight FlightBuilder() {
    return new FlightComparer( new Flight(),
        delegate( IFlight flight1, IFlight flight2) {
            if( flight1.Equals( flight2)) {
                return 0;
            }
            else {
                return -1;
            }
        });
}
```

The method FlightBuilder instantiates the type FlightComparer and passes in a new Flight instance as the first parameter. What is unique is the second parameter that expects a delegate. Instead of declaring a class with a method, an anonymous method is created, which performs the validation. An anonymous method is ideal because functors will be defined as delegates. The returned IFlight instance will have a correct hierarchy, and since FlightComparer does not allow access to the Flight instance there is no chance that the client can bypass FlightComparer and corrupt the data.

If, however, you're still uncomfortable with the use of the Proxy pattern, you can use the Flight class and have the property NextLeg use the delegate DelegateComparer directly. A proxy is advised because it makes it simpler to maintain and extend an application. From the client perspective the difference between the Factory and the Builder pattern is zero, so using a proxy is entirely acceptable.

The functor architecture looks more complicated than the following implementation, which is similar:

```
class Flight : IFlight {
    IFlight _nextLeg;
```

```
    public IFlight NextLeg {
        get {
            return _nextLeg;
        }
        set {
            if( !value.Equals( this)) {
                _nextLeg = value;
            }
        }
    }
}
```

In the set part of the property the method value.Equals is called. In the example, the return value from value.Equals should be a comparison of the data members' values. The value returned from value.Equals in this case is incorrect because the comparison is based on the reference information, not the data members of Flight. To have Equals return a correct value the Equals method has to be implemented. And if it is implemented, the GetHashCode method also must be implemented.

The return value of the method GetHashCode uniquely identifies an object with a certain state. If two different object instances contained the same state, then the GetHashCode method would return the same value. This carries over into the Equals method in that two objects that contain the same state are equal to each other.

What happens if the implementation of IFlight changes? The IFlight interface stored the legs using a linked list. If at some point a collection is used, the validation code remains identical but needs to be moved from one class to another. This involves a copy-and-paste operation. However, had a functor been used, then when moving the validation from one type to another you need only to copy the functor call. The functor implementations stay as is. In this situation a functor is the best solution.

The Closure Functor

The idea behind the closure functor is to be able to add an extra processing step when a specific logic is executed. For example, let's say that for a collection it is necessary to assign a parent-child relationship. When an object is added to a collection, a closure functor would assign the parent to the child object. A closure functor could also be used to perform logging operations.

The following is the definition of the closure delegate:

```
public delegate void DelegateClosure< type>( type input);
```

The delegate DelegateClosure<> uses Generics to define the input parameter, which represents the object to be manipulated. In the example of the running total, a closure functor would be used and not explained any further.

The Predicate Functor

Predicate functors are similar in some ways to comparer functors when testing an object for a go or no-go condition. The difference with predicate functors is that they return either a true or false value. A predicate functor tests an object to see if it meets certain conditions.

The following is the definition of the delegate for the predicator functor:

```
public delegate bool DelegatePredicate< type>( type input);
```

DelegatePredicate uses Generics to define the type that will be tested, and has a single parameter. An implementation performs some operations on the type, and returns either a true or false value.

Unlike other functors, predicate functors are usually chained together (using Boolean operators such as and, or, and not) to perform more-sophisticated tests. Consider the following Boolean and functor implementation:

Source: /Volume01/LibVolume01/UnderstandingUsingFunctors.cs

```
public class PredicateAndFunctor< type> {
    DelegatePredicate<type> _predicates;
    public PredicateAndFunctor( DelegatePredicate<type>[] functors) {
        foreach( DelegatePredicate< type> functor in functors) {
            _predicates += functor;
        }
    }

    private bool PredicateFunction( type obj) {
        foreach( Delegate delg in _predicates.GetInvocationList()) {
            if( !delg( obj)) {
                return false;
            }
        }
        return true;
    }
    static DelegatePredicate< type> CreateInstance(
        DelegatePredicate< type>[] functors) {
        return new DelegatePredicate< type>(
            new PredicateAndFunctor< type>(
                functors).PredicateFunction);
    }
}
```

The class PredicateAndFunctor<> has a private data member, _predicates, which represents an array of child predicates that will be chained together using the and (&&) operator. If any of the child predicates return a false, then PredicateAndFunctor<> will return false. The method PredicateFunction is the delegate implementation that iterates and calls in successive fashion the delegates contained within the _predicates data member.

In the example of creating the flight comparer delegate, an anonymous method was used. Because PredicateAndFunctor<> has state, a class instance is needed and the static method CreateInstance is used to instantiate the type; that, in turn, creates the delegate DelegatePredicate.

The Transformer Functor

Another type of functor is the Transformer functor. It takes one type as a parameter and uses a mapping to return some equivalent of the original type to a new type. The big picture idea behind a Transformer functor is to make it possible for a user to continue using one type that will be converted dynamically into another type. For instance, the Transformer functor is useful in the context of integrating a new system with legacy objects, or vice versa.

The following is the delegate definition of the Transformer functor:

Source: /Volume01/LibVolume01/UnderstandingUsingFunctors.cs

```
public delegate outType
    DelegateTransformer<inpType, outType>(inpType input);
```

The delegate `DelegateTransformer<>` is a .NET Generics type with two parameters, where the type `inpType` is the input, and the type `outType` is the output that the input is converted into.

Functors in Practice

Functors are easy to explain, and providing a reason for using them is not difficult. What is more difficult is actually using them. Using them can be awkward because of the separation of functionality between the functor and the type being managed.

I will use a movie-ticket application to illustrate the details of using a functor, interface, and implementation as a single solution. The heart of the ticketing system is `Ticket`, which represents a movie ticket and is defined as follows:

Source: /Volume01/LibVolume01/UnderstandingUsingFunctors.cs

```
public class Ticket {
    private double _price;
    private int _age;

    public Ticket( double price, int age) {
        _price = price;
        _age = age;
    }

    public virtual double Price {
        get {
            return _price;
        }
    }
    public virtual int Age {
        get {
            return _age;
        }
    }
}
```

Ticket has only two data members, _age and _price, which represent the age of the moviegoer and the price of the ticket. The age and price are defined when Ticket is instantiated. The properties Age and Price retrieve the values of age and price, respectively.

When selling movie tickets, ticket sales is an important statistic. Ticket sales indicate the popularity and success of a movie. In a traditional programming approach ticket sales are calculated by iterating a collection of Tickets. The total would be counted each time a ticket sales total is asked for. Another approach would be to use a closure functor.

The following source code calculates the total sales for a movie using a closure functor:

Source: /Volume01/LibVolume01/UnderstandingUsingFunctors.cs

```
public class TicketsBuilder {
    private class StatisticsCounter {
        private double _runningTotal;
        public StatisticsCounter() {
            _runningTotal = 0.0;
        }
        public void ClosureMethod( Ticket ticket) {
            _runningTotal += ticket.Price;
        }
    }
    public static IList<Ticket> CreateCollection() {
        return new ClosureAddProxy< Ticket>(
            new List< Ticket>(),
            new DelegateClosure< Ticket>(
                new StatisticsCounter().ClosureMethod));
    }
}
```

TicketsBuilder is a class that has a method, CreateCollection, that creates an IList<> instance. The method CreateCollection instantiates the type ClosureAddProxy<>, which implements the Proxy pattern for the closure functor. The parent collection for ClosureAddProxy<> is List<>. The delegate used for the closure functor is StatisticsCounter.ClosureMethod.

Like in the comparer functor example, every time an element is added to the returned IList<> instance DelegateAddClosure<> will call the closure delegate. Each time the closure delegate StatisticsCounter.ClosureMethod method is called, the input price is added to the total ticket sales.

The class StatisticsCounter.ClosureMethod is not entirely accurate, however. Imagine that a person buys a ticket and then asks for her money back or decides to watch a different movie. The ticket would need to be removed from the collection, and the total sales variable _runningTotal would need to be decremented by the price of the removed ticket. Even if it is impossible to get your money back, it is not possible to use such logic for all applications. The problem of the corrupted data needs be solved. Ticket sales can only be incremented because ClosureAddProxy overrides the methods that add elements to the collection. The solution is to use a closure delegate that overrides the remove-element methods.

The following is an example of two closure functors implementing the add-element and remove-element methods:

Source: /Volume01/LibVolume01/UnderstandingUsingFunctors.cs

```csharp
public class TicketsBuilder {
    private class StatisticsCounter {
        private double _runningTotal;
        public StatisticsCounter() {
            _runningTotal = 0.0;
        }
        public void ClosureAddMethod( Ticket ticket) {
            _runningTotal += ticket.Price;
        }
        public void ClosureRemoveMethod( Ticket ticket) {
            _runningTotal -= ticket.Price;
        }
    }
    public static IList<Ticket> CreateCollection() {
        StatisticsCounter cls = new StatisticsCounter();
        IList<Ticket> parent = new ClosureAddProxy< Ticket>(
            new List< Ticket>(),
            new DelegateClosure< Ticket>( cls.ClosureAddMethod));
        return new ClosureRemoveProxy<Ticket>( parent,
            new DelegateClosure< Ticket>(
                cls.ClosureRemoveMethod));
    }
}
```

In the modified implementation of TicketsBuilder, StatisticsCounter has two closure methods: ClosureAddMethod and ClosureRemoveMethod. The method ClosureAddMethod is used to increment the ticket sales, and the method ClosureRemoveMethod is used to decrement ticket sales. The method CreateCollection is modified to create two closure proxies: ClosureAddProxy and ClosureRemoveProxy. For each proxy the appropriate closure method is associated.

The calculation of the grand total for the ticket sales works. But there is a very big problem—TicketBuilder creates an instance of StatisticsCounter, but the instance of StatisticsCounter is not saved for reference. In other words, statistics are being generated but no client has access to those values. The solution for retrieving the total ticket-sales revenue is to create a property called RunningTotal.

When working with functors, remember the following points:

- Using functors does not come naturally because we developers are not wired to write code in such a structure. After you've written some functors it will feel natural.

- For most cases there are four types of functors: Comparer, Closure, Predicate, and Transformer.

- Functors are realized using delegates. The functors can be called directly in your source code.

- Often functors are used in conjunction with the Proxy pattern. If a Proxy pattern is used, you will need to define interfaces and/or abstract base classes.

* Functors make it possible to portably use specific application logic in multiple places without having to write special code to call the functors.

Avoiding Parameters That Have No Identity

Writing methods means using parameters, and that means the potential to make the mistake of using parameters that have no identity. Of course you shouldn't avoid writing methods, but be careful.

Let's start with a simple problem and provide a well-defined solution. The DateTime class is an example of a badly designed constructor that can be easily confusing as to what is a day, month, or year:

```
public DateTime(int year, int month, int day) {}
```

The compiler sees the declaration as

```
public DateTime( int, int, int);
```

If I wrote the following code for December 11, 2002, assuming an American date format, the compiler could not tell me what I did wrong:

```
DateTime date = new DateTime(12, 11, 2);
Console.WriteLine( date.ToString());
```

To make matters worse, the runtime does not even mark this as an error. Running the code yields the following result:

```
11/2/0012 12:00:00 AM
```

The generated format is Canadian formatting and the computer thinks the date is February 11 of the year 12 AD. I told you that the generated format is a Canadian date, but can you know that from the formatting? For example, the date could have been a US-formatted November 2. To know the answer, we would have to look at the day, month, and year members of the class.

The simplest solution to parameters with no identity is to do nothing and hope for the best. With IDEs like Visual Studio, writing good .NET documentation will generate the parameter definitions using IntelliSense. It is not always possible to convert the parameters into having an identity. If you do nothing, then you should convert the .NET documentation to generate the appropriate information that the IDEs will pick up.

A technical solution is to convert the DateTime types into enumerations, as follows:

Source: /Volume01/LibVolume01/AvoidingParametersWithoutIdentity.cs

```
enum DayEnumeration : int { }
enum MonthEnumeration : int {
    January = 1,
    February = 2,
```

```
        March = 3,
        April = 4,
        May = 5,
        June = 6,
        July = 7,
        August = 8,
        September = 9,
        October = 10,
        November = 11,
        December = 12
}
enum YearEnumeration : int { }
class FixedDateTime {
    public FixedDateTime(
        YearEnumeration year,
        MonthEnumeration month,
        DayEnumeration day) {
    }
}
```

The source code contains three enumerations: DayEnumeration, MonthEnumeration, and YearEnumeration. DayEnumeration and YearEnumerations have no values, and that is OK because none are needed. The enumeration definition MonthEnumeration could do without defined values as well, but I've defined some for convenience. The constructor for FixedDateTime uses the three enumerations in the exact same calling sequence as DateTime. The difference is that the caller of FixedDateTime would know which field is which. The following code illustrates how the developer could have easily caught the error using the enumerations:

Source: /Volume01/LibVolume01/UnderstandingUsingFunctors.cs

```
FixedMyDateTime date = new FixedMyDateTime(
    (YearEnumeration)12,
    (MonthEnumeration)11,
    (DayEnumeration)2);
```

As the code is written the int values are typecast from the int value to the enumeration, which can then be typecast back to the int type.

You may think the typecasts are neither legal nor helpful, but think again. It is perfectly legal to declare an enumeration and then use int typecasts. When you use the casts you will notice right away which field is the day, month, and year, and in the example there is a problem.

Using the enumeration to int and back typecast works only for int types. In the declaration of the enumeration, the base type of the enumeration was int, and that made the type compatible with the class DateTime.

Now let's look at a more complicated problem and a more complicated solution. The following source code is an example of a confusing constructor declaration using same types:

```
string message = "message";
string param = "param";
```

```
ArgumentException exception1 =
    new ArgumentException( message, param);
ArgumentNullException expection2 =
    new ArgumentNullException( param, message);
```

In the example there are two .NET classes: ArgumentException and ArgumentNullException. Both classes have a constructor with the same identifiers. The difference between the two constructors is the order of the parameters. This is confusing and a bad programming practice because there is no consistency in the parameter ordering.

What makes this an especially bad coding error is that the development environment cannot help you because the compiler sees the following constructor declarations:

```
ArgumentException( string, string);
ArgumentNullException( string, string);
```

The compiler sees two declarations that each use two string parameters. Fixing the ArgumentException and ArgumentNullException is difficult because the classes expect to see string arguments. Using .NET it is impossible to convert the string types into another type. If you have two buffers of arbitrary content, it is not easy to indicate to the compiler what the buffer's contents mean.

There is a solution and that involves wrapping a disposable type on top of the type that you want to improve. The following is an example implementation of fixing the ArgumentException using a wrapped disposable type that acts as a factory:

Source: /Volume01/LibVolume01/AvoidParametersWithoutIdentity.cs

```
class FixedArgumentException : ArgumentException {
    string _message;
    string _paramName;

    public FixedArgumentException() {}

    public FixedArgumentException
        MessageConstructorParameter(string message) {
        _message = message;
        return this;
    }
    public FixedArgumentException
        ParamConstructorParameter(string param) {
        _message = param;
        return this;
    }
    public override string Message {
        get { return _message; }
    }

    public override string ParamName {
        get { return _paramName; }
    }
```

```
    public ArgumentException GenerateBaseType() {
        return new ArgumentException( _message, _paramName);
    }
}
```

In the solution FixedArgumentException subclasses ArgumentException and implements the properties Message and ParamName. The idea is to make FixedArgumentException look and feel like an ArgumentException type. The FixedArgumentException constructor has no parameters because the parameter values will be defined using the methods MessageConstructorParameter and ParamConstructorParameter. Each of the methods returns a reference allowing the methods to be called using a chained mechanism. An example of using the explained methods follows:

```
throw new FixedArgumentException()
    .MessageConstructorParameter( "example")
    .ParamConstructorParameter( "no parameter");
```

In the code the throw and new keywords are used as usual when throwing an exception. But referencing of the methods MessageConstructorParameter and ParamConstructorParameter after the type instantiation is a new approach. The method calls are being chained together because the methods keep returning the current object instance. Using the methods results in a clear definition of the object's state.

For situations in which the object cannot be subclassed or made to look and feel like the object, the solution is to add a GenerateBaseType method. This would work for the DateTime definition because it is a sealed type definition. In the case of the FixedArgumentException, the client code would be modified slightly to the following:

```
throw new FixedArgumentException()
    .MessageConstructorParameter( "example")
    .ParamConstructorParameter( "no parameter")
    .GenerateBaseType();
```

In the modified code the last method call is GenerateBaseType, and it creates the type. The state of the created type depends on the chained methods that are called before calling GenerateBaseType.

When writing methods and constructors with parameters, remember the following:

- Having a parameter signature with multiple identical types can be a problem. Be cautious.

- The simplest solution to multiple identical parameters is to write .NET documentation for the API that will be exposed, allowing the development environment to pick up the information for IntelliSense.

- For int base types, you can use enumerations to distinguish parameters.

- For all other types, you can use disposal techniques to define constructor parameters.

- Using disposal techniques when defining constructor parameters can reduce the number of permutations and combinations for defining the state of a type. This is especially useful when the constructors are used for immutable objects.

- The disposal-type techniques work well for reference types, but are less efficient for value types.

Index

You Need the Companion eBook

Your purchase of this book entitles you to buy the companion PDF-version eBook for only $10. Take the weightless companion with you anywhere.

We believe this Apress title will prove so indispensable that you'll want to carry it with you everywhere, which is why we are offering the companion eBook (in PDF format) for $10 to customers who purchase this book now. Convenient and fully searchable, the PDF version of any content-rich, page-heavy Apress book makes a valuable addition to your programming library. You can easily find and copy code — or perform examples by quickly toggling between instructions and the application. Even simultaneously tackling a donut, diet soda, and complex code becomes simplified with hands-free eBooks!

Once you purchase your book, getting the $10 companion eBook is simple:

❶ Visit **www.apress.com/promo/tendollars/**.

❷ Complete a basic registration form to receive a randomly generated question about this title.

❸ Answer the question correctly in 60 seconds, and you will receive a promotional code to redeem for the $10.00 eBook.

2560 Ninth Street • Suite 219 • Berkeley, CA 94710

eBookshop

Offer valid through 4/23/07.

DATE DUE

AUG 1 2 2010

SEP 0 2 2010

JUN - 9 2011